ODYSSEY

A Psychotherapist's Journey Along the Cutting Edge

Victor Bogart, Ph.D., M.S.W.

Baskin Publishing Co., Eugene, Oregon

Published by
Baskin Publishing Co., Eugene, Oregon
© 1993 Victor Bogart
All rights reserved

Printed in the United States of America

For information, address Baskin Publishing Co.,
P.O. Box 7842, Eugene, OR 97401-0032

Library of Congress Catalog Card Number: 92-76171

ISBN 0-9635500-1-2

Author's Note:

To protect rights to privacy of actual individuals represented in the following pages, certain identifying information and names of living persons not in the public eye have been changed.

Acknowledgements

I am deeply grateful to the many who have contributed to the development of the Odyssey System and who have, in their own time and manner made their contribution to the ultimate writing and publishing of this book. I regret that it is not possible for me to acknowledge my debt to each of them by name but my appreciation of their contributions remain.

There are, however, some whom I can name and do hereby acknowledge:

My thanks to Michael Murphy for permission to quote a passage from his published article, *"Esalen: Where it's at"* (see pp 65-66). My thanks and appreciation to Julian Silverman, Claudio Naranjo, John Perry, Kasimierz Dabrowski, Wilson Van Dusen and Stanislav Grof for their contributions at the 1968 Esalen workshop, *Value of the Psychotic Experience*, excerpts of which appear in Chapter 11 and in the Appendix. My thanks, too, to W.W. Norton & Co., Inc., for permission to quote from George A. Kelly's *The Psychology of Personal Constructs* (see Appendix), and to Macmillan Publishing Co. for permission to quote from Marianne Moore's poem, *In Distrust of Merits* (p. 312).

My special thanks to my editor, Jean Bryant, whose critical judgment helped shape this book through numerous rewritings, and whose repeated exhortations to *Keep writing!* helped move the manuscript through difficult times toward a recognizable finish. But I also hold her free of blame for the final product inasmuch as she had no hand in the final editing; if she had, she would probably have exhorted me to rewrite the manuscript one more time. My thanks, too, to Gwen Rhoads for her technical assistance and cover design, and to Mike Scroggs for his proofreading of the final manuscript.

Finally, I wish to express my heartfelt gratitude for their sustaining friendship and support to Dan Parker, Joan Kerr, Pam Shaffer, John Schenkel, Hugo and Hanna Shane, and David and

Emma Eden. And to Charles and Suzanne Hornbuckle go my special thanks for making publication of this book possible.

And to Nikki, my partner and companion, I acknowledge my unending gratitude for her understanding and forbearance, her loving support, and her wise counsel through the long ordeal of bringing this project to completion.

Contents

Contents: 2

Contents: 3

Preface

I am a psychotherapist. But, of course, I am also much more.

All of us are multifaceted. We each know a variety of our faces, our masks, our personas, all of whom, depending upon the circumstances, are who we are.

This is a book about how my various selves and I have worked together to undergo much-needed transformation in times of trauma and great pain.

It is also a book about the art of expanding self-awareness to make possible the many shifts and changes that we must make if we are to hold to a growing path. So this book is both my account of my own personal odyssey and the story of my development of the Odyssey System – a persona-based way of helping ourselves to become more knowledgeable, more sensitive and more vigorously alive as we move along through our middle and later years.

This is a book that speaks to adults of all ages looking to understand and control the personal crises of mid-life and again as we transition into retirement.

And it also means to be a book that challenges those of my own later generation who contemplate surrendering to voices whispering that the time has come to turn down the flame and subside into a fading twilight with as little bother and embarrassment as possible. In the United States of America, most of us have grown up thinking that our watershed years are our sixties. If you're an average working male and you survive long enough to retire at 62 or 65, you suddenly lose your job, your work place and your identity as a productive member of society. The losses are hardly less cataclysmic if you're female. Of course you may gain social security, a lot of discretionary time, and what looks like a chance to do things you always wanted to do and didn't. But the loudest message is: *You're over the hill!*

This book is about discovering and claiming the new life that awaits you over the hill.

—VB

Prologue

The decision to write this book was made in a meeting of seven of my identified personas that took place on New Year's Day, 1991. Actually, the idea was proposed two days earlier by Sam, the one of my personas who is always thirsting to pass on what he regards as useable knowledge. We had come together for the first time in over a year. We used to meet regularly when we were actively working to explore and spread the Odyssey System. Then, on the next to last day of 1990, we met again to consider our future and Sam announced in a loud and clear voice:

It's time to write our autobiography!

The idea was immediately seconded by Leonardo who is always wanting to write a book of some kind. At the time it seemed like a fine idea. But the more time we had to think about it, the more imagination took hold and fears of horrible outcomes spewed forth. When we met again two days later, it was Althor who immediately gave vent to these fears by practically screaming:

For God's sake! An autobiography? That's scary! And, particularly in our case, it's a very dangerous thing to do!

I – and I'm Vic, the one in whose mind all of my personas

come to life – always know Althor's voice. It's pitched higher than the others and often is shrill with panic or breathless with fear. Althor is used to running scared when faced with the unknown. He is young and has worked very hard to win approval and to do the right things; but when things go badly or he doesn't know what to do, his impulse is to flee or duck and cover.

It was Sam who responded first to Althor:

Althor, I also have qualms. But I'm thinking that writing our story is our best option. It would get us back into doing what I like to do best — getting more deeply involved in our own search for understanding and sharing whatever we have to share with those who care to listen.

Why can't we live quietly? Althor shot back, his voice suddenly angry and bitter rather than plaintive. *I don't know about you, Sam, but the last three years have given me enough pain and suffering to last a lifetime. I don't want to lay myself open to any more shame and criticism, and spilling our guts to the whole world will do just that!*

Althor came to a sudden stop and Sam was quiet and thoughtful for a long moment. He cleared his throat and swallowed before replying.

Yes, there's risk. But I'm seeing some possibilities here that can take the risk out and leave us feeling good about ourselves. Let me list a few. First and foremost is the fact that in another 10 days Vic will be seventy years old. There are a lot of folks out there who are grappling with the same basic problem that he is: What should we be doing to make the most of the rest of our lives? I think that what Vic is going through – what we've all been going through, and how we handle the issues that face us – is relevant to anyone who cares to listen.

The second thing on my list is: We have a lot of skills, a viable mind, a reasonable body of knowledge, and a dollop of natural wisdom that we can bring to bear on this project. As the saying goes, we either use it or lose it. I can't think of a better project to force us to use it.

Sam paused, having forgotten the third thing on his list, but Leonardo, who was sprawled on the couch, sat upright and picked up the ball.

Well! I'm all for this project. I've almost forgotten what it feels like to be caught up in the excitement and tension of writing. I've been dying, or at least hibernating, while all of you were absorbed in licking your wounds. I've wondered if there would ever again be a place for me. Working on this project will be right down my alley. I can become one happy little phoenix. I'm all in favor and damn the risk!

Minnie, who gets off on doing housework and taking care of the rest of us, and Laura, who gets off on being sultry, both said they didn't care what we did so long as we were happy. Of those of us who were present, only Saul and Moishe hadn't said anything. Saul is the one of us who is most conscious of his age. Moishe, on the other hand, is ageless. He's our spiritual George Burns and is probably the one among us who comes closest to being a guru. But always with a sense of humor and a big grin.

Humor is transcendence in action, Moishe says at the drop of a hat.

What's with the hat? Who needs a hat? Only a bald dumbkopf needs a hat and then only when there's pigeons overhead.

That's Moishe. He's also very transcendental. I mean by that, he can detach and rise above whatever is happening down here at the worldly level and can tap into the realm of eternal truths more easily than the rest of us. Guru or not, what comes out of his mouth plays like vaudeville.

If you find the joke, you're halfway to heaven, he says. You figure him out.

Stop the funny stuff! I have something serious to say.

We all turned to look at Saul, the only one of us who looks like he's 70. Well, maybe 69. He was looking troubled.

If I'm going to stay alive for another 30 years I need something big and meaningful to get me involved and motivated. What we're doing now feels like hanging on. If we go on this way, I don't think it's going to hold my interest in staying alive all that much. I'll live as long as I have powerful reasons for doing so. Then I'll die.

The rest of us were silent while Saul looked down and stared at the floor in thought. When he spoke again he had come to a decision.

I can see the autobiography as a major reason for staying alive. It's going to keep us busy for the next three years, at least. I think it will help me feel good about myself. So I'm in favor of getting to work and saying whatever it is we have to say. And I also think that telling it honestly and autobiographically is the way we have to do it.

At this point it was clear that the group had lined up three-to-one in favor with three abstentions: Sam, Leonardo, and Saul in favor, Althor opposed, and Minnie, Laura and Moishe uncommitted. Now Sam became attentive to Althor who seemed to have withdrawn and grown smaller. When Sam spoke, his voice was gentle:

Althor, all of us have to agree on a project this big. We all have to commit to going ahead or not. You know it just won't work if we don't. Can you tell me what's in the way of your being able to make the commitment? Maybe we can all help to make it okay for you.

Sam continued to hold Althor in his thoughts as the younger man collected himself to respond. When he did, it was clear he felt backed into a corner and his words burst forth in spurts, like water from a faucet clogged with air.

I seem to be the only one who is really afraid... I see this as the stupidest and most dangerous venture we've ever tried... How many times do we have to go down in flames?...Why can't we just pull in our horns and live in peace?... What makes you think you have something important to say?... And who the hell really cares?... Taking all our clothes off in public is a terribly risky thing to do...

When the angry flow of his words ran down, Althor took some deep breaths and calmed himself considerably.

Sam, you said you could take the risk out of this project. If you can do that, then I'll reconsider. I want to know how you can do that?

The question surprised Sam. He didn't remember that he had said he could take the risk out exactly; more that he saw some possibilities of that happening. But now he felt challenged by Althor to assure that he could make the risk go away, and he didn't think he could do that.

Althor, my dear friend. Fear is something we all know. We all know very well how to see things in ways that lead us to feel frightened and unsafe. And we all know how much anguish we have experienced because we couldn't control how others were seeing us or what they were thinking about us. Pulling back and playing it safe makes sense while the wounds are fresh and in need of time to heal. But it's not a healthy long-term solution to life's problems.

Saul is right. We either Live – with a capital "L" – or we pass on. The question we have to answer is, what can we do to give our life a capital L? And I think the answer lies in all of us working together to achieve purposes that seem meaningful and worthwhile to all of us.

If one of us is afraid, then we all have to look at what's going on and come up with solutions that allow us all to move along. Together! If we don't do it together, it won't be done well, perhaps not at all.

Now, what I can promise you is that I will always be here for you. Whatever happens, we will face it together. You won't ever have to deal with anything alone.

Althor's head was down in his chest and it took a while for Sam to see that his shoulders were bobbing up and down and that he was sobbing. *Thank you,* he managed to say between sobs but otherwise remained speechless.

One by one, the others shared with him how much they appreciated and loved him and expressed their commitment to working together. When Althor spoke again his voice was very calm and he was surprisingly brief.

Thank you all, he said. *I love you, too. I'm not feeling afraid anymore. Let's do it!*

Chapter 1

I began to take my own impending retirement seriously when I turned 59. That was in January 1980.

The most subtle and far-reaching change in my thinking at that time was that I surrendered to the idea that I had better hold on to my job because it was too late for me to make a change. I had remained at Willamette Mental Health for more than nine years and the pull to abandon ship had been strong for some time. In earlier years when I felt myself no longer growing in a work situation, I would have pulled up roots and moved on. Now, the security of seniority and a vested interest in a retirement system anchored me. I felt trapped by the logic of survival and determined to stick it out as well as I could for the three years that separated me from early retirement. It was, I reasoned, a reasonable exercise in patience and the mature thing for me to be doing. Three years, after all, isn't very long. I had a respectable job, fair income, a modicum of status, and there was the guaranteed promise of release at the end of my sentence.

There is a distinction to be made between the work I did and the job I held. I loved the work. I endured the job. I had loved the job for a while but had come to feel more and more imprisoned by the bureaucratic web that entraps us all, and especially social service workers. By 1980, my job was a heavy burden. But it also allowed me to practice my work which I loved. The way I was choosing to endure the job was to detach as much as possible from it and focus as much as possible on the work.

At a deeper level, I can see in hindsight several long-held beliefs that fueled my dissatisfactions with my job. The most evident to me is that I never really believed and often didn't feel myself to be a committed authentic member of the mainstream. When I was nine, my family moved to Chicago from a radical colony in rural New Jersey named after Francisco Ferrer, a martyred Spanish anarchist educator. It was in Chicago that I first entered the public school system, and from then on I came to see myself as significantly different from most of my peers. I was suddenly an outsider being challenged with the enigma of making my way inside.

In a sense, I spent the next fifty years trying to understand the new rules of the game and figuring out where I could fit in. Throughout my adult years I continued to regard myself as a marginal member of society struggling to legitimate myself by gaining professional recognition and acceptance. But it was also more than that. I always strongly believed myself to be different and special, and I determined to have my uniqueness perceived and acclaimed. It was this belief in my uniqueness and my wanting to be acclaimed for it that I see as the second contributor to my dissatisfaction with the job.

On the other hand, I loved being of benefit to those with whom I worked and my job allowed me to do a lot of that. And here I can see operating another of my deeply held beliefs, namely, that my basic purpose in life is to be socially useful to the best of my ability. But perhaps this belief amounts to little more than an excuse to indulge my overriding passion. I am correct in speaking of passion here rather than belief. I *believe* in the essential goodness of people. I *believe* in their infinite wisdom and power to heal themselves. I *believe* that human potential is unlimited. Those are all beliefs. But I *love* people. I *love* relating to people with honesty and caring and the absence of authoritarian judgment. And I *love* to be instrumental in another person's opening up to their own flowering. Those are passions of mine beyond belief.

So here I was at my 59th birthday, still struggling in pursuit of my passions and professional legitimacy and acclaim. At the time, I saw myself as proceeding along two complementary career paths: On one path, I was hanging on to a full-time job as a psychiatric social worker for Willamette Mental Health. On the other, I was maintaining a small private practice counseling adults. I was bone weary of my full-time job while my private practice was much less burdensome and more nurturing. Looking down the two paths into the future, I could see a time when one would metamorphose into a guaranteed retirement income and I could expand the other into a magical new kingdom of my own designing. That made it easier to hold on.

I never much liked identifying myself professionally as a social worker. *Social worker* simply never matched the image I had of myself. *Psychiatric social worker* was more acceptable to me but I preferred to call myself a *psychotherapist*. I had chosen to become a social worker because that was the best available path to my becoming professionally qualified to work as a psychotherapist. But going for a master's degree in social work wasn't my first choice. That was back in 1964 at a time when I was teaching journalism to community college students in Longview, Washington. I had been in journalism off and on since World War II and, while I enjoyed teaching and relished my relationships with students, I was not relishing a long-term future as a journalism instructor and was casting about for a different career path. I was 43 by then and had accumulated enough practical experience and graduate courses to consider several options. Different options appealed to different parts of me, but the idea of becoming a psychotherapist was drawing all of me.

In 1964 Odette and I were three years into our marriage – a second marriage for each of us – and we were busy establishing our new family and shaping the substance of our lives together. One might say that our relationship was born out of psychotherapy. We met in 1960 at a singles party in Palo Alto to which each of us had half-heartedly accepted invitations. What we found when we got there was a hive of victims engaged in the pastime of blaming their ex-spouses for the failure of their marriages. Odette and I were the exceptions and we gravitated to each other, first in mutual support against the mob, then in burgeoning interest in each other. We ended up spending the night enthusiastically exploring our commonalities, our differences, and most of all each other's minds.

Among the things we learned about each other that night were that we had both been divorced about a year, had each spent two years in therapy, and had both come away deeply valuing the experience. We also learned that our respective marriages had lasted for 11 years, we each had three children, we both respected our ex-spouses, and we both accepted at least half of the responsibility for the failure of our marriages and subsequent divorce. And to top it off, Odette displayed a snappingly vibrant intelligence, a lovely deep voice, a direct manner of speech, and she was clearly the most magically beautiful woman I had ever met. For me, destiny seemed to be at work and I could see a door of future possibility swinging open. But at daybreak the door apparently got stuck in its hinges when, after a long breakfast at an all-night diner, I asked her for a date. She was, she explained, "still in another relationship." When we said good-by, her parting words were something like, "Don't call me, I'll call you."

Odette's allure for me was many faceted and not the smallest part of it was her attractiveness to men. Here was a mature, complex, intelligent, socially at ease woman who obviously drew men to her powerfully and naturally, like bees to a field of clover. I have rarely seen myself as more than moderately appealing to women and was half resigned to not making further headway in my amorous pursuit of Odette, so I was elated three weeks later when she phoned and the door opened again.

The unfolding of our relationship during the months that followed calls for more than summary treatment, for in the drama and excitement of those events can be seen the pattern of all that was to follow. But for now, it can suffice to note that in those months the flames of our mutual interest in the mysteries of psychotherapy were fueled, and that together we stumbled upon a whole new way of exploring and understanding ourselves and each other that has remained a major force in my life to this day.

So it was that four years later in Longview, it seemed the right time for us to move toward professional careers in the healing arts. I say "for us," because by then we had generated a vision of working together as a husband and wife psychotherapy team. One way of achieving that, we thought, would be with graduate degrees in psychology. But with three school-age boys and a two-year old daughter, we would have to go through graduate school one at a time and, because I was closer to getting through school than Odette, we decided that I would go first. So we piled our family into our old Volkswagen bus and drove off to visit some university psychology departments. We made trips to a number of campuses on the West Coast and in every case we ran into a stone wall:

...At 43, Mr. Bogart, you're too old to be admitted to our doctoral program in psychology.

...Your plan to someday work together as a husband and

wife therapy team is unrealistic.

...You don't fit the profile of what we're looking for in our graduate students.

We wondered if perhaps our dream, in 1964, was too far out in front of our time. In frustration, Odette and I sought out our dear friend and my former journalism advisor, Professor Phil Griffin, at the University of California in Berkeley. In his usual caring way, Phil supported us in our dream and pointed me in the direction of a master's degree program in social work.

By 1980 and my 59th birthday, I had been working as a psychiatric social worker for 14 years, the last nine for Willamette Mental Health.

Chapter 2

"Good Heavens! Who were you being in there?"

Odette and I had just emerged from an art gallery in Menlo Park into the bright sunshine. It was the springtime of 1960 and the springtime of our relationship. We were living together by then and excitedly continuing the process of unfolding ourselves to each other. Our first date some weeks before, a dinner date at a moderately-upscale restaurant, had been a near-disaster during which I failed miserably to live up to any of Odette's significant criteria for desirability. However, our future together was salvaged later that evening when we got carried away in the front seat of my 1956 turquoise and white Chevy station wagon and Odette accidentally sat on my glasses. That seemed to turn things around and, after another brief but agonizing wait, Odette called and invited me to dinner.

She was living in a small rustic cottage among the hills behind Stanford University with her three sons, Dennis, 10, Dean, 8 and Ian, 5. I arrived as Odette was burning the chops and the boys were raising hell with Dean attempting a coup de grace by throwing a chair into a glass door. I was superb. I remained calm. I swept up glass. I loved the burned chops. I pitched in and helped with the dishes. I comforted the boys and read stories to them at bedtime. I stayed the night. And by the time I left the next morning, Odette and I had decided I should move in with her.

The early weeks of our living together were dramatically enlarging and detailing my perceptions of Odette, and I struggled to gather in and absorb the unfolding, often-paradoxical dimensions of this complex woman. She was a devoted tiger with her children – and an indifferent housekeeper. She was comfortably self-disclosing and articulate – and deeply mysterious. She acknowledged a long history of intimacy with many men – and valued them all for how much she had learned from them. She was intellectually voracious and immersed in books – and an artists' model who was the first woman chosen by the nuns of a Catholic school for girls to pose in the nude for their students. She was scholarly and widely knowledgeable and literate – and had little formal education beyond high school. Here was a woman who continued to surprise me almost daily with her diversity.

Still, I was unprepared for what I experienced watching her in the art gallery on that Spring day in Menlo Park and it came as a shock. What I was reacting to was a transformed woman. As we meandered through the gallery, I was struck by her sudden differentness. This was not the Odette I thought I had come to know in our weeks together. Her face had changed. She carried herself differently. The quality of her voice was different and her manner of speech had altered. Inside the gallery I was almost speechless with amazement and curiosity. So it was that as soon as we came out into the sunshine, I blurted out:

Good Heavens! Who were you being in there?

To which she responded almost immediately with,

Oh! THAT was Cynthia.

And that was the beginning of the Odyssey System.

What is the Odyssey System? It's a way of conceptualizing ourselves as a community of sub-identities rather than as a single identity. Odette, for example, was also *Cynthia*. And, as the two of us discovered in the exciting weeks and months of mutual exploration that followed, Odette was also a host of identifiable and nameable others of all ages and characteristics. But not only Odette; I also was able to uncover, name and assume a variety of "me's." And it very quickly became apparent to us that this ability is universal. All it takes is a willingness to think of ourselves as different selves, all of whom share the same dwelling space and each of whom manifests through specific characteristic behaviors.

What we were discovering was that our different selves were the different masks or personas that we assumed in different situations and in response to different stimuli. And it was becoming apparent to us that each of our different selves, or personas, was a specialist of some kind. *Cynthia,* who emerged in art galleries, was adept at handling formal social situations and also flourished at posh parties and in conversations with maiden aunts over cups of tea and tiny cookies. *Lorelei,* on the other hand, was an innocent little girl who danced and smiled a lot and picked flowers. *Anne* was studious and a lover of books. *Carla* was a dark sensualist. *Helena* was a serene wise-woman goddess.

Robin was my little boy counterpart to *Lorelei. Sam,* my professor, and *Leonardo,* my poet, both of whom you met in the Prologue, also first came to light back then.

In all, as I recall, Odette discovered 16 different personas and I came up with six. But it wasn't just the number and varieties of sub-identities we were able to identify and name that excited us; it was experiencing the freedom to bring our diverse selves to life and give them expression. We had stumbled upon an easy way of making contact with and experiencing little known and unexplored aspects of our own infinite variety. It was as if the curtain was going up on a whole new performance in the theater of our personal dramas and we were being given new players, new scripts, new plots, and an unlimited horizon of new possibilities to play with.

That was in 1960, before The Beatles and just before the wave of experimentation with mind-altering drugs and new patterns for human relationships and being-ness that rocked our world and earned for itself the awesome honorific of an *era,* forever to be known in the minds of its survivors and their children as *the sixties.*

Interchapter 2+

SAM: *My God, Leo, it's sometimes hard to realize that was
30 years ago.*

LEONARDO: *Yes. And I'm having a problem writing
about all this that I need to talk about and I want
some feedback. What I'm trying to do here is to
emphasize the significant connections between
events across time, rather than present events
chronologically. I don't want to write this chronologically because our minds don't work that way.
Our minds work by connecting events in our lives
without regard to time. I can't bask on a sandy
beach on a hot day and not remember how intensely
good it felt to be doing the same thing when I was
14 years old at our summer home at Plage Laval
outside Montreal. The significant connections are
made without regard to when they happen. I want
this to emphasize the connections because I believe
it will all add up to a much clearer understanding.
Like an oil painting. Or a patchwork quilt.*

SAM: *Or like life. What I like about that approach is that I
think it's somehow relevant to a major theme of this*

work, *the process of transformation in late adulthood. I haven't thought this through. I'm just
hunching that it will work. Perhaps it's because our
late years are natural times for remembering and
making connections. Perhaps not. In any case, I
expect I'll get a lot clearer about all this as we go
along. But Leo, you said you're having a problem.*

LEONARDO: *Yes. Well, the problem is one of deciding
when to stop talking about specific events happening at a specific time, say in 1960, and when to
reconnect with another time, say 1980. The problem
is that there are many events occurring at different
times that need to be connected and I'm having a
hard time deciding which ones to connect and
when. For example, so much happened in the sixties
that needs to be told and it's going to take time to
do that. I'm not sure what to tell now and what to
leave for later.*

SAM: *Sounds to me like you're concerned that you may
leave important stuff out. Or that the reader won't
be able to follow, or maybe won't want to follow as
you zig and zag across time.*

LEONARDO: *Yeh.*

SAM: *Well, let's take the view that everything that needs
to be said will be said in time and that the reader
will either follow along or give up and go read
something else. Let's focus on doing the best we
know how with what we've got.*

LEONARDO: *Okay. I'll keep going. Does anyone else
have something to say?*

ALTHOR: *That's not the way the books that I've read have been written. It sounds so unorthodox.*

LEONARDO: *That's just the point. We ARE unorthodox! That's our central dilemma: our struggle with orthodoxy and our difficulty in fitting into it.*

MINNIE: *Yes. It's time to take a coffee break. We have some carrot cake left over in the fridge. I'll pop it into the microwave.*

Chapter 3

The first time I entered a state mental hospital in the fall of 1964, I was in a state of controlled terror, in fear that my disguise as a new graduate student from the University of Washington School of Social Work would be seen through. Surely any hospital psychiatrist (who, of course, must be able to tell staff from patients) would spot me for what I was and lock me up and throw away the key. My terror subsided in a day or two but not before it served its purposes.

My terror was, of course, at least reasonably well founded. I was to learn quickly that only superficial distinctions separate the hospitalized mentally ill from the rest of us, and most of the distinctions have little to do with what goes on in the minds of "the insane." On that day, I saw those distinctions evaporate. In the eyes of the hospitalized patients all around me, I recognized myself. In their bizarre and not-so-bizarre mannerisms and behaviors, I saw the "insanity" that lives in me. It wasn't *that,* that brought on my terror so much as it was my disbelief that my brand new "social worker uniform" would protect me from being seen through.

So what am I now able to see in the microcosm of my first day at Western State Hospital? For one, that I didn't then – and still don't – believe much in the relevance of the uniforms by which we separate ourselves from each other. The distinctions between ourselves and others are fabrications that we knowingly devise or blindly accept, usually out of fear. A case in point was the relationship between myself and one of the very first patients assigned to me, an elderly man named Nick Romanescu who, I was told, shunned people and couldn't or wouldn't speak. I felt a special connection with Nick from the first moment I saw him seated by himself in a corner of the ward's sickly-green common room. He looked like my father: same grey-blue eyes in a lined and chiseled face, same grey balding head, same short stocky build, same age. The resemblance was eerie and I had to keep reminding myself that my own father was alive and well.

My supervisor instructed me to "just spend time with him" and to offer whatever support I could. So in the months that followed, on each of my weekly visits to the hospital, I would check in with Nick and sit with him while he ignored me. Or I would trail after him while he silently walked as rapidly as he could through the wooded areas of the hospital grounds. Or I would talk to him assuming he might hear me and understand. And after several weeks, Nick seemed to be gradually accepting me into his world and a relationship seemed to be growing between us. For one thing, he was no longer ignoring me. Now, instead of my being an intruder on his walks in the woods, we were walking together, and our visits were becoming more amiable and friendlier for both of us. Still, he remained silent. Until one day he shocked me by turning to me and asking in clear but accented English, "Are you my son?"

Nick's question threw me for a loop; and it was more than just my surprise that he was speaking – and speaking English! I was well aware of some of my own feelings toward him, including my feelings of love and respect for this man whom I had to keep reminding myself was not really my father. What I did not suspect was that he was responding to me as if I might be his son! Here we both were, on the verge of dancing off together into "another reality" in which we both could live out our respective fantasies of the father-son relationship we might each still be wishing for. And who was leading the dance and who was following? Was Nick responding to my "unconscious" son-like behavior by trying to fit me into his world in the role I seemed to be playing for him? Was I "over-responding" or counter-transferring in response to my own unmet needs for a father I never really quite had? Was Nick reaching to fill a void of his own? Were we both trying to reach through the barrier of our formally-defined roles to a more primal father-son kinship that exists between all males of older and younger generations? Any or all of the above?

One of the lessons I was learning through Nick, or perhaps being reminded of, was that the barrier that separates is not a barrier but a sieve, or a gate that remains closed only temporarily. Whatever "reality" we happen to be subscribing to in this moment is only separated artificially from alternative realities. The reality of me as a neophyte psychiatric social worker was separated from another reality of me as Nick's son only by an array of mumbo-jumboisms. Not that the mumbo-jumbos don't have their own justifications. Of course they do. Without them, the structures supporting our lives would melt in disarray. Nevertheless, they are only constructs — that is, sets of beliefs reinforced by codes of behavior — that serve as social conveniences. And because the existence of any particular "reality" depends upon a belief in it as "more real" than some other reality, its existence is only as sturdy as the fabric of beliefs and behaviors that supports it.

What I was learning from Nick was that there wasn't as much separating the two of us as I had imagined there would be between a hospitalized patient and his social worker. Despite the separation and distance resulting from hospital rules and social conventions, we had created some deeply-felt connections, commonalities and sharings. What I was learning was that a magical thing can happen when formal reality with its prescribed social distances dissolves enough to allow for compassion and authentic human exchange. As the boundaries of formal reality are allowed to dissolve, doors can open into alternative realities that are also very real.

I think that alternative realities are subjectively real for us because each reality reflects aspects of the multifaceted belief system to which we happen to be wedded. Falling in love offers a sharp juxtaposition typical of the alternative realities I am talking about here. Most of us know the contrast between the states of being "in love" and "out of love" as remarkably poignant — soaring as opposed to earth bound; feeling at-one with our beloved as opposed to feeling despondently alone; singing songs of love as opposed to singing the blues; and so forth. Each of the two states has its own experience and its own validity. Each state reflects aspects of ourselves that are very real.

But the totality of who we are or believe ourselves to be must have room for both states. To be sure, being in love and being out of love can be seen as a single flowing process in the same way that the tide comes in and the tide goes out. But, particularly when we're young, our experience leads us to believe that there are walls around the states of being in love or out of love that make them separate realities. In point of fact, many of us come to feel, particularly when we are no longer young, that the walls have become insurmountable.

Back there in the fall and winter of 1964, I was already charting a path in my relationship with Nick that would lead me as a future therapist to focus at least as much of my attention upon the walls as upon what was transpiring within the particular realities they seemed to surround. Looking back from the vantage point of 1991, it is possible for me to see my development as a therapist as one long sequence of experimentation and revelation in the art of what I regard as "wall management." Wall management pays attention to the condition of the particular walls that I and my clients have erected around our respective realities. It considers how steadfast the walls are, and how successfully they are holding off the pressures of alternative realities threatening to break through. It acknowledges and respects all of the realities that are to be found within the walls. And it leads to decisions about helping clients to strengthen particular walls, or restructure them, or render them more permeable, or dissolve them altogether. And, as I have tried to practice it, wall management attempts to teach the art of wall management to my clients to whatever extent they wish.

Interchapter 3+

LEONARDO: *Sam, I think we're losing our audience. I don't think most folks will follow all this stuff about wall management. Isn't there another way of talking about it that will make it clearer?*

SAM: *Sure. Suppose we use ourselves to make some points. The only reason you, Leonardo, or I, Sam, exist at all is that Vic has created a "reality," as he is using that word, in which we can materialize.*

ALTHOR: *Of course, we don't have physical bodies the way Vic has.*

SAM: *That's not quite true, Althor. To some extent you take over Vic's body when he assumes your persona in the world. Well, maybe not to the extent that the face of Althor that we know and love is the same face that Vic's friends out there see.*

LEONARDO: *Thank God!*

ALTHOR: *Oh, I don't know. At least I'm not a wild-eyed Italian who hasn't had a haircut in thirty years!*

LAURA: *How about me? Here I have this svelte body and Hedy Lamar face that have been going to total waste. I wish Vic would undergo a sex change so I could materialize.*

ALTHOR: *Thank God it's too late. If he were to get one now you'd come out looking like Grandma Moses.*

LAURA: *I could get used to that.*

SAM: *Okay, Okay. The point is that we exist as separate identities only because Vic has created, first of all, a reality in which all of us are able to emerge; and secondly, some smaller and separate realities within which each of us comes to life individually. Now, to pursue this a little further: When Vic materialized you, Leonardo, he created for you a reality in which you get to play out Vic's own aspirations to be living a creative and artistic life. It just so happens that, for the most part, his artistic aspirations get expressed through writing; but your name suggests that it could just as well happen through painting, or sculpture, or invention – although I don't remember Vic ever inventing anything.*

LEONARDO: *How about the Odyssey System? Isn't that an invention?*

SAM: *Yes, I suppose one could think of it that way.*
Good point. But to get back to the 'walls' thing:
Just as you, Leonardo, are an expression of
Vic's artistic longings or dreams or whatevers,
I, Sam, am an expression of his intellectual
dreams and strivings; and Althor is an expres-
sion of his desires to belong and to be accepted
in 'formal society'; and Laura is an expression
of his sensuality and the feminine aspects of his
sexuality; and so forth. It is only within the
context of each of these separate "realities"
that we exist. And what separates us from each
other is only a barrier of some kind that Vic is
calling a wall, but you can call it anything you
like. And the wall's function is to act like some
kind of container that holds the particular
"reality" within which we can take form and
manifest.

LEONARDO: *So, all it takes for Vic to switch from*
being me to being you is to leap over the wall
that separates my reality from yours?

SAM: *Exactly.*

ALTHOR: *Okay, I'm understanding what you're*
saying so far, but I still don't get what he
means by wall management. That sounds even
more complicated to me.

SAM: *It is more complicated. That's because it covers*
a lot more territory and gets to be a lot more
detailed in actual practice. But I can give you
an example of wall management that will be
easier for you, Althor, to grasp. Do you re-

member how you were created?

ALTHOR: *Well, I'm not sure how much I actually remember but I've been told about it a lot.*

SAM: *Well, for the benefit of our readers, you are a merging of two younger personas, one of whom was named Arthur and the other was Albert. As little boys and young children, Arthur and Albert each had separate characteristics that had a lot of meaning at that time. But as they came to adulthood, they found more and more similarities and fewer differences. It was then that they decided, or Vic decided, depending upon how you want to think about that, to merge into a single adult persona named Althor.*

ALTHOR: *And the wall management part?*

SAM: *...was simply turning the two walls around Arthur and Albert into a single wall around you, Althor.*

ALTHOR: *And how was that done?*

SAM: *By combining the two contexts within which Arthur and Albert existed separately into a larger single context that allowed the "reality" of you, Althor, to emerge.*

ALTHOR: *I think I'm understanding but I'm having trouble with your use of the word "context." What I understand you to be saying is that a* context *is the environment within which something happens that is a product of that environ-*

ment. Like I happen only in the <u>context</u>, i.e., the environment of a particular state of mind that Vic generates that you and Vic are calling a particular reality.

SAM: *That's right.*

ALTHOR: *But I'm still not clear on how you get from two contexts to a single larger context.*

SAM: *By going from "either-or" to "both-and." Whenever we have to choose, we usually think of having to choose <u>either</u> this <u>or</u> that. But we have another option of shifting how we're thinking about the choice so that we come up with a way of being able to choose <u>both</u> this <u>and</u> that. And this particular kind of shift in thinking is the basic mechanism involved in the act of transcendence. Of course, we didn't know any of that back in 1964. In fact, we didn't really learn that until our historic acid trip in 1968. But that's another story.*

Chapter 4

Most of my memories of our two years in Seattle, from 1964 to 1966, have dwindled and faded over time from scene-length scenarios to snips and snapshots: ...Odette and I in the early morning in our VW Bus, usually in a cold rain, dropping Teddie off at her baby sitter, getting Odette to her job at Group Health, and my going on to campus to attend classes... Picking up Dean and Ian in late afternoons from the Wallingford Boys Club and their ricocheting intense voices – enthusiastic, or wound down, or unhappy, or joyful – reporting on the latest events happening in their crowded lives... All of us around evening mealtime in our two-story frame house on Eastern Avenue North in the U-District – the bustle of meal preparation, the singing, the recounting of the day's experiences, the sharing of concerns, the sharing of dreams... The sharp-sweet mixture of pride and apprehension with which I watch our beautiful four-year old Teddie squealing with excitement in Dean's lap as he drives his recently-acquired moped up and down the street... All of us partying with friends in evenings filled with music and dance and intense conversations about all sorts of exciting and important things.

Of those years I have no sad or unkind memories. It was a time of reveling, of growing and learning, of planning and working toward futures holding only promise of good and of fulfillment. It was a time of exciting new beginnings. It was a bountiful time.

The dramatic sense of destiny that had powered Odette's and my relationship during our first year together was being re-charged in Seattle, largely, as I see it, because we were once again on our vision quest. An early vision during our first year together was that someday we would go public and do exciting things with our discoveries and fresh ideas about multiple personality theory. We had both read the book and had seen the movie, *Three Faces of Eve* [1], and while we were greatly moved by it, we felt that our own experiences were at least as remarkable as Eve's. Still, we did not generate specific plans to pursue it in any practical way, and the vision remained an intriguing sidelight while I pursued my master's in journalism at Berkeley and then taught community college classes in El Centro and then in Longview.

In Seattle, however, all of that was changing. We were again pursuing our early dream of becoming psychotherapists and, while we were not yet formulating specific plans around our interest in persona work, at least we were moving in a promising direction. And there were additional connections being made with some of our other earlier interests. But I want to talk about these using a different metaphor.

We are being carried along through life by rivers and streams of thought. We go about our daily lives expressing through our many behaviors our thoughts, our ideas, our beliefs, our secrets. These inner thoughtways of our minds shape and direct who we become and what we do in the outer world.

I am fascinated by the geography of the mind – not the physical placement of organs, not the anatomical structure of the brain, but the mindscape as it would look if the substance and patterns of our thinking could be seen as waterways. If such were possible, we might see rivulets of familiar and comfortable thoughts feeding into quiet streams flowing into more deeply channeled rivers emptying into self-satisfied lakes of established assumptions and beliefs. Or perhaps, springs of fresh new ideas feeding upstart burbling brooks tumbling into enriched ponds burgeoning with new concepts. And one might ask: What deeply channelled rivers of entrenched ways of thinking are there to be seen? And, what dams of old assumptions are keeping new streams of would-be discovery from flowing through the infinitely rich mother lode of our experience?

If such mindmaps could be drawn, I'm sure that the map for each of us would be complex and changing and uniquely our own. That no one else's mindscape is identical to one's own can make for intense feelings of differentness and loneliness, but oh what joy when we find powerful similarities with another's! And that is certainly one way of viewing the connections Odette and I were making during our early years together.

Back in 1960, during our first year, Odette and I were sharing and exploring a number of the major waterways of the mind that had drawn us together. One of the big ones was an obsessive fascination with the spoken and written word. And in my mind's eye, I can visualize how this particular waterway developed for each of us.

Odette was born into a tragic marriage doomed by abandonment, alcohol, and other assorted instabilities. Deeply scarred, she was raised by her maternal grandmother, a high school teacher, in a household of maiden aunts steeped in literary tradition, precise manners, and tightly controlled emotions. In a childhood rocky with repeated back and forthings between her wounded adventuring mother and her pained caring grandmother, books took on special meaning. In what could be seen as a strategy for survival, Odette learned to withdraw into the magical worlds that opened for her among the pages of books. As she matured, she became adept at finding not only the books, but also the minds that could supply her with the emotional support and the intellectual nourishment upon which she thrived.

In some ways, Odette and I had similar childhood experiences. My own parents divorced, a year or so after I was born. Shortly after that, my mother went into nurse's training at Beth David Hospital in New York City and, until she married again when I was five, I was boarded out to a kind and loving family of musicians who raised chickens near Stelton, New Jersey. My mother came to visit on her days off. I don't remember my early childhood as particularly traumatic or deprived; my early memories are filled with sounds of violins and pianos practicing, clucking hens, crowing roosters, and warm caring voices. But there were also persistent bed wettings and nightmares. And there is one line from a small child's record my mother bought for me that I used to play over and over on my small wind-up gramophone. I can still hear the male singer's scratchy quavering voice as if it were playing now. He is singing a song about a miller who lived on the River Dee, and the last line of the refrain goes:

I care for nobody
no, not I,
and nobody cares for me.

Nature and the outdoors fed the developing waterways of my mind during the early years and it wasn't until adolescence that a passion for the music of language awakened in me. Then it came in a romantic rush of Shelley and Shakespeare and Jack London and my own laborings to capture the essence of my own tempestuous risings and fallings in poems of easy rhymings and excruciating searches for just the right word – very much like seeking out the one itchy spot in the unreachable middle of my back, the scratching of which would undoubtedly trigger endless orgasms of ecstasy. Later, when I was called upon to choose a career path, I struggled between creative writing and the more practical path of engineering, and for a number of years engineering won. But after three years in wartime

England – where military duties were punctuated by repeated baskings in the theaters and concert halls of London and Cambridge, and by a re-reading of Tolstoy's *War and Peace*, and by much writing in a journal that has long since disappeared – an engineering career no longer held my attention. But, Capricorn that I am, I still could not free myself for a starving-garret life as a poet, more's the pity. So I eeny-meeny-miney-mo'd my way into journalism and fell in love with it.

Thus, Odette and I came together with shared mindstreams committed to the world of words. And we shared a love of drama and an enduring sense of specialness, the belief that our lives were meant to be filled by special things happening for us. And, of course, we shared the new streams of a rapidly burgeoning fascination with psychotherapy and its promise of making growthful things happen in the mysterious entwined realms of the *intra-* and the *inter*-personal.

All of these mindstreams were active during our first year together when we learned of some work being done at Palo Alto's Mental Research Institute, a few miles from where we were still living in sin, as it were. Two of the MRI group, Virginia Satir and Gregory Bateson, were later to assume significant roles for both of us, but we didn't meet either of them at that time. Nor did we rush down to MRI's offices to explore what was going on. Instead, we read and studied the reprint of an article given to us by a friend who was more familiar than we were with the work being done at MRI. The article, *Toward a Theory of Schizophrenia* [2], was written by Bateson, Don Jackson, Jay Haley, and John Weakland – all members of an MRI group researching communication patterns among families in which one member was hospitalized as schizophrenic. The article discussed research findings indicating that the consistent sending of conflicting verbal and non-verbal messages by parents played a role in the formation of schizophrenic behavior in their children.

The idea that persistent double-binding communication within one's family of origin has the power to drive one crazy made a lot of sense to Odette and me, and Bateson's article quickly became one of a number of articles and books that nourished the flow of our interest in psychotherapy. Another was Virginia Satir's book, *Conjoint Family Therapy*. [3] Published in 1964, it was based on her experiences at MRI where she had developed a brand new approach to working with all the members of a troubled family sitting together in the same therapy session. Both Bateson's and Satir's work emphasized the pivotal role that communication plays in mental illness among troubled families.

In Seattle, at the School of Social Work in 1964-66, these mindstreams – these two themes of family therapy, and the role that communication plays in mental illness – strongly influenced the direction of my graduate work. I was able to orchestrate my professional education around them, and a number of experiences broadened these streams in my consciousness. I remember most:

• Satir's visit to the School of Social Work and her demonstrations of conjoint family therapy. I recall how moved I was by the sensitivity, warmth and exquisite skill of this lioness of a woman. Not only was Satir a model of excellence in the new world of family therapy, she was also a psychiatric social worker who gave me a vision of the profession as operating on the cutting edge of therapeutic innovation.

• My weekly trips for two days of internship at Western State Hospital for the mentally ill during the first year, and to a child guidance clinic in Everett, Washington, during the second.

• Working for the Northwest Family Research Institute during my second year where I spent most of my time researching and writing my master's thesis and digging more deeply into the growing body of literature on family therapy.

I saw it all as drawing me closer to the goals I was setting for myself.

These days, in 1991, the school of social work is housed in a sleek, modern brick building of the sort I associate with insurance company regional offices. Back then, the school was housed in a remodeled church that was warm and friendly and the folks inside impressed me as dedicated to compassionate service. I felt myself to be in the right place. I made friends quickly and I easily found those members of the faculty whose needs to teach best matched my own needs to learn. I did not have to stretch the system or go outside of it to organize my learning around the dual themes of family therapy and the role of communication in mental illness. My teachers saw what I wanted and helped me get it. At least up to a point. None of them ever gave me my head completely. Every one of them insisted that I also learn what they felt I would need to know to function professionally as a psychiatric social worker. They did their jobs well.

But a quarter of a century later, I found myself asking if I had learned as much as I would need to survive.

Chapter 5

And now come the golden years. The years of magic. The years of dreams materializing. The years of pain. The sensuous years.

I had never lived in southern California before we moved there in 1966, but for Odette and the boys, our move was a homecoming. Odette was an almost-native southern Californian, having been taken to live in Glendale with her grandmother shortly after her birth in Boston, Massachusettes. Odette grew up being passed back and forth between the contrasting worlds of ordered life with her grandmother and chaotic life with her mother. And while mother and grandmother were sharply divided in values and life styles, both were ferociously committed to a passion for books and learning that yielded a rich nurturing broth for Odette's growing mind to feed upon.

Not long after she graduated from high school in 1947, Odette married Owen, an ex-navy pilot, and moved to Santa Barbara where he was pursuing a master's degree in geology. For a short time, she attended evening classes at a nearby junior college but it quickly became a time for growing babies as the boys began making their entrances one after the other, as legions of babies were doing with such determination in those years after World War II.

When Owen finished his master's, he went to work teaching in community colleges and Odette graduated to the status of faculty wife, first in a county seat in the Sierras and later in an oil field town in the southern San Joaquin Valley. It was there that their marriage crumbled, and Odette piled herself and her three boys into her VW bus and drove north to the Bay Area where she set up house in Los Trancos Woods behind Stanford.

Now, in '66, they were back in southern California and the six of us were living in a rented house on the beach in Ventura, south of Santa Barbara. It was there that the boys discovered The Beatles. Before long, The Beatles, and Donovan, and Peter, Paul and Mary, and Simon and Garfunkel, and all the others – but mostly The Beatles – were playing the music and creating the rhythms to which all of us were learning to dance our lives. The sensuous magic, without which *the sixties* would be no different than the years before or since, flowed; and in varying degrees, we all learned to release ourselves into the moods and messages of the music.

But that didn't happen all at once. Much of the first year we focused on learning how to become Californians again and adjusting to all the newness: warm bright climate, blue skies, palm trees, new schools for the kids, new job, new status and income, new neighbors, new friends. And there were adjustments to make to the ambiance of southern California, which I found exhilarating with fresh vistas around every bend and beyond every rise. So much to explore. So much to discover.

Five mornings a week I drove the 20 miles south along the freeway to the sprawling California-Spanish style campus of Camarillo State Hospital. I had been recruited by Camarillo several months before my graduation and I was pledged to remain on staff for two years, the prescribed internship required for ACSW certification. Membership in the Academy of Certified Social Workers is the ticket to professional advancement, to state licenses to practice on one's own, and to whatever other treasures one might find within the profession's store of goodies. It is also the public's guarantee that ACSW social workers have completed a two year master's degree program and two more years of post-graduate work under an approved ACSW supervisor.

I chose Camarillo because I saw a state hospital for the mentally ill as providing the in-depth experiences I needed to further develop my new professional skills. The primary assigned role of social workers at mental hospitals like Camarillo was to prepare patients for placement in suitable living situations upon their release back into the community. The secondary assigned role was to offer emotional, psychological and social support to patients and their families. My own agenda, which was consistent with both assigned roles, was to advance my skills in the subtle practice of deciphering and unlocking the jammed machinery of psychological and social functioning.

So it was with high motivation and enthusiasm that I threw myself into the many learning opportunities available at Camarillo. There were weekly medical staff meetings where experts lectured on the various forms of mental illness, on the physiology of organic brain syndrome, on the effects of this or that medication, on the pros and cons of electro-shock therapy as a treatment for involutional melancholia, on the latest research findings of this or that behavior-modification project. There were numerous seminars and demonstrations of experimental work being done with different populations of patients. There were weekly meetings of the social work staff that I still remember as among the least dreary of the seven hundred or so I was to attend over the next fifteen years. Probably because they were among my first. Perhaps because I was most eager to learn. And, of course, there were all the lessons I was being taught daily by my assigned patients and their family members.

Of the workshop presenters, most were recognized experts in

their fields who drove up from Los Angeles each week to lead training seminars. Two of them, whom I still regard as primary teachers of mine during my Camarillo years, were Walt Kempler, psychiatrist, and Lewis Yablonsky.

Yablonsky was a sociologist and author associated with Synanon, the heroin addiction treatment center in Santa Monica staffed by recovering addicts. I already knew of Yablonsky and Synanon through his book *The Tunnel Back*. [1] At Synanon, it seemed, a powerful magic was being brewed by recovering heroin addicts who were successfully helping their brother and sister addicts to rid themselves of their heroin habits. Before Synanon, nobody was being very successful in treating heroin addiction.

Yablonsky's workshops were not about Synanon, however. They were training sessions in psychodrama, the powerful form of group psychotherapy which Yablonsky had learned from J. L. Moreno who pioneered its development in the 1930s. [2] Simply put, psychodrama helps participants to probe and act out hidden motivations and feelings through dramatic role playing. At Camarillo, Yablonsky was teaching us how to use psychodrama as a form of family therapy in which family members acted out their own roles and those of other family members in situations of family conflict. While Yablonsky's Camarillo workshops were feeding my continuing interest in family therapy, they were also rekindling Odette's and my curiosity about Synanon.

Santa Monica is an easy drive from Ventura, and Odette and I visited Synanon several times in '66 and '67. We found it to be both a treatment center for heroin addicts and a courageous experiment in communal living. Synanon was a self-contained community in which addicts were given the chance to exchange their loyalty to heroin for loyalty to the Synanon community. Synanon accepted entire families as well as individuals and couples and, so far as we could see, it functioned as a participatory democracy in which all of its members were held responsible for every aspect of their own and the community's functioning.

I don't think I've said much, if anything, yet about my deep longing to belong to a community. Sometimes I associate my longing with feelings of being suspended in a warm protective womblike environment. Sometimes I think of it as purposefully pursuing common goals with others whom I trust and care about. Sometimes I think of it as spiritual communion. Sometimes as joyous dancing. Sometimes as a meditation.

This longing for community has manifested at various times in my life, like a whale surfacing to breathe and re-invigorate after long submersion. My own particular whale was once again renewing itself with the breath of life in our visits to Synanon. It was destined to do so again.

Chapter 6

For me, our visits to Synanon were stirring memories of community that I trace to my childhood in Ferrer Colony. When I was five, my mother married Bernard Shane and I have memories of my mother coming to take a bewildered me from my family of musicians; memories of walking with father Izzy to the tar-papered chicken coop out back to say good-by to our chickens; of hugging good-bys to gentle Izzy and to my warm and caring mother Rose; of my own mother holding my hand and our walking away from the white frame house with its green trim, down the cement path to a waiting car on the unpaved country road out front.

And suddenly there are six of us living as a whole new family. That must have been in 1926.

Actually, all of us children had been living within a few miles of each other before we came together as a family, but I don't have earlier memories of having met Bernard or his children. Evelyn and Hugo had been boarding with a family in Ferrer Colony at the time I was living with the Weisses in nearby Fellowship Farm. My older brother Lutz had been living at The Living House, a boarding house for children attending Ferrer Colony's Modern School whose parents, I guess, were living in New York City. Bernard, like my mother, was also living and working in New York. And like my mother, he made the trip to Stelton to be with his children as often as he could manage. He and my mother met on an occasion when both of them were visiting their kids and he offered to drive her back to New York in his car. After that, I suppose, nature took its course. I say "I suppose" because as a child I could never imagine nature taking its course with any of my parents. I barely can even now.

For the next five years I lived in a very special world, far removed and very different from the other world out there. I remember my world as more like a mood, a quality of the spirit, a mosaic of vignettes, fairly brief, almost like snatches of dreams remembered, bright with sounds of voices and people gathered together in sunshine.

Perhaps if I browse for a while among the vignettes, the mosaic will become clearer:

...I remember learning how to draw my first star with a crayon. I was in what must have been a pre-school class being held at the Living House where my older brother had been boarding before we all came together. That was when I was still too young to attend the Modern School. I was fascinated by the stars my teacher drew on our papers to reward us for good work. I don't remember what the papers were about – probably exercises in drawing numbers and letters of the alphabet – but I was fascinated by the way she drew those colored stars so quickly and easily.

I don't think it took me very long to learn how she did them, and learning how to make stars like that myself may well rank as one of the most rewarding experiences of my life. It still gives me satisfaction to be able to draw stars quickly and well. Counting all my doodling in lectures and classes and staff meetings, I estimate I've racked up more than a hundred thousand reasonably well-formed five-pointed stars over the years. When the achievements of my life are toted up for my final weighing-in, I hope all those stars won't be overlooked. I may be needing them.

...I remember being taught with the other children at the Modern School how to build canoes using strips of wood lathe to make the skeleton and then covering it with canvas and painting it all to make it waterproof and bright. And I remember with what happiness and ferocity we all paddled our canoes in the dammed-up pond which was the school's swimming hole – playing Indians on the warpath.

...I remember a somewhat-older me type-setting by hand a poem I had written for the school magazine. My memory also has me taking my turn at a foot-operated printing press. I can see myself feeding a single sheet of paper onto a face plate that opens in front of me while two black rubber rollers swing up to roll across a green-inked round steel platter high up on the press. And then the rollers swing down pressing fresh green ink onto the type which had been set and locked into its page frame. And then the rollers rise up out of the way and the face plate closes to press the blank sheet of paper against the green-inked type. And then the face plate swings open again to reveal the marvel of my green poem on a freshly-printed page ready for plucking.

I don't remember the poem. I wish I had a copy of it now to check against my prideful feeling that it must have been pretty good. Funny, I've never thought until now to include it among the meager library of my published works. Along with my collection of five-pointed stars.

...I remember Hugo and me and Davy Freedman who lived next door digging our way to China in the grassy field alongside our house. We got down deep enough to where we could almost pull our heads below ground level before we lost interest for some reason or other. I think we were probably distracted by Alice Frumkind who lived in the house on the other side of the grassy field. Alice always came to play with us every chance she got and her mother kept calling her back home with high-pitched cries of, *Elkelleh, come here right this minute!* I don't know what her mother had against her playing with us but we never got to know Elkelleh very well. Ah, destiny. Another road not taken. It might have led to our joining Alice in wonderland. As it was, we never even got close to China.

...I remember being consumed by my first love. I suppose I was sevenish and she was my age and plump and blond and totally beautiful. At the Modern School, all us kids – I imagine there must have been thirty of us – would jump and splash and dive and swim in the dammed-up pond on hot Summer afternoons. Two of our teachers, Billie and Zack, swam with us and made sure we were safe. They wore swim suits – or at least I think they did because I would remember if they didn't, and I don't. But the rest of us were naked. And that's when I fell in love with blond, curly-haired, round faced, adorable Jerry Axelrod. In the one clear memory of her that I have, she is standing on the wooden plank of a diving board in all of her golden splendor ready to jump in. That's it. No memories of ever playing with her or talking to her. Only of her on the diving board and of me dreaming about her for the next thousand years or so.

...In my memories of the Modern School there are no grades and no classrooms. There's a large outdoor deck, large enough for a hundred people to mill around on. There's a large assembly hall for meetings and lectures and dances for grown-ups and their children. There's a library with books about children having wonderful adventures, and history books full of lithographs of warriors and the terrible agonies of ancient battles with people having their heads chopped off. There's a print shop, and a carpenter shop, and a weaving shop with looms, and other shops I can't identify. There's a large rectangular playing field out back with white goal posts where Big Jim Dick – who came all the way from England, and who, with his smiling wife, Nellie, were the school's principals – taught us how to play soccer. And, of course there's the swimming pool that was formed by damming the brook that winds its way behind the school at the bottom of a grassy tree-lined gully.

I have no memory of being taught how to read and write and do arithmetic and learning about geography. It seems as if we just absorbed all that stuff along the way, somehow, while we were playing and making things and experimenting. And being free to be children growing.

...I remember sitting with my mother on the back steps of our house in the warm sunshine. She is shelling peas... I remember lying on my back in the tall grass of the field next door and seeing heroic faces of men and rolling shapes of elephants and lions among the mounds of white cumulus clouds drifting overhead... I remember trees: the big weeping willow on the front lawn, the apple trees out back, flowering trees in spring, golden trees in autumn... I remember our grey and white cat Chauncey, and collecting and candling eggs from our flock of white chickens that lived in a clean, two-story chicken coop out back that my father Bernard built.

...I think I remember when my father Misha and his new wife Sophie and their little son Tudor – who I learned was my half-brother – came to live in Ferrer Colony. I remember more clearly walking to their house on my way home from school on some afternoons and visiting with them.

...I have memories of grown-ups arguing over how best to build a world where everyone "gave according to his ability and received according to his needs." I remember their passion, their kindness, their loving intent. I remember their reverence and respect for us children.

...And I remember my brother Lutz and me having our pictures taken for passports when it looked like one of us would be going with my father Misha and his family to live in Russia. As it turned out, Lutz went, and I got to go to New York to see all of them off on the huge ocean liner, *Majestic*. And I remember my disappointment at being left behind. That must have been in 1930.

...And I remember a year later when we drove the graveled roads of Ferrer Colony for the last time. Bernard and my mother and Evelyn and Hugo and I piled into our black sedan with our packed suitcases and boxes of belongings, and we had gone some distance down the road when my mother remembered she had left the tea-kettle sitting on the stove and I was told to run back and get it. I remember running very fast. I remember my fear that once again I might be left behind. But I wasn't, and the curtain dropped on my world as I had always known it.

Those are the vignettes. Bits and pieces of a mosaic. And what can I say of the mosaic itself? Certainly that it still persists for me, like a village scene by Brueghel hanging in some museum whose message to me is: *You are that which you see here, even though you may wish to deny me!* Theme music, sweet and melodious with few dissonances that I can still sometimes hear and occasionally dance to when my life is going right. A mosaic of another world, a *Once upon a time...* world that shaped me before turning inside out, leaving me gasping for breath in Mrs. Charbonneau's fifth grade class in Eugene Field Grammar School on Chicago's North Side.

I can see some important ways in which I've been gasping for breath ever since.

Interchapter 6+

ALTHOR: *Which one of us was the little boy who experienced living back there?*

SAM: *That was Robin.*

ALTHOR: *Why isn't he here with us now?*

SAM: *Well, there's no reason why he can't be here, if he
chooses to be. I suppose we might ask him if he'd
like to join us.*

ALTHOR: *Okay. Robin, are you there? If you are, will
you join us?*

At this point, there is an appropriate pause that is long enough
for Robin to pull himself together, as it were, and to bring himself
onto the scene. When he appears, the others see him as a little
freckle-faced redheaded boy with an overbite and an "outee" belly
button and no clothes on. Then all of a sudden he transforms into
Moishe, the old wizard who looks and sounds like George Burns.

MOISHE: *Hey you guys! Why don't you pick on somebody your own age?*

ALTHOR: *I wasn't trying to pick on Robin. I'm just curious. I'd like to get to know him.*

MOISHE: *Well, he doesn't have anything to wear so he can't come!*

> *Okay, so that's a joke. But I don't think he should come because coming here would spoil him and I don't want him to spoil. Besides, he's already here.*

ALTHOR: *What do you mean, "he's already here"? I don't see him.*

MOISHE: *Okay. So you can't see him. But every time you pet a kitty cat and melt inside a little, or turn into jello when a baby smiles at you, that's Robin.*

ALTHOR: *Oh. Alright. But I don't understand why coming here would spoil him.*

MOISHE: *Because he chose to diversify.*

ALTHOR: *WHAT?*

MOISHE: *Diversify. He chose to let go of his identity as Robin and to grow up into the rest of us. Well, mainly into Leonardo. The free spirit, the artist, the lover of life, the poet, all of that in Leonardo comes from Robin. And Robin also has grown up into me.*

ALTHOR: *Into you?*

MOISHE: *Oh yes, me, the cosmic jokester. I remember*

*the time when I – I mean when Robin – was five
years old and Lutz was teaching me to read.
He'd read a sentence from this story book about
this little boy in a forest and then he'd have me
read the sentence after him. And Lutz would read
a sentence with the word 'forest' in it, and every
time it was my turn, instead of saying 'forest' I'd
say 'woods' – because that's what I was used to
calling a whole bunch of trees. And Lutz would
point to the word 'forest' and spell out f-o-r-e-s-t
and repeat, 'forest', and I'd spell out, f-o-r-e-s-t
and repeat, 'woods'.*

    *And I remember the time I was in front of
my father Misha's house and old Hyppolite
Havel came by in his great white beard and his
great white robe and he greeted me in German
with, "Wie gehts?" which is something like,
"How ya doin, kid?" Of course, I couldn't
speak German and I couldn't speak Yiddish –
which might have led me to understand the
German – so I answered: "Which gates?"*

Moishe bursts out laughing and everybody else moans in
feigned agony. And then Sam clears his throat rather stuffily a
couple of times for attention.

    SAM: *If I may, I'd like to come back to the mosaic we
were talking about earlier. Remember, we left
Vic gasping for breath in Mrs. Charbonneau's
fifth grade class in Chicago?*

Actually, that is Sam trying to be not-all-that stuffy, after all.
But when none of the others laugh, or do anything in particular, as
if they don't realize that he is trying to lighten up a little, Sam

regresses into his normal professorial mode.

> SAM: *We've described the mosaic of our Stelton child-*
> *hood in terms of several metaphors: a painting*
> *by Brueghel; harmonious theme music; a "Once*
> *upon a time" storybook of usually happy end-*
> *ings. And all these metaphors fit. They describe*
> *Robin's life as he experienced it. What I'm*
> *seeing is that they also describe a life style that*
> *we have never completely abandoned. Whenever*
> *we've thought we recognized it happening*
> *somewhere in the world, we've been drawn to it,*
> *like homing pigeons turning homeward. That's*
> *what drew us to Synanon, and to the practice of*
> *conjoint family therapy, and to Esalen. And*
> *that's certainly what our Odyssey System is all*
> *about. We – who are Vic's family of personas –*
> *are re-creating in our relationships with each*
> *other, Robin's Utopia, where our arguments*
> *always lead to peaceful solutions, where har-*
> *mony reigns, and where everybody loves chil-*
> *dren and, most of the time, each other.*

> MOISHE: *Oy vay! Minnie, where do you keep the bi-*
> *carbonate? Sam, next time you give a speech, let*
> *me know ahead of time, so I can take a powder*
> *before instead of after.*

Chapter 7

I first met Walt Kempler at Camarillo State Hospital in the fall of 1966, a few months after I joined the hospital staff.

We had settled into our three bedroom one-story house on a long stretch of white sandy beach within a stone's throw of the Pacific Ocean. Living on the beach in Ventura was the best of all possible worlds. For all of us, as I remember it. Certainly for me. Being able to swim in the ocean, to walk or run the beach outside our door with the surf and the sea birds calling; to turn my back on civilization and feel the infinity of waves rolling in and abandoning themselves in wild matings with gleaming stretches of golden sand waiting naked beneath them and sliding exhausted back to sea, hissing softly. And all the time the southern California warmth; and the feeling that nowhere else on earth could life be as good as it is right here, right now. And always, the future looked even brighter.

I was drawn to Walt as powerfully as I have been drawn to any of my mentors across the years. I was in my mid-40's when we met, just launching on my new professional track, and actively seeking established teachers and models to help me formulate and grow my new professional persona as a psychotherapist. Lou Yablonsky might have become such a teacher for me but I limited his role to what I could draw from his book and psychodrama workshops. I saw him as a sociologist with great strengths in psychodrama and the sociology of Synanon, both of which I had great interest in but neither of which were front and center on the stage of my attention. Walt Kempler, on the other hand, was a psychiatrist with great strengths in precisely the areas of my strongest desires to grow: the practice of psychotherapy with individuals, groups and families.

I first came to know Walt at his Thursday afternoon workshops at Camarillo where he demonstrated and taught his own particular brand of family therapy.[1] What held my attention immediately was his warm and direct style of relating to the families he worked with, particularly the children. Walt loved the children and treated them with the regard and affection I myself have always felt towards them. And there was another quality that came through in his work with families that challenged me: the extent to which he shared with them his feeling responses of the moment. He seemed focused upon a clear intention to be genuinely himself.

Walt's family therapy emphasized authentic encounter as a valuable therapeutic strategy. Being authentic is risky. It means sharing honestly the feelings and perceptions that you are experiencing without regard to whether they are negative, positive, or indifferent. It means taking responsibility for knowing your own feeling responses. It means not hiding behind your therapist's mask. It means challenging the family members you're working with to be authentic with you and with each other. It means understanding, believing and trusting in the correctness of the process because your authentic responses will often trigger angry attacks from seemingly-helpless clients. But if you persist on the path of authenticity, the aroused anger of seemingly-helpless victims can break through the illusion of their helplessness and reveal their power to confront their own situations with courage and honesty.

That's the theory in a nutshell. Of course, nutshell descriptions of psychological theory are always oversimplifications that leave out much more than they include in. Usually left out is any reference to the substrate of knowledge and understanding that shapes the clinician's appreciation of the moment. Walt, for example, in his honest sharing of his feelings with his clients, understood precisely what he was doing and the theoretical and practical reasons for doing it. That is the substrate that I'm referring to as left out of the nutshell: the distilled considerations of a mind that has actively engaged in working its way through baffling complexity to clear understanding. Clear understanding must always be the therapist's Holy Grail.

It wasn't long before my own search for the Holy Grail had me commuting to Los Angeles one evening a week to the Kempler Institute on Wilshire Boulevard to attend Walt's therapy group. There were usually about eight or ten of us, a mixed group of trained therapists and not, sitting in a rectangular room with Walt at one end. My memory holds few details of names and faces and who said what to whom, but the common theme was that we were all confronting troubling issues in our personal lives. Again, authentic encounter – the honest sharing of each person's own particular *I and Thou in the here and now* – was what we were being challenged to strive for.

While the principle of authentic encounter guided us in our relationships with Walt and with each other, it also applied to our relationships with the "significant others" who populated our personal worlds. These troublesome companions of ours are often our parents, lovers, wives, husbands, friends, enemies, or therapists. And while we tend to think of them as separate from us – existing only 'out there in the real world' – they are also our fanciful characterizations dwelling in our minds. It's as if we reshape them all into players for the motion pictures we create in our inner world and project onto the mind-screen of our intra-personal drive-in theater.

In the end, we are looking at ourselves in a mirror. *I have met the enemy, and they are us,* says Pogo in Walt Kelly's comic strip. *There never was a war that was not inward,* writes poet Marianne Moore.[2] *Mirror, mirror on the wall,* says Snow White's wicked step-mother.

I don't suppose it's easy for any of us to examine closely what we see in the mirror on the wall inside our minds. It's even more difficult to reveal to anyone else *all* of what we think we know of ourselves. Fear rises up to cloud our judgment – fear of the consequences, fear of our imagined pain, our shame, our rejection, our dishonor, our banishment. So, we usually end up conning ourselves, finding ways to avoid looking too closely, to avoid sharing too much.

For reasons rooted in my own fear of imagined consequences, I have always found my own therapy to be very hard work. This has been true for me both before and since I became a professionally-trained therapist. Professional training and experience have given me tools, expertise, knowledge, language skills, awareness and a more sophisticated appreciation. Over time, these have allowed me to reduce much of my burden of fearful secrets. But I am yet to be delivered from my fear of total revelation, except on those wonderful occasions when I've transcended to a higher reality where none of my fearful concerns hold any meaning.

Deliverance from fear has always been a primary goal of my own psychotherapy. I am reminded of Althor's outburst in the Prologue: *For God's sake! An Autobiography? That's scary! And, particularly in our case, it's a very dangerous thing to do!* So long as Althor believes that to be the case, he continues to experience fear and awful anticipations. His fear incites him to a self-defensive stance in life, and to commit his personal resources to preparedness against an imagined fate worse than death. Fear urges him to withdraw, to shrink, to cripple himself in a cold war against imagined enemies.

Althor is not alone. Indeed, all psychotherapy directs much of its attention to the question: How best to deliver us from fear? Psychotherapies differ from each other in their reasoning, in their approaches and in their methods; but their basic assumption is the same: *We are usually better off without fear than with.* I say *usually* because our fears also serve valuable purposes. For example, while Althor fears the consequences of writing this book, Sam, Leonardo and Saul fear the consequences of *not* writing this book. Perhaps none of them would budge if fear were totally absent. Fear can stimulate our moving in a right direction, just as it can get in the way of our being able to move at all. How we respond to fear is a choice we have to make, but fear is a useful force. At the very least, it grabs our attention and lets us know: *There's something going on here!*

Enough of that for now. I want to shift the focus on those southern California years and pull back the camera from Walt's therapy group to a larger frame. Viewed more broadly, I saw myself as an eager member of an advancing horde of adventurers carving out new territory on the expanding frontier of a New World of Psychotherapy. It was a time of innovation and radical change in psychotherapeutic thinking; a time for feasting in any of the many accessible banquet halls of clinical knowledge and experience. I was operating on the principle: the more I eat, the more I will digest, the more I will grow.

So it was that my commuting trips to LA increased in frequency and expanded to include my own small family therapy practice and a place on the part-time staff of the Southern California Counseling Center, a non-profit agency providing affordable low-cost counseling on La Cienega Boulevard.

About the same time, Odette and I were involving ourselves in new and exciting adventures in Ventura and Santa Barbara.

And somewhere along in here I bought a brand new Datsun silver convertible that turned my commuting into fantasy trips of flying my Spitfire among the Heinkels and Messerschmitts in the skies over war-torn England. Pure fantasy, of course, but I made it somewhat real by taking flying lessons at an airfield in Oxnard and occasionally flying low over our Ventura beach home in my Cessna.

Flying is exactly the right metaphor for that time of my life. Perhaps for all of my life. I do not stay rooted in one place for very long without some vital organs within me dying. So I flew along the freeways, I flew the skies, I flew into new experiences, into new experiments in living – all the time trusting that the wings would hold and the engine would keep running.

Chapter 8

While I was pursuing excellence as a therapist along the formal paths of professional education and work experience, Odette was developing her own array of skills by following her interests and her intuition. How deeply one plunges into any experience makes for the difference between passing fancy and passionate commitment. Odette was a deep plunger. She plunged into the ocean of the written word and fell passionately in love with the poetry of May Sarton, Theodore Roethke and E.E. Cummings; the mystery novels of Dorothy Sayers and the romance novels of Georgette Heyer; books on philosophy, cybernetics, epistemology, and existentialism by Teilhard de Chardin, Martin Buber, Paul Tillich, Henry James and Gregory Bateson. She plunged into art and music and fell in love with Rudolph Klimpft, Claude Monet and Bessie Smith. She plunged into her relationships with everyone she met and, I think, fell in love with most of them. In sum, she plunged into life and made every experience significant. Including, fortunately for me, our marriage.

I learned a great deal from Odette because we shared. We shared being both teacher and student to each other. We shared what was happening to each of us as we moved along our often-separate paths. We shared our readings, our writings, our learnings. And we shared a commitment to honest communication and to working through whatever difficulties we encountered. Of course we argued and quarreled and fought a lot, but the communication was there and no argument remained superficial for long as we dug and grappled for clarity at the deepest levels of our respective understandings.

The truth is, her understandings were often deeper and better formulated than my own, perhaps because of her deeper immersion in relevant literature, perhaps because of a more vigorous intellect. As I experienced Odette, she flourished magnificently in her pursuit of Truth and Beauty. And because we shared, I flourished along with her. I chose Odette initially because I saw her as a highly intelligent, sensitive, passionate and powerful woman, and I knew I would be pressed to overcome all of my own limitations to remain in the ring with her. I don't recall a moment when I haven't seen the two of us in this way. And it is a fair assumption to say that this quality of relentless pursuit on both our parts was the engine that drove our marriage. Often for better. Sometimes for worse. Always loaded with drama. Never ordinary.

It was in our marathon weekends in Ventura, Santa Barbara and Ojai that Odette and I first began working together professionally as the husband/wife therapy team we had envisioned becoming years before.

In 1967, marathons were rapidly gaining popularity as a new form of brief pressure-cooker group psychotherapy for basically healthy adults. From ten to twenty persons, looking for relief from emotional battering of one sort or another, would sign up for a weekend marathon to be held in some pleasant environment, such as a large private home or a quiet resort hotel. When competently led, marathons were proving to be particularly effective in helping participants push their way through painful psychological barriers.

I first learned about marathon groups from two clinical psychologists I had come to know at Camarillo, William Wells and Margot Robinson. Both Bill and Margot had trained as marathon group leaders under Fred Stoller, the originator of marathon.[1] The marathon idea grew out of Stoller's experiences in a sensitivity-training laboratory in 1963 and, during the next three years, he and George R. Bach developed the form and procedures.[2] By the time I learned about marathon groups from Bill and Margot, they were conducting their own, mostly in the Los Angeles area. When they invited Odette and me to join forces with them and – after suitable training – expand operations northward to Santa Barbara, we leaped at the opportunity. The four of us adopted the name Marathon Associates, opened a business checking account, put together a brochure with a schedule of upcoming events, and sailed in.

What I remember most about marathons are the beautiful people we got to know. And, because the marathon process has a way of making all of its participants beautiful, we came to know a lot of them.

They arrive between 6 and 7 on a Friday evening, generally in pain, feeling alienated, fragmented or meaningless, and looking for relief and answers. They come singly or in pairs, carrying bags of food and belongings. The instruction sheet which they received in the mail, along with their receipt for the money they sent earlier with their filled-out registration form, advised them to bring comfortable clothing, food for the meals they will be sharing and a sleeping bag, should they choose to not sleep in the available beds in rooms set aside for each of the sexes.

Most of them are meeting us and each other for the first time. We greet them, take care of unfinished financial matters, give them name tags and directions to kitchen, bathrooms and sleeping quarters. By 7, most if not all have found their way about, have stowed their gear, and have staked claim to a sitting place in the large room in which we will be spending most of the 25 hours of scheduled group time over the next two days. Some are already getting acquainted with a person sitting next to them. Others sit silently, containing their thoughts and apprehensions, watching, waiting.

I rein in the group's scattered attention with bits of information designed to set the stage for the weekend production about to unfold: schedule of meeting times, breaks for meals, housekeeping dos and don'ts. Then, an explanation of the ground rules by which all of us will be conducting ourselves. The rules are few and simple.

"The First Rule," I say, "protects your right to privacy. Whatever you choose to share about yourself is privileged information. The First Rule is that each one of us will respect the right to privacy of all of our fellow group members. What you share in the group, stays in the group. Any questions about the First Rule?"

Questions lead to clarifications. When these are completed, I go on:

"The Second Rule is that each of you is entitled to share – or not share, if that's what you choose to do – your personal stories in your own way and without interruption. Nobody gets to play 'psychotherapist' to anyone else – no diagnosing of one another's problems, no psychological theorizing, no prescriptions, no mind games. We can listen. We can ask questions to help us understand better. We can share our own experiences. We can share our feelings.

"The Third Rule helps us do a better job of abiding by the Second Rule, and it is this: Each of us takes responsibility for our own feelings and observations by introducing them with the personal pronoun 'I'. 'I think...' 'I feel...' 'I see...' and so forth."

My introductory talk takes 10 or 15 minutes. Odette follows by leading us in an ice-breaking exercise through which we all learn something about each other and begin to let each other into our lives.

For the next five or six hours, those whose shell of resistance has worn thin enough, assume the burden of revealing their story and their pain. Usually, their words and tears are met with understanding ears and comforting hearts. Often, a story ignites another in a similar vein. In those first hours, the process is slow. The bud that is this newly-forming group uncurls itself gradually, petal by petal. By bedtime of the first evening – around midnight or later – enough of the flower is revealed to reassure the facilitators that this organism will indeed bloom and thrive and pollinate.

At Saturday morning breakfast, put together by volunteers, there is some laughter and a growing sense of family warmth and acceptance. Then it's back to the second work session where more stretched souls take the plunge and in taut voices disclose their personal agonies.

Over lunch, people are drawing together in little clumps of sharing and intimacy.

In the early afternoon, Odette leads us in a trust-building exercise known as a blind walk. You do it silently and in pairs, and you take turns. One of you puts on a blindfold and your partner leads you around to explore different places and things – flowers, fragrances, moss, cold running water, a bird's nest, some things you can't quite figure out. Blindfolded, you have to trust that your partner will take care of you, and pretty soon, it's okay. After a while, you can run together and it's okay. I remember a blind walk on a beach: it felt so good to be running blindfolded on the sand with my partner's hand in mine, and laughing, and smelling the salt air, and feeling the wind, and hearing the sounds of the waves, and letting loose of my distrust. It's all so different when you can't see.

Then, it's back to work again, and more participants share their personal agonies, and the sense of this group as safe and nurturing spreads and deepens through the late afternoon, and through the Saturday evening meal and the late-evening session that follows.

By Sunday morning, all but a few are released, and in the remaining hours, most of those will work through whatever keeps them from opening up. By 5 o'clock Sunday, the group is a close-knit joyous collection of unburdened souls, ready to face the prospect of renewed, invigorating life.

Our marathon experiences proved to be powerful and productive for most participants, but they also created problems. By the time the weekend was over, most everyone felt born anew and launched onto a whole new sea of life, as it were. There was an expectation that the future – now that they had moved beyond the limitations they had brought with them on Friday evening – would also be limitless. But their personal worlds – their work and social situations – had not transformed along with them, and by Tuesday or Wednesday, a number of them were already "coming down" or "crashing," as the new language of the time referred to it.

After our first few marathons, we became increasingly concerned that the weekends might not be altering outlooks and modifying behaviors in as enduring a way as we had hoped. It might even be that, for some participants, the net effect would be disillusionment and a breakdown of belief in a better future. So, we instituted what we called *minithons*, an optional series of 5-hour follow-up sessions held a week apart. We reasoned that in their minithons, weekend graduates could continue to support each other as they worked to integrate the lessons of their marathon experiences into their daily lives. And if they wished to continue their group beyond the minithons, they could go on together as a support group on their own. That arrangement seemed to work very well.

I said earlier that what I remember most about marathons are the beautiful people we got to know; many whose names I've forgotten, and others with names like Don and Flo and Robin and Penny and Hoddy and Margaret and Ed and Jean who came to marathon weekends concerned for their marriages and who remained in our lives for years after as enduring friends.

And one other, whose name was Mario.

Chapter 9

I can visualize Leonardo in medieval garb sounding a fanfare on a long-shafted trumpet with purple banner hanging, then striking a pose and announcing loudly to an audience:

And now, onto this crowded stage of the Golden Years, enters Fritz Perls the Wizard, and his troupe of players from the magical kingdom of Esalen de la Grande Sur.

Or something like that. And for all us loyal citizens of the human potential movement, Esalen *was* a magical kingdom. Or at least a great center of learning where a constant stream of magicians came to expand awareness and the mind of man and where, in the process, magic often happened.

Listen to Michael Murphy, writing back in 1967, about the learning center he co-founded: [1]

Esalen refuses to subscribe to any dogma – in philosophy, in psychology, or in religion – and for our seminars and encounter groups we bring in leaders from every field to contribute their own approach to the precarious condition of being human.

*A weekend seminar with B.F. Skinner, the developer of
operant conditioning, will be followed by a series of workshops with a Protestant theologian, an advocate of LSD, a
Carmelite monk, an existential psychotherapist, the president
of the American Psychological Association, an historian, an
authority on ESP, a Zen scholar, an architect, or a Hindu
mystic. Skinner, Harvey Cox, Alan Watts, Father William
McNamara, Rollo May, Abraham Maslow, Arnold Toynbee,
Gardner Murphy, Shunryu Suzuki, Buckminster Fuller, and
Hraidas Chaudhuri all have participated in the work at
Esalen. Part of the excitement at Big Sur comes from the force
of encountering the leading exponents of varied points of
view.*

Odette and I made our first trip to Esalen sometime in late 1966
or early 1967. I remember vividly the first time we walked into
Esalen's large rustic dining room and this bald-headed old man with
scraggly white beard and eyebrows was sitting at this table looking
at us and his eyes locked onto Odette's and after a long moment her
body trembled and her eyes filled with tears. He waved to us to join
him and we sat down across from him and Odette said to him in a
voice filled with emotion, *I've been waiting all my life for someone
to look at me like that!*

In the exchanges that followed, Odette confessed to never
having known her own father, and Fritz Perls, the originator and
developer of Gestalt Therapy and Esalen's resident guru, responded
with, *I'll be your father*, and a healing pact was made. Not many
days or weeks later, a deeply hurt and angry Odette told me that
Fritz had violated their newfound father-daughter relationship by
making a sexual overture of some kind. As a consequence, Odette
dismissed Fritz both as father and possible teacher. But that was not
true for me.

Fritz rocked the foundations of my being more than anyone I have known before or since. To me – particularly to the little boys still living somewhere inside of me: my own innocent playful Robin, my sad fatherless Arthur, my insecure Albert – Fritz was the fearful patriarch, the all-wise Father I secretly longed for. Just as Odette was longing. And note the deifying F in father, as in *Our Father in Heaven ...Fritz the Father*.

It's easy for me to trace the roots of my deifying fatherization of Fritz to my Stelton childhood. In my mind, Fritz *belonged* there. To my little boy Arthur, Fritz was the saintly white-bearded Hyppolite Havel he met at my father Misha's gate. And he was also Moses who had gotten the word straight from God on Mt. Sinai to give to all the members of the tribe; and for all my being a reluctant Jew, I am still a member of the tribe. At Esalen, I felt as if I knew Fritz from some misty place in my past and here he was re-emerging into my present. Not until I learned that during my Stelton years he was still in Germany was I rationally convinced that Fritz was not in my childhood. Irrationally, I have never been convinced.

While my little children alternately basked and trembled before *Papa Fritz,* my adult personas – Sam in particular – were soaking up all the Gestalt Therapy they could from *Teacher Fritz.* And Fritz was a powerful teacher. There were evening demonstrations of Fritz working his magic on anyone with the courage to volunteer for a turn on Gestalt Therapy's unique piece of furniture, the *Hot Seat.* There were 3-day and 5-day workshops to attend and, between sessions, Fritz could often be found hunched over a chessboard, or somewhere on the grounds, or in the hot tubs. In the absence of any of the above, he was always available between the covers of his books.[2] For a span of about three years, I trod all of these learning pathways as often as I could manage.

Briefly put, Gestalt Therapy is a mechanism for transcending whatever horns of the particular dilemma one happens to be caught upon. *Gestalt* is a German word that means *an organized configuration or pattern.* When we resolve a dilemma, we bring closure to an unfinished situation – an incomplete *gestalt* – by forming a new understanding in which old "facts" are rearranged in a whole new configuration. All of our problems are unfinished situations – incomplete *gestalten* – which are capable of being resolved by the formation of whole new understandings.

We all know what it feels like when an unfinished gestalt is completed and a new understanding happens. If it's a big one, the experience of completion can be quite blinding. Suddenly everything is seen in a new light, through new eyes. When Archimedes suddenly understood the principle that explained why his soap was floating in his bathtub, he had just completed a new gestalt that led to his immortal exclamation: *Eureka! I've found it!* History records countless such transformative moments.

In Gestalt Therapy we work through our unfinished business by arguing with ourselves out loud. The arguments inside our heads are brought out of the closet in the form of opposing sides who set about thrashing out their differences. Fritz's names for these internal adversaries of ours are *Topdog* and *Underdog.* Generally, *Underdog* gets to sit in the *Hot Seat,* a three-legged milkmaid's stool, while *Topdog* occupies a chair next to Fritz. Under Fritz's direction, you move back and forth between chair and hot seat as *Topdog* and *Underdog* talk, yell, scream, badger or plead with one another. What usually occurs is that *Topdog* and *Underdog* are unable to resolve their differences *at that level of thinking;* they reach what Fritz calls *an impasse.* It is at the point of impasse that a breakthrough becomes possible, leading to new awareness. The old situation, the unfinished gestalt, gives way to new understandings and fulfilling feelings of self-satisfaction at a job well done, and, before long, the next batch of unfinished business readies itself to seek out the spotlight of your attention.

Let me draw your attention to the obvious similarity between the two-chair *Topdog-Underdog* structure in Fritz's Gestalt Therapy, and the multi-chair, multi-persona structure in the Odyssey System. What I did, some years later, was to take Fritz's structure and adapt it by adding chairs and opening up the dialoguing process to include as many personas as needed. I will be saying more about this later. Back there at Esalen, I could see the outlines of this potential application of Gestalt Therapy and it sharpened my fascination with Fritz's therapeutic style and technique and intensified my emotional bonding to him.

During 1967, Odette and I attended several weekend workshops at Esalen together and Mike Murphy's creation quickly became a magnet that drew us into its warm spiritual heart. I have clear memories of a workshop in sensory awakening led by Bernie Gunther and a workshop for couples led by Gerry and Sally Smith; of daytime hours of sharing and learning, and of long evening hours of deep relaxation and sometimes probing, sometimes languorous conversations in Esalen's famed sulfurous hot tubs, above the cold cobalt waters beneath the stars, where mixed bathing and nudity were a preferred option for most of us. Among my clear memories are a host of tender, joyous scenes and warm-hued, fresh, discovering moments.

Esalen was – still is, of course – a 250-mile drive up the coast from Ventura, a drive that took us northward on Highway 101 to Santa Maria and San Luis Obispo and then onto two-lane Highway 1 to Morro Bay, on past Hearst's Castle, then winding beside the rocky shoreline to the Big Sur country. It took us about seven hours in our 1966 green and white Volkswagen van and we'd usually stop in Santa Maria for lunch.

There came an occasion in the fall of '67, on our way home from Esalen, when we stopped in Morro Bay and spent an afternoon visiting with Mario, whom we had come to know in one of our Santa Barbara marathon weekends. Mario lived in an A-frame house that was clean, tasteful and simple. Odette fell in love with it. So stopping at Mario's instead of Santa Maria became a pleasant habit. And not much later, there were occasions when I would come home to our beach house from Camarillo, or Los Angeles, or my flying lessons in Oxnard, and Odette and Mario would be lying or sitting on the sand together, talking intensely or reading. So far as I knew, there was not much other than the growing friendship that the three of us shared.

Sometime early in '68, Odette expressed an interest in attending a 5-day training workshop at Esalen in sensory awakening to which Mario would also be going. I would not be able to go because of work commitments. So the three of us agreed that Odette would fly up to San Luis Obispo on Sunday morning, Mario would drive the two of them to Esalen on Sunday afternoon for the workshop, and I would meet them at Mario's house on the following Friday evening after the workshop ended . And that's what happened.

It was understood that they would be sleeping in separate quarters and I kept under wraps whatever concerns and fantasies I may have had. Until Thursday evening. During the first four days of their workshop, I focused on work and my parental responsibilities. Then on Thursday evening, I went to see the film *Camelot* and my world exploded and crumbled before my eyes. In a blinding flash I saw myself and Odette and Mario up there on the screen as Arthur, Guinevere and Lancelot. The irresistible forces that were compelling this mythical triad in their fateful intertwining dance were also compelling the three of us. I *knew* – in my bones, without the slightest doubt – that Mario and Odette were in love and were sexually involved. Or as Fritz would say in his uncompromising directness: *They were fucking!*

I can hear Fritz saying straightforwardly, without any particular emotion: *"Fucking* is an activity. It's what's happening. You think of it as great or awful or healthy or sick, but it's all *fucking."* I am still not completely comfortable using the word that way; I am more comfortable using it as an expletive in anger. But what I was experiencing back there in the theater, and all the time I was driving north to Mario's house, and while I was wandering aimlessly through Mario's house waiting for them to return, was not recognizable to me as anger, but as apprehension. And deep shock. And anguish. And as an overwhelming need to know.

You've been sleeping together, haven't you?

They were still coming through the door when I confronted them. And, still standing in the entry way, Mario looked at Odette and Odette took a long moment before replying:

Yes. ... And if you'll wait until we get inside, we'll explain how it happened.

So I listened and asked questions as they explained how the reservations person had mistakenly put them in the same room. And how Mario had wanted to be reassigned to a different room. And how Odette reassured him it would be okay to share the room and respect each other's privacy. And how appropriate Mario was being. And how drawn to Mario she was. And how she couldn't sleep. And how by Wednesday she couldn't stand it any more and confessed her need to him. And how he resisted. For a while. And how much she loved Mario. And how much she still loved me.

And the three of us spent the night sharing our anguish and our concerns. And exploring our options.

Interchapter 9+

HAWK: *Cuckold! Why didn't you bust Mario in the jaw, grab Odette by the hair and drag her home where she belonged? And why didn't you confront Fritz and give him hell for making a pass at your wife? What the hell was wrong with you?*

SAM: *Hawk! Where did you come from?*

HAWK: *Never mind that. Just answer my question!*

SAM: *Well, it's just not my way of dealing with situations like that. Why didn't you? You're our military type, our George Patton. You're the one who should have been able to pull off that kind of macho response.*

HAWK: *Maybe. But I wasn't there. I retired at the end of World War II. We're talking here about the sixties and you were all espousing Down with War and Violence, and Up with Love and Peace, and Let's Hear It for Sexual Freedom. None of you had the guts to react with violent outrage when you got kicked in the balls. If I had been there, I would have beat the shit out of these guys who fucked with my woman.*

SAM: *Bullshit, Hawk! That's just a copout. You were there. We know who was flying the Los Angeles freeways in his silver Datsun Spitfire shooting down Messerschmitt 109s. Maybe you're only a fantasy warrior, a Don Quixote. My guess is, you just weren't strong enough to take over. I think your head got in the way of your gut and you came to the conclusion that this wasn't a battle you wanted to fight.*

HAWK: *Alright smart ass! So now that you've explained my response, how about explaining your own.*

LAURA: *IF YOU BOYS WILL SHUT UP FOR A MINUTE, I'D LIKE TO PUT MY TWO CENTS IN!*

That's better.

Now. While both of you were being concerned about your manhood, whatever that is, I was finding love. In everyone and in everything. For me, all of our relationships with all the people we came to know in Camarillo and Santa Barbara and Esalen and everywhere else were love affairs. I felt a lot of loving from everyone I met, and I felt myself loving back. And that's true of my relationships with Fritz and Mario. And, most of all, it's true of my relationships with Odette and with our kids.

Now, I know you regard me as rather passive in a languorous and sexy kind of way, and I can be that, and I can get a lot of pleasure out of being languorous and sexy. But I also know what's good for me and what isn't. And if I have to, I can fight like hell to protect what's good for me. And having you boys get into pissing matches with Mario and Fritz over who gets to win Odette was definitely not in my interests. If it was at all possible, I wanted all of our needs to be met and our differences to be resolved in ways that drew us together, not tore us apart.

If at all possible.

I believed it was possible.

I believed it could happen.

I needed to give Love a chance.

So I did.

Chapter 10

I have difficulty getting into who we were being in the 60's with my 90's consciousness. My 90's mind has a tendency to view who we were being somewhat critically, almost with a sense of shame, as if we were guilty of having committed gross sins. My 60's mind got somewhat brainwashed in the reactionary waves of the 70's and 80's and is still in process of recovering. It is more nearly correct to say that back there in the 60's we were all being essentially courageous, wholesome adventurers who were rejecting the conforming respectability and boredom of the 50's, exploring fresh frontiers, experimenting with new life styles, spurred on by a more forgiving humanistic idealism and a psychedelic revolution in consciousness.

So it was that Odette and Mario and I rejected a more orthodox Draconian solution to the problem of, *Now what do we do?* and agreed to explore alternatives to traditional marriage. As a first step, we agreed to loosen the constraints of monogamy and accept intimate relationships with selected others. We would not regard Odette's and Mario's relationship as a clandestine affair; we would legitimize it in our restructured marriage and would do our best to integrate it into our lives.

Early in '68, Odette began spending three days a week with

Mario in Morro Bay. And I became sexually impotent with Odette. And I began a search for new partners, partly in hopes that my persistent flacidity was not generalizable to the entire population of available women. I make a joke. Of course, I did not experience it as funny.

For a time, we seriously considered the possibility of group marriage. We read books, like *The Harrad Experiment* by Robert Rimmer, which purported to be an account of a group marriage of three heterosexual couples.[1] We attended a Rimmer workshop at Esalen and looked more closely at the possibilities of a *ménage a six*. We talked to potential partners. I went so far as to invite a dear friend, for whom I also felt a strong sexual attraction, to join us. She, wisely I'm sure, declined.

Let me take a step back and examine the canvas before I splash more lurid colors and shapes onto this almost frenzied painting.

As we moved forward into 1968, it was becoming more and more clear to Odette and to me that our marriage, probably our life together, was coming undone and that we were scrambling to find the best possible paths forward. I'm sure we loved each other. I'm sure we both hoped to save our marriage. I'm not sure either of us believed we could. Nor am I sure of the extent to which we were responding to the pulls and uncertainties of our mid-life crises – I was now 47 and Odette, 36 – and *Seven Year Itch*-iness for which our marriage statistically qualified.

Still looking at the canvas several steps removed, I can see that by early '68 some of the burdens of our marriage were overwhelming Odette, and that falling in love with Mario was her relief valve, perhaps her escape. I, on the other hand, was so caught up in my pursuit of dreams of professional excellence and glory that I wasn't home very much; literally and figuratively.

One of the heavier burdens that Odette and I never dealt with successfully, in spite of our highly developed communication skills, was the one of financial responsibility: Who's responsible for bringing in the paychecks? Who's responsible for paying the bills on time? Who's responsible for balancing the budget? We were clear enough on the question of, Who brings in the paychecks? That was my responsibility. But beyond that, things got fuzzy, and money was always a concern that neither of us dealt with at all well. Nor did our money problems surface in all the sharing and self-disclosing that we practiced in our work with other couples.

So over the seven years of our marriage, the burden of unsolved financial problems grew heavier for Odette. Not for me, so much. *Not* dealing with finances reinforced my addiction to the belief that the problems didn't really exist. Or, if they did and I didn't pay too much attention to them, they would go away. And suddenly, in the spring of '68, they did. Or there was the illusion that they would. Odette came into an inheritance.

By then, I was only a few months away from completing my two years at Camarillo State Hospital and I was looking forward to new professional horizons with my hard-earned ACSW journeyman's credentials in hand. I had no clear future planned or visible. The old commitments to job and marriage were all coming apart. Nothing was holding together for very long. And the disintegration was happening within our family, as well. Dennis was about to graduate from high school and go off on his own. Dean and Ian wanted to finish high school in Ventura, while Odette and I had no clear idea of where we would be in September.

All of the ingredients for an explosion were coming together. Perhaps in hope we would all land safely on the other side, Odette decided to use her inheritance to make the explosion as grand and glorious as possible.

So we developed a plan and put it into operation. I say *we* with some qualification. It was Odette's, not *our*, inheritance and there was never a question of who controlled its fate. Odette put the money into her own bank account, wrote the checks, monitored the expenditures, and so forth. Still, I was involved in the decision-making process and I most certainly participated in enjoying the benefits.

So we paid off all our debts, thinned out our belongings, and made arrangements to store what was left.

Dean and Ian would be spending part of the summer with their father, Owen, and after long talks with everyone involved, we made arrangements for the two of them to live in an apartment of their own in Ventura so they wouldn't have to switch high schools in the fall.

Teddie would come with us.

We were pulling up stakes with no plans for what lay beyond other than to clear the deck for a fresh start along new paths that were not yet clearly visible to us. To help bring the new paths into focus, we would spend the summer, or a big part of it, at Esalen.

Interchapter 10+

HAWK: *"not yet clearly visible,"* my ass! *It must have been clearly visible! How could you not see that you were dismantling your marriage and setting it up for Odette to switch husbands?*

SAM: *Well, you're right Hawk. We could see that. But by then it felt inevitable and that the only option to which Odette and I could agree was to play it out in style.*

HAWK: *Really? I bet Odette had plans! She and Teddie would be living in that little dream house in Morro Bay with Mario, and you would be out on your ass because you didn't have the balls to stand up and fight for your marriage.*

SAM: *C'mon Hawk, it takes two to make a marriage work.*

HAWK: *Yeh. And it takes two to make a marriage not work. How come you didn't put up more of a fight against it's not working?*

SAM: *I don't know. Odette and I had a special kind of relationship. We both really believed that adults need the*

*freedom to make their own choices, and that certainly
includes with whom they choose to live their lives. I
still believe it.*

LEONARDO: *"He who chooses, chooses what is given." I
remember Odette quoting that line from a poem; by
Theodore Roethke, I think.* [1] *If I understand the
point of that line, it's that you can only choose from
among the possibilities that are presented to you.
What you're implying, Hawk, is that by not putting
up a fight, we were withdrawing ourselves from the
marriage and that left Odette without the option of
continuing to choose us. And if she saw Mario as a
choice, that left us out and Mario in.*

LAURA: *Boys, boys, you're being much too logical again.
What was happening was the playing out of affairs
of the heart. You're forgetting that Odette and I –
and I mean me, Laura – are intensely romantic
when we're turned loose. You're forgetting the
tradition of romance that helped make our marriage enriching and fulfilling. We just hit a place
where that was drying up. And Mario, and the hot
baths at Esalen, and all the little adventures into
group marriage or whatever, were our ways of
trying to revive the romance that had always been
central to our relationship, the glue that held it together.*

*We were being pulled by the drama of it all. The
play's the thing! You play your part and you do it as
well and as truthfully as you can. What else matters? Really. And in that sense, Leonardo, we were
choosing what was given to us to choose.*

I love my personas. They do such a good job of making sure I don't fall into the trap of examining all this personal history from a state of singlemindedness. Each of them sees truth through their own eyes. Together they give me a multi-lensed advantage. My overall vision may still not be entirely clear but it brings me closer to a truth I can comfortably share with you. A truth I can live with.

SAM: *On behalf of all of us personas, thank you very much. But there is another important element that is still being left out of the picture of our spring of '68. We mentioned that I would be leaving Camarillo State Hospital and that we would be spending a big part of the summer at Esalen. We haven't mentioned the linkage between those two events. That linkage was very important to me, Sam – the professional, the psychotherapist.*

LEONARDO: *Yes. You're right, Sam. The linkage is that Esalen would be offering a five-week series of workshops and seminars on the theme,*

THE VALUE OF THE PSYCHOTIC EXPERIENCE

Led by an All-Star Cast of Presenters

Featuring the Brightest Star

on the Leading Edge of the Psychiatric Firmament

the One and Only

RONALD LAING!

SAM: *Dammit man! Stop hamming it up! This is important stuff!*

LEONARDO: *Okay, then, you tell it.*

SAM: *Okay. Well. ...Let me see. Okay. Here goes:*

> By then, I had been working for three years – count-
> ing my practicum year at Western State Hospital –
> with hospitalized patients diagnosed with one form or
> another of psychotic disorder. I had become very
> familiar with the medical establishment's view of
> psychotic behavior, which, generally, was to label it
> "sick" and attempt to reduce the symptoms as quickly
> as possible so the patient could be returned to some
> level of "normal functioning." The standard means
> for getting rid of "craziness" was to tranquilize the
> patient into a deadening stupor by the application of
> anti-psychotic medication. If medication failed to
> achieve the desired result, there were other proce-
> dures to be considered, such as electro-convulsive
> shock therapy (an oxymoron, if I ever heard one).

> In three years of working with the hospitalized
> mentally ill, I had formed opinions critical of the
> established medical approach to psychotic behavior.
> So, obviously, had Ron Laing and those others who
> would be holding seminars and leading workshops at
> Esalen. Here were psychiatrists and others who would
> be exploring positive aspects of the psychotic experi-
> ence. I was ready for that. I had learned much of what
> state hospitals had to teach me about the nature and
> treatment of severe mental illness. Now, I was ready to
> expand the frontiers of my own understanding. I was
> ready for the next step.

> It turned out to be more than a step. It turned out to
> be a cosmic leap.

Chapter 11

I can see the Esalen Summer of '68 as if it were a full head of hair that left alone tangles in a random web or blows luxuriantly in the wind. Combed and organized it presents an arranged look designed for comfort, or to please, or to selectively mask and reveal the native experience. The native experience of the Esalen Summer proceeded with an order of its own; it wasn't all random chaos. And in retrospect, I am drawn to seeing all of the experiences of that summer of '68 as woven together – a combing and dividing and braiding together of three plaits of hair.

In one plait are gathered all the organized learnings: the month-long program of workshops and experiences exploring new paradigms for understanding altered states of consciousness. Here were the times for drinking from fresh pools of knowledge about positive transformations to be found in psychosis, acid trips, shamanistic rituals and religious awakenings. Here were gathered the psychiatric revolutionaries who were challenging orthodoxy and redesigning how we ought to be thinking about losing our minds.

In a second plait are gathered my personal journeys into the labyrinths of my mind brought about by my own curiosity and my seeking after deeper truths.

And in the third plait is the continuing story of Odette and me and Mario and our interwoven strivings, longings, fears and conflicts – all of which you may regard as foolhardy, vain, courageous, out of control, or typical of the times, depending upon inclination and the phase of the moon.

Because all three plaits go a long way toward explaining much of what has manifested in my life since the summer of '68, I have decided to treat each plait more or less separately, in the order presented above.

However, some of my personas are not in agreement.

LEONARDO: *I'm not happy with leading off with plait #1, the story of the workshops. We've got an awful lot of material there. I imagine it may be attractive to therapists and other folks who are comfortable with psychiatric-type stuff, but I think we're going to lose a lot of folks here. I can see a lot of readers losing interest, or maybe not understanding the technical stuff and dropping off like flies.*

SAM: *Well maybe we can present it in a way that will allow readers to pick out what interests them and hop over what doesn't. I feel very strongly that we have to include the material that's relevant to the issues we're concerned with. We've got about 50 or 60 hours of audio tapes that we recorded during those workshops and seminars. That's a lot. It would take seven or eight working days of uninterrupted listening just to hear them all.*

There's a lot of solid information here. We

*were on the threshold of revolutionalizing our
culture's understanding of mental health and
mental illness. Psychiatric breakthroughs were
happening right and left. These tapes record some
of our leading visionaries who were exploring
new possibilities for psychotherapy's tomorrow.
What makes it doubly important is that we are
now living in their tomorrow. I, for one, don't
believe our nation's mental health institutions
have paid proper attention during the past 23
years. I think they've turned a deaf ear. And I
think the people have a right to know.*

LEONARDO: *Goddam, Sam, you sure pontificate when
you get the chance.*

> *So you have an axe to grind. You think the
> mental health establishment has turned its back
> on the psychiatric revolution of the sixties and you
> have an obligation to rally 'round the old flag.
> Well, I'm more interested in holding to the pur-
> pose of this book. This book is our story; and I'm
> not sure that a chapter full of other people's
> quotes has a proper place in it.*

SAM: *Well let me put it to you in another light:*

> *All of the "other people's quotes" that I've
> selected for inclusion here are also expressive of
> my own belief system. I identify strongly with their
> words, because they articulate the matrix that was
> shaping me. The therapist that I have become over
> the years still holds to the values and beliefs
> encoded in their words. In that sense, their voices,
> as presented in these pages, are extensions of my*

own. They are autobiographical. Well, quasi-
autobiographical.

LEONARDO: *Okay, Sam. You win this round. I'm*
willing to give it a try. But I warn you, if it's not
working, I'm going to blow the whistle.

It's a fair and mild late Friday afternoon and you have just driven down from San Francisco to Esalen. You have been looking forward to participating in this month-long series of workshops, *The Value of the Psychotic Experience.* Other commitments kept you from attending earlier sessions, but now you have been able to get away for this one, the third weekend seminar.

You've parked your car in the lot overlooking Esalen's rustic buildings and the blue Pacific, walked downhill to the office, confirmed your room arrangements, checked out the dining room, and made your way to the cabin you'll be sharing with one or two other friendly people, just like you.

Now, you are finding your way to the meeting room where the workshop for which you've registered will be getting off the ground. Below you, the ocean is shifting from blues to greys and sweeping gentle waves shoreward. You can hear their muffled encounters with the rocks at the base of the cliffs that are defending this rustic resort from the sea. Warmth and anticipation unfold within you.

You find the redwood meeting room and take a seat among some fifty other friendlies, many of whom are bubbling with their neighbors. You introduce yourself to the dark eyed, raven-haired woman sitting on your right and her words of response, "Hi, I'm Greta," are joined in your awareness with those coming from the front of the room where a slender athletic-looking man of medium height, probably in his early forties, is making introductory announcements:

> *...the baths on the men's side are reserved for this group from 11 to 1, both tonight and tomorrow night.*
>
> *If in the midst of all this activity, you have time, there'll be massage available for which you can sign up in the office. And, it's not exactly the ordinary run-of-the-mill massage kind of experience. So, I recommend it.*
>
> *Gia-Fu Feng will be doing Tai Chi Chuan on the deck by the pool at 9:15 tomorrow morning. It's a form of meditation in action.*
>
> *The meeting tomorrow morning here will be at 10:00. That's all of the mundane business and these gentlemen will take you on the rest of this journey.*
>
> *I introduce to you, Julian Silverman, our coordinator and master of ceremonies for this series of workshops.*

Suddenly, Leonardo interrupts the flow of words with the blast of a shrill whistle and the personas are back to arguing the direction this chapter is to take.

LEONARDO: *Hold it, Sam! I'm seeing another ten thousands words of quoting these guys and I don't think most of our readers are going to stay awake for all that psychobabble.*

> *Now, I want to hear what the rest of us have to say about this. Let's get some consensus on what*

*we're going to do with this chapter. Let's start
with you, Laura, and then continue on around.
Where are you on this issue?*

LAURA: *Well, speechifying bores me. I guess I'm not all
that interested in listening to these guys pontificate. Sam, I really don't care about the technical
stuff – all those words that begin with psycho:
psycho-this and psycho-that. I want to hear more
about people and where they are in their relationships. I want to get on with the love interest.*

MINNIE: *I agree with you, Laura, but I'm also interested
in striking the right balance. Elements need to be
in right balance with each other if this book is to
represent us fairly. Unfortunately, my sense of
what's balanced isn't reliable when it comes to all
that psycho-stuff. Maybe Sam has more that ought
to be said to provide the right balance.*

LEONARDO: *Minnie, what Sam has, in all those long
monologues by the workshop presenters, are their
truths. Sam wants to use them to try to
communicate our belief system to the reader. He's
having them parade their thoughts and words
before the readers and claiming them as our own.*

*It feels to me like an attempt to evade the hard
job of speaking for ourselves. I don't like the feel
of it. I'm not sure it's honest. And I don't think our
readers are going to buy it.*

ALTHOR: *I'm confused. I think that you, Sam, are thinking there are some real important points that you
want to make but I'm not sure what they are. Is*

that so? And can you say what they are?

SAM: *Yes, I think I can.*

In the first place, I think it's important to clarify – for ourselves and for our readers – the network of beliefs that have been directing and shaping our lives. Back there in the summer of '68, when we were relative newcomers in professional mental health circles, our belief systems were in the throes of being reshaped and refined by all of our experiences.

It happens that the people at the seminars – Silverman, Perry, Naranjo, Grof, etc. – did a wonderfully articulate job of spelling out their perceptions and beliefs, particularly with regard to the whole mental health scene.

It also happens that there was a remarkable fit between most of what they had to say and my own perceptions and beliefs, at least to the extent that I had formulated them at that time.

As a consequence, the workshop facilitators were extending my own beliefs in directions they were already prepared and predisposed to go.

I can agree that most of our readers may fall asleep over long quotations that are of little interest to them. On the other hand, there are going to be some readers who will be interested in hearing what these representatives of psychiatry's cutting edge were saying back then.

*So, I propose that we put the transcript of
their conversation in the Appendix. Those who are
interested can turn to it. Those who aren't, won't.*

*Now: I also agree with you Leonardo that we
need to be speaking for ourselves and not letting
others speak for us. And the best way I can think of
to do that is to point out some of the important
connections between what was being said in those
workshops of '68 and our own subsequent elaboration of the Odyssey System. And, without further
ado, that's exactly what I'm going to do.*

LEONARDO: *Hold it! What about a vote? What about
decision by negotiation and consensus?*

SAM: *Later, Leo. I'll write it first and we can agree later.*

On Individual Differences...

<u>JULIAN SILVERMAN in '68</u>:

*There is no such thing as schizophrenia; there are
kinds of madness. We can describe the kinds of madness
only when we understand what individual differences are
all about, and how they can be conceptualized in a substantive way. Otherwise, we keep on getting involved in all of
our garbage of "my thing is as good as your thing" or
whatever.*

*There's been no adequate conceptualization until now
of the nature of an individual difference between normal
people and psychotics. One of our programs is to describe
as adequately as possible the nature of individual differ-*

ences. Once one accepts that one lives in a different space
than an other, one does not put one's own thing on another
as easily. One respects much more the nature of difference.
...We really do have separate and distinct ways of experi-
encing ourselves and each other.

SAM in '91:

The Odyssey System conceptualizes individual differences in a substantive way by invoking each individual's
operational array of personas. Odyssey's practice of *Multi-*
loguing empowers one's array of operating personas with
voice and legitimacy, with self-awareness, and with shared
responsibility for the welfare of the human organism in
which each of them plays an important part. Multiloguing
provides the expressive tools through which personas learn
about themselves and each other, and about their potentials
for growth and change. In multiloguing they practice self-
expression and mutual respect and caring. And, they learn
how to negotiate their disagreements and work out solutions that are acceptable to all of them. In short, they learn
how to work together to channelize their shared organism's
behavior in the world through a sharing of, rather than a
wielding of, power.

With regard to individual differences of which Silverman speaks: the more clearly the range and depth of an individual's aspects are revealed through the elaboration of
his personas, the more individual differences can be noted
and catalogued, assuming one wishes to do so. In my own
experience, no two individuals have ever generated identical arrays of personas, which leads me to conclude that
persona arrays are highly individualized, like fingerprints.
Toeprints, too, I guess.

I'm getting off on a little mind game here which goes something like this:

Assume that you and I each have 20 personas with whom we can establish a working relationship. Assume, also, that each of our 20 personas can be represented by one of our fingerprints and/or toeprints. Each of yours is different from each other, as is each of mine, as are all of ours. That's 40 identifiable patterns of difference between the two of us. If there are five of us – as in the average nuclear family – we've got 100 identifiable patterns of behavior. Thinking like that can lead us to one huge number of recognizable individual differences in a hurry. And what I find so exciting about the Odyssey System is that *all of these individual differences are workable with.* We're not just talking *theory* here; we're talking *usefulness.*

On Opening up to Wholeness...

JOHN PERRY in '68:

> *Analytic or therapeutic progress, in essence, is one's opening up to one's unrealized and unrecognized aspects of oneself and getting out of the blindness of the ego which needs to defend itself against all of them.*

SAM in '91:

Odyssey's *raison d'etre* is the opening up to as many of the unrealized and unrecognized aspects of oneself as one is able to manage at any particular point in one's movement toward wholeness.

Odyssey's process of Multiloguing draws one inevitably into discovering and clarifying aspects of self that are more readily accessible to consciousness. Usually, these previously hidden aspects arrive as new personas. This can happen either entirely on one's own initiative or with the gentle guidance of a non-assaultive facilitator.

Odyssey's *Journeying* process, on the other hand, provides a means for exploring the deeper labyrinths of the unconscious. In Journeying, one enters a self-induced trance state and goes on an inner journey with one's own working cast of personas. The journey's progress is chronicled by a *spokes-persona* whose task it is to narrate the events of the journey as they occur. In this way, a team of one's own personas ventures in the realm of personal myth and metaphor and returns with treasures of information that can prove useful in the organism's pursuit of wholeness.

JOHN PERRY in '68:

Another aspect about wholeness: As one opens to the other possibilities within, one at the same time is opening one's receptivity to those things outside and in other people. The negative side is that if we are closed to these things within ourselves, we are closed to these things on the outside and in other people.

SAM in '91:

I couldn't agree more. An assumption made by the Odyssey System is that each person's perception and understanding of external reality mirrors his or her inner reality.

I dislike you because I see you as a reflection of an aspect of me for which I have grown a distaste, not because I see you as you know yourself to be.

If you mirror hidden aspects of me that I secretly long to incorporate into my being, I'll probably fall head over heels in love with you. Or, more accurately, my *idea* of you. You are, after all, just an incidental vision of mine through which I am achieving a pleasurable ecstasy.

If, on the other hand, you mirror many aspects of my own for which I have developed significant degrees of acceptance, fondness and respect, then I am likely to love you in ways that honor us both. If we both do our jobs well, our respective perceptions of each other may even come close to approximating our respective understandings of who we experience ourselves to be.

WILSON VAN DUSEN in '68:

The degree of freedom varies in a system. Where you have something that is unconscious, it's an interference and the degree of freedom is less. Where it becomes conscious, the degree of freedom is greater. Wholeness means greater freedom to choose and to interact.

SAM in '91:

I like Van Dusen's operational definition of wholeness.

In Van Dusen's terms, the various processes that are the Odyssey System all focus on maximizing the degree of freedom with which the systems – that are each of us – operate and interact with our worlds. Odyssey generates greater freedom to choose by opening up a wider range of options, by increasing the clarity with which the options are perceived, by working through the internal ambivalences that frustrate one's power to choose among them, and by enlisting more of one's total awareness and resources toward the successful pursuit of chosen outcomes.

JOHN PERRY in '68:

I think this is why we need each other: One ego can't contain so many paradoxes and so many opposites. It's as if you cannot have a complete experience in consciousness with all the contrasting outlooks, and contrasting ways of orienting. And so, we come into contact with other people with different points of view. And then, the wholeness seems to be as much a matter of what goes on between us and others, as it is a matter of what goes on between us and ourselves.

SAM in '91:

True enough. Still, by articulating our individual arrays of personas, we can expand our ego's ability to contain and manage paradox way beyond what we might otherwise do. An expanded versatility with the world of paradox and opposites certainly can never do away with our need for relationship and interdependence. But it can raise the level at which we interact and relate enormously.

On A Medical Illness Model v. A Problem-Solving Model...

JULIAN SILVERMAN in '68:

The notion of disease is a very interesting notion. Sickness – mental illness – is a metaphor, like all other metaphors. Like bravery.

Do you know what bravery is? I can describe bravery to you. I can tell you about the guy who goes out and fights the lion, or he goes and stands in front of a tank and he has a grenade, and he does a lot of things. Okay? Now we can summarize these behaviors. And we can say "this is a brave man". But "bravery" is <u>not</u> what he <u>did</u>.

And being "mentally ill" is <u>not</u> what a guy <u>does</u>. A guy might be saying funny things; he might be posturing in a funny way; he might be hallucinating, whatever that is. He might be having certain kinds of notions about what's going on around him that are different from the ordinary, whatever they are.

The notion of mental illness is a selling of a particular way of dealing with people who don't conform to the expectations of the community ethics. "They're 'funny' – and we've got to keep them under control."

And so, somehow or other in ages gone by, people got together and decided that, since the mind is where it's supposed to be at, and people are "ill" in that the memory is impaired, or the thinking process is impaired, so let's call them "ill". And we'll put 'em in bins. And we'll have certain people control them. And who are the people to control them? Well, it used to be the priests, and we used to have inquisitions. Now we have other priests, and they wear white coats, and they say who's sick and who's not.

But the metaphor "mental illness" doesn't tell you: "It's <u>as if</u> he is ill." "It's <u>as if</u> the mind is ill." It says: <u>"That guy is sick!"</u>

Where is the sickness? Ahh! We've been looking for it! We've been looking for it in the biochemistry. Can't find it.

We find funny things, you know, like a famous neuro-
psychiatrist said, "For every twisted thought there's a
twisted molecule." But so far, not so good.

What I'm trying to do here is to sell you a whole batch
of little funny tidbits, an argument which goes against pre-
vailing notions of mental illness; prevailing notions of the
debilitating, destructive value of the psychotic experience.

The psychedelic movement – the schizophrenia-type
doctors who have gone into and worked with psychotic
episodes – tell a different story. And that story has to do
with the notion of inner space versus outer space. Which is
a very non-scientific kind of a statement to make because in
science you can't talk about "inner," since "inner" is not
observable and testable and, therefore, not "science."

...I've been trying to present the little tidbits that say
"No" to the existing format and suggest that we have to get
out of the conventional psychiatric stance into a different
way of experiencing madness.

We're going to drop the illness model here, and we're
going to start talking about a problem-solving model.

There are certain kinds of notions each of us has
about where to go in the culture. You learn about that from
momma and poppa, and the school, and people on your
job, and your elders. They tell you how to answer the basic
questions of your existence, and what you define yourself
as. So those are the things that tell you you're cool.

But you're not cool. You're a drag. You can't function
properly. You're not a good mate. You're not a good
provider. You don't do the things that are basic expecta-

tions of you in relation to your community.

What do you do now? Well, I gotta have something!
I'm not nothing!

The answer is that you problem-solve. There is an
automatic, built-into-the-nervous-system type of process for
getting answers to these insoluble questions. And they
involve going into a different psychological space.

<u>SAM in '91:</u>

Ah, Julian, I love you!

As I have been pointing out, going into a different
psychological space and problem solving is what Odyssey
is all about. It works with – as you say, Julian – our *auto-*
matic, built-into-the-nervous-system type of process for get-
ting answers to these insoluble questions. That explains, I
believe, why most folks find the Odyssey system so easy to
get into. We all recognize our various aspects, our personas, unless we are so rigidly defended against them that we
see them as dangerous demons who must not be let out of
the closet in which we imprison them. And our personas
turn out to be an excellent collection of problem solvers,
once we give them the opportunity and the right tools.

And what I love most about the whole process is its
empowerment and dignity. When you empower your personas, they will transform you and dignify your existence.

Chapter 12

Now to the second plait to be combed and gathered for braiding: my personal journeys into the labyrinths of altered consciousness in search of deeper truths.

Here again we are fortunate to have the recorded observations made at the time. We can go back to July, 1968, and hear for ourselves – see for ourselves, if we have the gift to conjure up the scenes from the brush strokes of language. Much better, I think, than sitting here in 1991 and generating a version of events that took place 23 years ago based on my own imperfect memory. Certainly more direct and honest. At least you can judge the quality of the original cloth and make of it what you will.

So join me as I turn on the tape recorder and we can attend.

This is the journal entry for Sunday, July 7, and I'm picking up on what I've just written. Let me read it and see how it sounds:

This is the first entry in my journal since our two months at Esalen's Post Campground has gotten under way. I have a tape recorder all set to go next to me, the intent being that if I come to a space where talking rather than typing seems better suited to the recording process, I can switch.

Everything is new. The typewriter is brand new. The portable tape recorder is brand new. I'm sitting in a brand new 1968 VW camper on brand new pillows to bring me up to typewriter height. When I move my hand too far to the left, the world of sound around me is burst open by the brand new clanging of brand new camel bells hanging from one of the old items which feels ludicrously out of place here, the rod end of a two-piece bass fishing rod that I've carried with me from some past-life I can no longer remember, or rather, wish to.

Outside, Dennis is probably sitting and reading but I can't see him. And probably listening to Donovan on a stereo recorder, not new. And Teddie has just slid into view on her bottom, skidding or inching across the dirt floor of the campsite. And now she's gone again.

In re: What's new? There's such a conglomerate of new things and experiences that I'm going to slip to the tape recorder now to try to put it out that way.

Now, I am no longer reading.

Among the new things I want to record are the experiences of this weekend, which included attending a college type seminar on psychosis. It's significant that I forget the precise title of the seminar, but it was Julian Silverman and Wilson Van Dusen talking about "Blowout" centers, about theory, about creating new models for understanding and treating "schizophrenia." And I've had so much of talking about things, that I spent much of the time not physically present there. On the weekend I also went about doing, rather than talking about doing.

Yesterday morning I started out with a massage from Dick, in which he tried to unravel the knots and pains and tie-ups that accumulated, or that I had built up, during the previous time away from Esalen. It was much harder for me this time to "go with" Dick. I had forgotten how to breath, it seems. During the massage, we talked a bit, with Dick telling me that he saw my groin as cutting off my balls, and he offered the interpretation that I have cut off my balls as a self- protective mechanism against Odette. And we talked about this for a while. And I really didn't want to go back to that seminar for more talking about. And Dick was saying that I was one of the nicest guys that he had ever known and that he hated to see me do this to myself. And then we talked for a while some more.

After the massage, Dick and I went up to his room with Tina, who is also a massage therapist, and we had breakfast and smoked some hash. And smoked some marijuana. And that's the first time I ever smoked grass. And like nothing was happening to me, except I experienced a slowing down, and a ... "vagueness" is the word that comes to mind. But it's hard to put words to that experience.

And then it was time for Dick to go down and do a massage and I didn't want to stay alone with Tina, and commented on that, saying I felt uncomfortable staying because I didn't know where it was at for them, in terms of my staying or not staying. And so Dick and I went down to the baths and I went into a tub. And it was then that things started to happen.

I lay on my back in the hot water. And I was practicing being able to float and matching my breathing to my rising and falling in the water so that I could stay with just my nose above water with the rest of me immersed. The technique involves breathing in as I'm going down, and out as I'm rising, so that my buoyancy from the intake of air counteracts the going down, and I don't go down enough to put my nose under water.

And while submerged in this way, I could hear Dick and the others talking in the tub. And at first, the sounds were outside the water coming in. And then, I became aware of the fact that they really were coming from underneath the water. And I tuned in to that underwater world of sounds and vibrations. And I went deeper and deeper into it. And I was on my way.

I can't now recall much of that experience because there were so many others to come later. But I remember coming to the surface and sitting up and telling Dick that I was going back down to return to my trip and I wanted him to know so that someone would be there to pull me out if that became necessary. By which I meant, if I sink, I don't want to drown. From that point, I went on to about a five-hour trip, not all in the water.

I think it's important to record as much as I can about the total experience, and I want to do it by picking up pieces of it, fragments, which I will call "notes." For example:

Note: It was that first shift in perception having to do with moving the sounds from outside of the water to inside the water and then moving my attention to inside the water, that, in a sense, characterizes the whole trip. The trip became a maze, or a chain of shifting perceptions. For example: later, when I was sitting on a massage table and looking at the ocean breaking onto the rocks, there was a particular set of rocks down in front of me, the largest of which transformed into a long sequence of different shapes – animal, bird, reptile, lion, crocodile, all kinds of shapes. And what triggered the movement from one shape to another was my own ability to shift perceptions – to make some kind of perceptual shift happen.

Note: A major factor which had to be overcome, or side-stepped, or dealt with in order to facilitate perceptual shifts, was the element of fear. Or psychic pain. Or tendency to avoid going into a space. And I found myself dealing with it. And by "dealing," I mean involving my cognitive processes in a loose way so that I was paying attention to my internal processes, as well as to my perception of external events. And where I found myself avoiding going into a shift in perception, I would make the cognitive choice to move into that space, and to face the fear, or become one with the fear. And this process seemed to open a perceptual door, so that a whole new chain of perceptions and experiences opened to me. I found I could repeat this process time and time again. And the feeling was — is — that an infinite variety of experiences are available, if I but have the know-how to open doors to these new worlds.

Note: This whole trip carried me into a world in which I had never been before. I don't know if grass is supposed to be a hallucinogen, but I had an amazing variety of visual experiences which, I think, would fall into what we normally categorize as hallucinations. It was like I was the subtle director of an infinite stage, on which I could permit to be created a variety of scenes, images, colors, movements, and relationships among elements on the stage from which new meanings emerged for me. By "new meanings," I mean to say that I would have clear flashes of *knowing* the meaning of my own experiences. I felt certain that this knowledge is recoverable, can be used, communicated, learned, and that it need not remain in another world of experience — locked away in some closet to which I can only have access through some chemical agent.

The quality of the trip, for me, was identical with the quality of trips which have not been drug induced. The major differences are that I am less interruptible on a chemically-induced trip, and that the intensity of the experience is much greater, as is the ability to make perceptual and experiential shifts while in the middle of a trip.

Before I went on the trip, I was talking to Dick about the extent to which my thoughts automatically shut down my tripping ability. The problem of talking about an experience, for me at any rate, is that my mind is busy trying to translate raw experience into words, and this mental activity leads to a splitting away of my mind from my body. I mentioned to Dick that it's as if there is a single mind-body connection, or circuit-breaker, which is triggered out by words and results in mind-body splitting. Perhaps it is not reasonable to expect I could ever maintain myself on a trip for long because this connection would "cut out" the instant I began to comment about, or interpret, the experience that I was then undergoing. I said that I felt that the answer lay not in trying to keep the circuit from cutting out, so much, as in learning ways to reduce the frequency of cut outs, and increase my ability to reconnect the circuit.

For example, as I talk about yesterday's experience now, I am in a narrower perceptual field than I was during yesterday's trip, or than I could be now if I stopped talking and focused on my experiencing in this moment. I am sitting with my legs crossed and my arms folded, and my field of vision is relatively narrow, and the spectrum of colors that I see is relatively small. But when I let go and defocus and see from a relaxed stance, I can begin to see/hear a more expanded world; I see more light, more darkness, more variety of color, and hear sounds of which I was previously unaware – not with the intensity with which I can see and hear on a trip, but further along the continuum.

There's Teddie half way up the hill in her white slip, her hands in front of her, and her shoulders moving. She's posturing or dancing or posing or meditating. And I am waving. She does not wave back but turns away. And now, she's stretching. And dancing. And doing her thing. And coming back down the hill. Dancing and singing her way down the hill. Very free. Very free. It's that kind of freedom, I think, that characterized the trip, for me.

Note: One of the characteristics was that I was physically in a catatonic state. There was no need to move my body. And I have no way of knowing how long I held any particular position. Time was lost. It's a timeless space. Or a different time dimension. I had no way of being able to tell time, except for the fact that it was daylight. But when I became conscious of time, I couldn't tell whether it was daylight of the same day or daylight in another day.

Note: In terms of Blowout centers and appropriate techniques for guiding people through trips... Interruption for Teddie who wants to say hello ...

Hello. Is it on?

Yes, it's on.

Why'd you say, 'interruption for Teddie?'

Well, because I was in the middle of a sentence. ...

I was about to say that from the time I went into the trip until the very end, I had the sense of having guides there with me. I can't know for certain because I haven't checked it out, but it's obvious to me that Dick had spread the word to Esalen staff, or certain members of Esalen staff, and there was always somebody with me, yet not making direct contact with me. They would talk and laugh, or carry on their conversations, or sing, or play musical instruments, all of which enabled me to feel safe, to feel surrounded by people who cared, and who encouraged me nonverbally to go through the experience, and who provided the security of knowing that I was in a safe place. I cannot be certain of the number of people or their identity because I didn't leave my trip very often to check on external reality. During the course of the five hours, if that was the time span, I "came back" a number of times. On one or two occasions, a staff member – like Paul, who's presence I acknowledged – would ask if I was in an okay place, would ask if I was on a good trip. And when I let him know I was, that was the end of that, and I went back, and he went somewhere. But someone was always there.

One of the most significant-to-me happenings was when Fritz came and sat on a massage table next to me and talked, not to me but to someone who was there. He read a poem which he had apparently just finished writing, and I had the feeling that it was my poem and that he wrote it for me. And I "came back" immediately in response to Fritz's voice, and Fritz read that poem to people who were close by so that I heard him read it on three different occasions. He never acknowledged my presence, never hinted that he was concerned about me, yet I felt his concern. And at one point when I reached for the poem, he ignored me. But then he went, I guess, for a massage with Ida Rolf and he left his jumper on a hook nearby and very carefully put the poem in a pocket. And it was there. And I went to it and read it. Several times. Took it out of his pocket and read it. Had no feeling of shame, or guilt, or that I was doing something naughty – I was aware of not feeling that. And then I read the poem again and put it back in the pocket. And I took it out one other time, later, while he was still gone, and read it again, and put it back. And I cannot now remember it all, but I can remember pieces. I can remember the first two lines, and the last two lines, and they spoke to me loudest. And the first two lines were:

In and out the garbage pail

I put all my creations.

And the last two lines were ... well, I can't remember the last two lines now, but the sense of them – of the last stanza in which there were four lines – was to the effect that it's time to end the re-studying of data, to end dealing with fears, and

Create a new gestalt

For my remaining years.[1]

It was particularly pertinent to where I was in that space, and particularly pertinent to my dilemmas of these days.

Chapter 13

And now another eight days of the Esalen experience have passed. Yesterday, a Sunday, appears to have been a remarkable day, according to the audio tapes. Sometime during the day, Odette and I had a huge fight, which I honestly cannot, in 1991, remember, but which, according to the record, must have been a doozy. And in the evening, I went on my second marijuana and hashish assisted journey into altered consciousness.

And now, through the magic of tape, we begin to weave together into a single braid the three plaits of my full-headed Esalen Summer: the first plait of my learning from the organized workshops; the second plait of my questing after truths lying masked or hidden in the labyrinths of my unconscious processes; and the third plait of my tangled struggles for clarity and a right path in the matter of my marriage and the relationships between Odette and Mario and me.

This is Monday morning, July 15, 1968. I'm sitting in my camper with the shades drawn all around. It's 10 minutes of eight. I'm parked on the third level at Esalen. I'm sitting on a bed. Smoke is rising from a cigarette that I didn't even know I lit. This is the second cigarette since sometime around 10:30 last night, a point at which I was pretty far out, and I heard Dick's voice a long way off saying, "Why don't you stop cigarettes and turn to a pipe." At some level I made a decision to go along with that – to stop smoking cigarettes and turn to a pipe – but at a deeper level, I was aware that I was only going along with it, buying the idea. And while I felt I was making the decision mine, it was not entirely. And I'm sitting here knowing that I do have the power to make that choice. But the power feels not total, as though I'm weakening it out of the same kind of shit that keeps me from being able to *go anywhere with* the anger, rage, hurt, which I feel over the me/Mario/Odette scene. And it hit me, just before I turned on the recorder, that I use this head-trip about my hurt feelings and my rage to blot out the positive things that happened last night. Only this time I'm not blotting them out. At least not yet.

It's crazy. Among all of the things that I have in this camper, I can't find an ashtray. Okay, so I'll do without ashtrays. And I just had a struggle over putting this cigarette out in a little Welch's grape juice jar. There was something symbolic about that for me. It's like the difficulty I'm having putting my penis into a vagina. But I did it.

I'm sitting here trying to choose between staying here at Esalen and driving off. One of my thoughts has to do with whether driving off would be avoiding the inner journey and going for the outer. And I was wondering if there is really a difference as far as I'm concerned. I've been on the inner journey – particularly last night – and this morning I'm still with it. But now I have nowhere to go and no one out there to turn to. And I know that's an illusion. The world is full of people. But there's no point in going to somebody else until I've really come to me. I'm thinking: I'll just drive and keep talking into the tape recorder and getting to a place, maybe up in the Sierras, where I can spend time recording and typing and going with wherever I'm at.

I just put the camper bed up and I seem to be making the decision to leave here. Still, the question came up again: Am I running away to avoid facing the fear? And I want to say that last night I faced all the fears I could find in that trip. I experienced death, I experienced a coming alive again, I experienced myself as being in many ancient places and as many ancient things. I've been a falcon, I've been a serpent, and it felt good. As a serpent, I felt loose, lithe, my body just flowing snakelike, my vertebrae and my whole body liquid. And I experienced many other things: God, great white light, myself rising, projecting, moving into areas of fear and into the dark places, and moving through the dark places up and out into a great bright light. Rocketing myself into orbit, into space.

The one area where I hang myself up still, are my feelings re Mario and Odette. It seems that what I have to do is *not* do in that area, more specifically to *not* wipe myself out. I'm wanting to work very hard to stay with this and to *not* run away from it. And that's an inner journey. It doesn't matter where I "go" in the outer.

So, there's this need to journey alone and that's why I'm pulling out of Esalen. I need the freedom to be able to move away from the things that I'm attached to. I have a little sticker that Teddie stuck on the wing window with scotch tape yesterday that says: *Do your thing!* That's what I'm doing now – knowing I can come back.

I'm pulling away from Esalen, going up the long hill heading south. Before I left, I let Dick and Tina know that I'm leaving, and we had good talk and it feels right. That was a good trip last night. I really did go through so many places; I don't know how to recount them all. Except by beginning to recount.

I'm driving up a long hill on Highway 1 alongside the coast and the ocean is flat and grey with light places in it and kelp beds down below, and there's a long deep ravine opening to the water, and I can look back and see Esalen rising on a hill. And I can come back.

I'm now about five miles north of Morro Bay on Highway 1 and I can still see the ocean. I stopped for breakfast at a pancake house at Hearst's Castle. It's close to two hours since I left Esalen.

At breakfast, I was reading Vivekananda who says that our one great sin is *weakness* – thinking weakness, experiencing weakness, out of which come all the other sins, such as causing pain to oneself, and inflicting hurt on others, and wiping oneself out, and not being able to do one's thing in the world. All of these come out of weakness.

A big part of this trip for me is getting into the habit of being strong in the world – regardless of where in time/space I happen to be, or the nature of the world in which I happen to find myself. This is my world, all of it. These are my people, all of them. What I do with my environment – the way in which I perceive it, the particular grid through which I see it – can either feed my sense of being strong and alive and moving in the world, or it can feed my sense of being weak and helpless and inert.

I'm now driving by a sign that says *San Jacinto Avenue*, and this is Morro Bay, and the sun is shining and I'm driving down a four lane divided highway with a center strip of brown grass and brown sand, and to my right is the ocean with white breakers rolling in. It's a beautiful day and Morro Rock rises facing me like a huge half shell with scalloped ridges. This is Mario's country. But it's really my country, too. This is all my country.

Someone, I guess it was Maslow, pointed out that we are always looking at the here and now through a rear-view mirror. Julian brought it up again last week – that one can only report on one's experiencing of the here and now by looking into the rear view mirror in which the here and now has just slipped by. One is always reporting in a new here and now.

This was very vivid to me last night in the beginning of my journey. I was conscious of my voice reporting on what was happening, but the moment my voice was out, it went zooming off into another dimension, and I had the sense of being both here and now and aware of my voice receding in the rear view mirror as I was driving away from it, separating from it in time. The act of separation was being magnified far beyond what I usually experience. I felt as if there was an infinite gap between my here-and-now impulse to record and the hearing of my voice through my ears. From the moment I moved to record, to the moment my voice shaped in my vocal chords and emerged from my mouth there was an infinite time-lag, an infinite space.

It's now 12:15 and I'm on Highway 101 somewhere south of San Luis Obispo. Ocean's no longer visible, sky is blue, white cumulus clouds are frothy puffs dotting the sky. Looking south, it's overcast down toward Santa Barbara. I'm driving through rolling plains country with rising rolling hills in the background and fields in the foreground with cut grain lying golden in the sun. And beyond, green hills and cauliflower trees. There were cows in the field but I don't see them now.

There's a parked two-tone car, another car broken down. And I'm on El Camino Real. *Nipomo exit, 1 mile.* There's a sign: *39 Miles to Anderson's Pea Soup Restaurant in Buelton.*

One of the reasons for wanting to tape is my need to note and affirm my here-and-now experiences. It's not enough to hold them in my head. They don't carry over. But I can get them out through this tape. There is a feeding of my strength that comes from recording what I'm going through; I can go back and hear it again and enlarge on it, or modify it, or do whatever I want with it. There's a feeding of my strength that comes from experiencing my stamp in the world, from being able to see it, hear it, touch it, rather than carrying it all inside of me. I am living in the world and I have to make my impression in the world, whether it's simply a footprint in the sand, or a recording, or whatever.

This is the Santa Barbara county line and Santa Maria city limit. Santa Maria exit on my right: *Welcome to Santa Maria, Next Five Exits* and a great big rocket in the middle of the sign.

This is my world, too. I tend to look at it through a perceptual grid that makes my stomach hurt. Maybe I can learn to look at it in another way. But my foot presses down on the accelerator and I want to run, drive faster and faster. And that's not the answer. Not the answer.

I'm just yawning like mad! Mad yawning.

And that reminds me of something I did with a word last night. Dick said that about every half hour I would issue forth with a one-sentence phrase or comment, and I remember doing something with the word "unbearable." Unable to bear. Unable to carry, unable to give birth to, unable to go naked – these are all meanings of un-bearable. And they're all statements about a state of being. Unable to be bear-like. Honey bear. Grizzly bear.

We are imprisoned by the meanings we read into the words that we use. We're trapped by the language. But we can learn to modify the language, learn to shift perceptual frames – like doing a figure/ground reversal to expand and enlarge on the levels of meaning, and to open to different, contradictory, non-sense meanings of the words we're using. These all are doors to freeing ourselves from the prison of our own words.

But there's another world without words, a wordless world of experience. Last night's journeys were word-less by and large. It is my own choice to use words to comment on my wordless experiences that puts words into them.

With respect to last night's journey: One of the things that I learned was that my body-stiffness – my aches and pains, my inability to move – are all my body responding to head trips. It's not just physiological, because when I experienced myself as a serpent, or as a great bird, or as one of the witch doctors or tribal chiefs or warriors or priests in ancient lives, my body was lithe and loose. Particularly as a serpent, I experienced my body as being completely fluid and was able to move my neck and spine and my whole body as if it were liquid, even though I was only sitting. There was no impediment. I experienced my body moving this way. And I got feedback from Dick to the effect that that is what was going on, so far as he could see my movements.

Which, of course, validates all that Bernie Gunther and the other mind/body workers are saying. I come to this because I was somewhere thinking about the need to blow one's mind in order to get out of one's familiar, established mind sets and into an experiential here and now.

Last night's journey got going with my seeing shapes – demons, monsters, beautiful shapes – in the silhouette of the trees at Esalen outlined against the sunset sky over the ocean. That's where I started tripping as I was able to move into the shapes and just go with the experiencing of them. It was truly beautiful. I didn't come up against any particular demon that was so fearful that I backed away from it. Not at that point in time.

It was later that I moved into experiencing death. That was catatonic. My whole body went cold and dead and I experienced it all. I was able to move into death and stay with it, and I came out somewhere – emerged, transcended, reborn out of it in some way. I really cannot precisely say at what point the emergence occurred, or precisely what stimulated it, beyond saying that it was my willingness to move into experiencing death that enabled the rest of the journey to go on, and to come out the other side. To come out to joy, to transcendence, to a sense of being infinite, to being whole and alive. Alive. Very much alive.

Among last night's experiences was one in which I was being scalded and burned and consumed by fire. I can relate it to a time when the underside of my left arm was accidentally scalded by boiling water. Or, so I've been told. This must have been prior to age two. My arm still carries the scar but I have no conscious memory. I relived it last night, the part of burning up, of being consumed by fire from which I emerged into a very holy place. Like being able to move out and be in touch with God, the Infinite, and to rocket myself, to power myself by my own drive into infinite space. Very much like a rocket ship going up.

The one place where I went back in, time and time again, in hopes of going through something but failing at that, was in the realm of my feelings about the me-Mario-Odette relationship. That simply was impenetrable. And I think it was because of the way in which I was posing the question. It comes back again to the nature and the limitations of the problem solving process. The solutions that we find are dictated by how we pose the question. I posed the question from the vantage point of, *How can I get out of my experiencing pain and grief and remorse and rage and hostility and anger?*

There is no answer at that level because the question is irrelevant. It is irrelevant because to pose the question in that way yields no answer of a growthful sort. A more productive path is to acknowledge that my feelings are not relevant, *not reverent* – of me, of others, of my place in the world, of those I really love and care for – and to move into another dimension with it, and to not hang up at that level of question asking.

The application of this knowledge is, of course, a different matter.

Monday evening, five minutes after six, and I'm driving through Sutherland, five miles south of Santa Barbara on my way to Ventura. In Santa Barbara, I had the bus given its 600-mile check and a piece of the tail pipe that fell off was replaced. I also spent about an hour with Penny. Over a glass of wine, I shared the nature of my trip right now and how it's going. Robin came home about 15 minutes before I left. So I spent about four hours coping with the world out there, and I feel pretty good. It was a strong, confident me that moved through the four hours. No sweat, no anxieties, no hassles.

I called the boys from Robin and Penny's and talked with Ian.

He and Dean seem just fine. In Ventura I'll drop in and see them and maybe make a phone call or two, and maybe take care of a few other items. I don't think I'll spend the night there. If I do, I'll have more business to take care of tomorrow. I think I can just go on without doing that.

I have no clear notion of where I'll spend the night. I don't even have a clear notion of where I'm going. I might stop in LA and perhaps see Lee, or check in on Diana, or I might even bypass LA and curve around and go into the Sierras. I really don't know. I'll let that happen as I go along.

The camper is riding beautifully and it feels very nice. I have a secure feeling in this camper. It's a nice home.

Twenty minutes to nine, Monday, the same day. I've just left Dean and Ian at their apartment in Ventura and they are well. I'm driving down 101 headed south, and I'm going to take the Santa Paula freeway to Highway 99, and then turn left on 99 to Bakersfield, and head up the valley, possibly to Sequoia National Park which I've never seen. It's almost night now. The sun is down and it's that time when the sky turns slate grey and the trees turn dark green. Headlights are necessary, but you can still make out cars and everything else.

In Ventura, I did some shopping at Thrifty Mart, and that was a real hassle: shopping where Odette and I have so often shopped together. Shopping has always been for the family. I was struck by pangs of loneliness which reawaken old fears and memories of being alone in the world. It surprises me how quickly I get sucked into it. It is a weakness trip, and yet it's hard to shift from seeing the experience through that screen that has me feeling anguish and loneliness. It's a weakness trip because implied in it are all kinds of statements to the effect: *I've really had it with Odette, and with Mario, and there is no more family for me, and I am alone in the world!*

And this is not where it's at. Not unless the fight that Odette and I had yesterday has solidified her need to have me out of her life. That's a possibility that I simply cannot act on at this point in time. We just have to wait and see. I don't think that's what's going to happen but even thinking about it is senseless. I am here and now, and I'm on the Santa Paula freeway, and I'm driving through groves – they look like orange trees but I don't think we have oranges this far up, more probably lemons. And it's a nice part of the road and there are hills off to the left with lights on them and this is good. This is my world, too.

I'm on Highway 126 to Interstate 5 and Bakersfield. I'm purposefully avoiding Los Angeles. Highway 126 is not well traveled. Bakersfield will give me a spot of hot desert valley, maybe around midnight or early morning. Driving through the valley at night is something I've always enjoyed. Tomorrow, I can be up around Merced or Fresno, and into one of the state parks or forests up there. Probably Sequoia. I've never seen that. I really don't want to get too far away from Esalen. I want to be able to come back without too much hassling. And if I go off to New Mexico or Arizona, it's a long haul and I'm afraid I wouldn't have time. All of this is to do my thing. We'll see what lies ahead. ...

This is Saticoy, or the turnoff to Saticoy. I've never been down this road before. Wait, I was – one time with Odette; we were on a trip to catch up on things a number of years ago. We came through this valley on our way to Ventura and Santa Barbara. It's 10 miles from where I've been living for the past two years and I haven't been down this road in all that time. ...

Going through Fillmore. Palm tree lined streets, main drag, kind of warm. Can't see much of Fillmore. It's obviously a rancher type town. There's a car wash with two girls washing a car. I really oughta go and wash mine, maybe strike up an acquaintance. An EastSide Market over there which is open. It looks pleasant enough. And the palm trees are the great big tall ones that rise up 60-70 feet. Maybe not that high but they give that impression. A clean pole with a tuft on top.

Tee-ta-ta-tummm.

Tee-ta-ta-ta-taa, tee-ta-taa, Tee-tum.

Eleanor Rigbeee.

[Vic's singing, if one could call it that, continues for a long spell as a home-grown medley of 60's tunes with lots of *Beedlyaaa-bebumbums.* and *boom-biddleyadaas.*]

The singing reminds me of pieces of my journey last night when I was being a warrior, many long-time-ago centuries, some other civilization – Oriental, Indian, African, something – and there was a feeling of rhythm, rhythm, rhythm, and drums beating, and playing and singing and chanting. I don't remember any particular style, or quality of the music, except warlike with a deep gut rhythm.

The tires on the road have a rhythm – *bumpa bumpa BUMpa bumpa - bumpa bumpa BUMpa bumpa* – and the wind is a high resonant over-riding *whee-eeyee-eeyee.* Like the sound of a train clacking over the rails. There's something very primitive about that beat. I'm sure it has something to do with why I like to drive, and why I like to drive at night because it blots out the sharp corners of the visual world, and it leaves room for things to happen.

My life has been punctuated by night trips in cars. It was one of the things that I used to turn on to when I was hitch-hiking in my teens. I loved to travel at night. I preferred traveling at night. And loved riding in the big transport trucks that have an incredible rhythm of their own. When I was younger, I longed to be a truck driver – an ambition that never got fulfilled. It's the rhythm that grabbed me – the hours of being swept along by the rhythm of the road. And the engine. Diesel engines have a powerful rhythm of their own.

It was a poetic experience. There was mystery about it. I'm sure it had something to do with putting me in touch with my sense of the infinite, linking me to cosmological time, to time in another dimension, to another universe of experience.

One way of looking at my life is in terms of my drive to be in touch with the infinite. There is a word which constantly recurred in the workshop to describe this quality of experience. What was it? Oh yes, *numinous*. Numinous experience. It has been very strong in my life. And, yes, it has been subverted and squashed down. No... it isn't that *it* has been, it's that *I* have permitted it to be. And I suppose I have been looking for ways to see my wife ... wife ... Let's continue that sentence: *I suppose I have been looking for ways to see my life ...wife ... as a unified thing.* ...That brings me to tears. ...That brings me to tears.

And that's probably really the strongest bond that exists between Odette and me. We both have this deep sense of being related to the cosmos, to infinite time, of both being priestly, noble, God-like, and of having a sense of being in touch with that.

This is Highway 99 coming down the Grapevine. There's a big overhead yellow sign: *Next 5 miles - 6 1/2 percent grade - Downhill - Trucks Use Low Gear.* Elevation 3,000 feet and going down. Big sign: *Bakersfield 35 miles, Sacramento 313.*

Moving along at 65 miles an hour and I feel like I'm flying my Cessna 150. Well, there's a trip! I'm tempted to call the tower for permission to land this thing.

Something broke back there. That sounded bad. Something dropped and broke. Hmmm. I guess a bottle of liquor. I have a feeling it was the box with my shrine things in it. I hope nothing... I was going to say, I hope nothing meaningful got broken, but maybe there's no such thing as broken.

The highway is really divided at this point. I can see a long line of trucks and cars moving up the grade toward LA about a mile away from me on my left. Lights in the night. Night lights. Service stations: *Shell, Texaco, 76 Union.* And the sound of my camel bells *jinglingelinkelinkelink.* And the wind's whistling sound, and the steady thrum of rubber on concrete.

This is Bakersfield. Sign: *Ramada Inn - 4 Miles.* That triggers memories – like the coffee shop back at Castaic Junction where Odette and I usually stopped, coming over the Grapevine; it's a coffee shop that has much meaning for her because, before she ever knew me, she used to go there to meet one of her teacher-lovers. And the Ramada Inn here in Bakersfield is where Odette and Teddie and Dennis and Dean and Ian and I stopped on our way down from Washington, and spent a night there, and had a great meal there in the Spanish Galleon dining room.

I get caught up in thinking about Odette back at camp and me here. It takes me out of here and now and gets me to wishing I were there with her. And thinking that these days we could have been sharing together are not days of sharing.

And there's Ramada Inn. And I can see from here the row of rooms where we stayed. And I'm gonna turn off 99 and check the damage in back. There's a sign: *Porterville - Sequoia Park - North 65 - Exit 1 3/4 Miles.* I think I'll take that. I'll check the map and see where it goes.

So, I'm going to Porterville. I checked the damage and it was a box, not of the shrine things but of a set of small liquor glasses. Three of them remain unbroken, so that's not bad. Porterville is 45 miles, Sequoia Park is 105. I should be able to make Sequoia Park and then maybe hole up there tomorrow and just continue to work on this trip, rather than drive more. The time is 11:30. Sequoia Park is probably two, two-and-a-half hours away, which should put me there 1:30 or 2 o'clock. That should be okay.

I've been sitting here thinking that there really are meanings to draw from the experience of the box of glasses falling. That I consider the breaking of four or five liquor glasses relatively unimportant does not wipe out the significances of the glasses breaking at the time they did, and in response to where I was in my head, and what I was saying. Meanings are there to be drawn. One can do that with any module or segment of experience. The meanings to be drawn from any moment of experience are infinite. And that's something I want to be more aware of. There's a phrase on the dust jacket of a book about *The Book of the Dead* – let's see, what was the phrase? Having to do with mind expanding, but the word was not "expanding". Umm - *dilating!* Mind dilating! Exploring the meanings of experience is mind dilating.

There's a huge orange half moon rising to my right – an almost unbelievable moon. The bottom is cut off by the hills so it looks like a segment of an orange rising, or like a giant elbow macaroni. Ridiculous to try to describe the damn thing. Now it's coming up over the hill BIG and orange. Looks like it's not a moon at all but something... I think I'll stop and take a look at it when I get a chance.

I'm parked at the side of the road. The night is balmy and the sky is loaded with stars, and the moon has shrunken in size but it's a half-orange moon. I walked around a bit and there are warblers and crickets in the fields making music. It's really lovely here.

While I was out there I was reminded of a piece of my journey last night. As I went through experiences, I very often came out with some incredibly amusing and insightful observation that broke me up. And just now, while I was outside, I was doing a backbend and I was reminded of this place in the middle of my back that always itches. And on one of my trips last night, this particular spot was not only itching but felt very solid back there, like there was a metal plate. And I leaned back in the chair and spread my arms out with my head back, and then it occurred to me that another way to scratch the middle of my back was not by reaching behind me and scratching, but by doing it from the inside. And it worked! And it just broke me up. If you have an itchy place you can't reach from the outside, you can get to it from the inside. I travelled through my body and back to that little spot and scratched it. And that was a wild experience.

I'm 33 miles from Sequoia National Park on Highway 198, and

it's 1:25 a.m., Tuesday morning of the second day. The moon is straight ahead and fairly low in the sky. This is becoming mountainous country and I can see the hills, the mountains, all around. And stars are in the sky and it's a very lovely night for driving. The moon is lighting the sky so that the mountains stand out very clearly. They're not high towering mountains yet, more foothills. Immediately below and to my left, there's a lake and the moon is reflecting off the water and it's very lovely. It's not a round lake. The shore juts out at a number of points and makes it look even more intriguing.

Now the road winds and I'm negotiating the curves with my left hand and holding the mike with my right.

And now the moon is turned around so that it's off to my left, oh, about 20 degrees high. The highway's in very good shape.

Whoopsie doo, there's a camping area!

I've pulled into the camping area and I'm parked for the night. I'm on the lake shore with the mountains rising all around. Scraggly gaunt oak tree here in the campsite. It looks like it has no leaves at all, just a bare skeleton against the stars in the blue sky. And the stars are very bright, and the half moon is immediately behind a trailer in the next campsite. The hills rise all around and the crickets are singing and it's quite mild. And it's time to turn in.

It's 10:30 a.m., Tuesday, the second day and I'm pulling away from the campsite. The lake is Lake Kaweah on the map. Bright blue clear sky, and the sun is shining. The road goes around the lake, so I'm driving along the other side of Lake Kawea which, as I said last night, is not round but shaped somewhat like a long, crooked finger.

There's a hawk or vulture soaring in the sky overhead, and I'm coming over a rise, and I can see the Sierras now, rising high with what looks like snow on top.

Now the road is following a river bed which has some water in it, and there's a car way down there with the trunk open, and a single figure, a man, standing between the car and the edge of the lake. And two green outhouses.

The countryside is turning into trees and stream beds and lots of uncultivated natural growth. The green of the grass is very bright. There are houses scattered about but they haven't destroyed the natural scenery. And right now, on my left, a green draw with trees lining both sides and a backdrop of rolling hills rises up steeply, at a 30 or 45 degree slope, and I can find all kinds of incredible shapes in them.

And that's what happened to me last night, in the dark. There was enough moonlight, and the sky was light, so I was able to ... there were two giant ... Oh! There they are now! Wow! Two magnificent godlike women lying down, and I can see one with the Sierras behind her, a woman lying on her back, and I'm looking up her armpit over her face, and her body lies down toward the left, her legs are apart, and she's wearing a flowing skirt, and that was one of the figures I saw from the campsite. But I wasn't able to see the Sierras behind her. And another woman! Sharing the same head but lying in the opposite direction and going away. And her breasts are very prominent, and she has her right knee raised. There are so many women lying in these hills, it's like a valley of the Gods, where they sleep. The Bedroom of the Gods. And a lot of huddles. A lot of bodies close by, so there are family groups. And it just kinda blows my mind.

This is Sequoia Park, and I paid one dollar for a one-day, overnight camping permit, and I'm going up a long winding road into the park toward the various campsites. It's all very lovely. I'm in a long line of cars moving up the road, going slowly uphill. The trees are no longer just green but rust-colored and olive and bright green and reds and oranges. And down below a stream flows and forms into pools with green and black and turquois and white water cascading over rocks.

It's 3:25 in the afternoon of Tuesday, the second day. I want to read a poem I just wrote. The title is, *I sit at a campsite table amid.*

> *I sit at a campsite table amid*
> *towering sequoias reaching trembling fingers*
> *skyward quivering in touchtalk with the wind.*

> *I sit with my Olympia portable typewriter*
> *and my Sony solid-state 4-track servo-controlled*
> *   portable tape recorder*
> *trying to find God with my head.*

> *The Sequoias*
> *mindless stretch their spines through timeless space*
> *touching God both inside and out*
> *feeling unity of self with self*
> *unity of self with wind and light and dark*
> *unity of self with stars and sun and moon*
> *unity of self with the infinite*
> *stretching rolling waving in timeless space.*

> *My mind struggles and gasps through pain*
> *a mechanistic time driven tangled circuitry*
> *gasping sticky messages*

to sterile metal fingers striking black symbols on white
     paper

in search of God.

But not always.

Sometimes I transcend to mindlessness
and God is here there everywhere in me and in my
          oneness
with All.

I am the serpent
dancing the slow liquid dance of adoration
of serpentry
and All.

I am the falcon
seeing without judgment through unscreened eyes
all life

and no dichotomous death

or pain

or anguish.

I am the ancient warrior king priest Godself
in ritual to life
that is All

and in every thing and place.

I am twentieth century man

dying through numberless deaths
to be reborn
in joy
in love
with life.

Yet pain and anguish catch me up still
and I writhe in mind-inflicted agony
cut off from you my fellow gods

slipping from memory

to ache

to anguish

again to death

with only a mindhope
that again
beyond death
lies life.

This is 6:30 in the morning of Wednesday, the third day.

I left Sequoia National Park around three o'clock this morning and I'm on highway 41 between Visalia and Paso Robles, on my way to Paso Robles, where I will call Mario to find out where Odette is and how she is doing. I am very concerned about Odette ... about our relationship ... about me and Mario. And I'm having trouble not thinking about that, not being worried. I have trouble not feeling shaky in the knees and scared. Every once in a while I feel confident that the three of us can go on together. But my memory of the fight Odette and I had comes back and I have flashes of the enormity of that, and my worry and concern return. Now I have to know where things stand. And I am longing to be with her.

I still have mixed feelings where Mario is concerned. When I'm feeling strong, I want for the three of us to be able to love each other and go on. But there's too much that's unknown right now. My world is being massively shaken and I am not able to sustain going ahead and doing my thing so long as I am being caught up in wondering about Odette. And caring about her condition. And caring about where I stand with her. These things weigh very heavily.

I've been able to go through the feelings of weakness and grief and come out feeling more whole, and that's been a help. But I'm not able to *not* care about my relationship, about my love for Odette, about the fight we had, about her turning me off for good and all. Which may very well have been the direction in which she's moved out of the campground scene on Sunday. I can't know. And I have to find out.

And at this point, the batteries powering the tape recorder give out and the metaphor to be found in that casts a long shadow forward.

Chapter 14

It was over.

I don't think I feel much of anything about it now, after all these years, except a lingering sadness. I don't remember much of a scene, or even a trumpet-sounding *dénouement*, only of a clearer understanding that our marriage and our experiment with communal living was at an end. And, that after Esalen, Odette would be going off to live with Mario.

Well, there's a bright side to everything, I suppose. Even to the end of a basically rewarding and productive marriage. But, of course, there is never really an end to anything. Its effects go on and on, reverberating down hallways of endless time. Every act of closure, every death, echoes on forever. Somewhere. The bright side for Odette and Mario was, no doubt, the opening up of doors to a promising future borne on the wings of love. Or so I imagined. The bright side for me was to be released from uncertainty and doubt.

And, in time, from pain.

It was over.

I believed I could learn to accept that and go on.

Most immediately, going on meant finishing out the last of the Esalen workshops in the *Value of the Psychotic Experience* series. After that, I would have to find a job. And during my last days at Esalen I met a man who was shortly to become instrumental in my undergoing a radical shift in the system of logical thought that structures how I go about the business of thinking and understanding.

Al Kraft was not an unheard-of stranger to me when we met one afternoon on the deck at Esalen; his name had come up in workshops as a psychiatrist who had been researching the therapeutic uses of LSD. It also turned out that the Krafts lived in Menlo Park on the San Francisco peninsula, and that Al's wife, Pearl, was acquainted with Odette through mutual friends.

Al and I formed an immediate bond, partly, I think, because he was a naturally warm and caring human being, partly because of our shared interest in altered states research, and probably because of a sense of brotherhood stemming from our belonging to the same generation of erstwhile East Coast Jews of the non-practicing sort.

During our conversations at Esalen, I told Al of my experiences with marijuana and hashish and expressed my interest in trying LSD. Al responded by offering to serve as guide on an LSD trip provided I prepared properly for the journey.

The first of my preparations, he explained, would be to clarify for myself my purpose in going on the journey. What was I hoping to accomplish? What were the questions for which I would be seeking answers?

A second preparation would be to develop the mind set that no matter what transpired in the course of my journey, no matter how scary it got, no matter how terrified I became, that I would resolve to not back away from whatever was about to happen. In other words, that I would commit to saying "Yes" to every step on the journey.

There were additional preparations to be made of a more mundane sort. I was to come with recordings of my favorite music to accompany me on my trip; I was to be dressed in loose, comfortable clothing; and I should be prepared to spend about 12 hours voyaging in another reality.

We agreed that I would come shortly after the Esalen workshops ended and I was invited to pull my VW camper into their driveway and camp out for as long as I wished.

I had little difficulty with any of the preparatory steps outlined for me by Al. My two previous trips into altered consciousness had given me confidence in my ability to "go with" whatever negative experiences I might be facing. The musical accompaniment would consist of an assortment of my favorite symphonies and concertos – Beethoven's Sixth *Pastoral* Symphony, Mozart's 40th in G Minor, Tchaikovsky's 1812 Overture, and a Beethoven Violin Concerto.

With regard to Preparation #1 – clarifying my purpose in taking LSD – it was easy for me to identify my own fear of death as my greatest concern, notwithstanding the numerous "other lives" I had already experienced during my two previous trips. There was something about my fear of dying that I saw as crippling in its effects. It was as if my fear was so deeply imbedded in my psyche that it twisted my personality in ways I didn't understand but knew I greatly wanted to be free of.

So it was that I turned up at Al and Pearl's house in Menlo Park about two weeks after our meeting on the deck at Esalen. A day or two later, in the early morning of still another sunshiny California day, the three of us drove to Al's spacious and comfortable suite of offices in downtown Menlo Park. To assist as guides during the 12 hours of my journey, Al had enlisted the services of two additional professionals, both psychologists whose names I don't remember. A pad was spread on the floor with a pillow for my head. The twin speakers of a stereo tape player were placed on each side of the pillow. The tapes of music were stacked in the order I wished them to be played. And I was reassured for the dozenth time that my guides would be with me at all times to help as I might wish.

My memory is that Al then extracted some liquid from a small bottle labelled *Sandoz: lycergic acid dyethylamide*, added a touch of *amphetamine sulphate*, poured the mixture onto a cube of sugar, which he then offered to me on a silver platter, saying, *May the God spirit within you grant what you wish.* Well, he may not have said those words, exactly, but I certainly felt his reverence and support for my embarking on a spiritual journey of the soul. So I stretched out on my back, placed my head on the pillow between the stereo speakers, closed my eyes, and allowed the music to fill and swell the thousand spaces in my sponge of consciousness. And then I was being pulled away from the world I had known, and I was being sucked resolutely backward in time.

My first experience was one of sliding backward through the stages of my life as I have known it, regressing and shrinking into childhood and then infancy, and then being drawn backward through a birth canal and a uterine existence where I continued to shrink and then disintegrate and dissolve until my essence was contained in two miniscule particles that whirled away from each other in opposite directions across the vastness of space, held together only by a slender thread, a silver filament that stretched across light years of distance, threatening to snap, until the two tiny particles of my essence slowed their motion and then hung in balanced terror on opposite walls of the universe. And then, slowly, they began to move, drawn together by the stretched-thin silver filament, in the same way that a stretched rubber band finds its strength and overcomes the forces that had been pulling it apart. And as my tiny particles of essence were reducing the vast spatial distances between them, they gathered speed and momentum, until, at long last, they came crashing into each other, erupting in a blinding nuclear explosion that hurled me breathless into an earlier life.

And thus the pattern was set in which I lived through countless lives, leading to countless deaths and countless hurlings across the universe and back into countless explosions opening into countless new births. A continuing cycle in which each new birth opened into a different life that preceded the last one in historic and geologic time. My memory of my countless lives and deaths has dimmed over the years but some vivid images remain – particularly of my *French Period* in which I spoke the language fluently, romanced prolifically, and fought and died, sword in hand, many times over. In time, my regressions through past lives took me back to the Ice Age where I lived through a long sequence of lives in never ending struggle against bitter cold, until the ridiculousness of my insistent returnings to an ice-clad world struck me as a great cosmic joke that warmed me in my own laughter.

There is a constant theme that ran through it all. Each life was a struggle between the polarities of life and death, war and peace, valor and cowardice, ice and fire, health and sickness, plenty and starvation, victory and defeat, light and darkness, good and evil. And suddenly, at the end of my 12 hours of eternal battling between the polarities of human existence, an illuminating understanding of the meaning of it all overwhelmed me with its total clarity and I exclaimed for all about me to hear:

There is no such thing as a dichotomy!

The words don't quite say it correctly. They are a shorthand for the fundamental truth that was revealed to me by virtue of my countless turnings on the wheel of my lives. Of course there are dichotomies. Each of us can think of dozens in the span of a minute or two. We are used to recognizing dichotomies because, indeed, our thinking processes operate by noting differences between and among events. The actual events themselves – night and day, for instance – can also be seen as differing aspects of a more comprehensive event, like the full rotation of the earth about its axis. So night and day, and all other dichotomies, are conveniences that we structure with our minds. But they are ALWAYS differing aspects of the same phenomenon. We often forget that truth, particularly when we attach our emotions and our loyalties to *this* side of a polarity and in opposition to *that* side.

What I meant to be declaring when I burst out of my 12-hour journey with the declaration, *There is no such thing as a dichotomy!* was that I was seeing a natural law in operation, which I call *The Law of Transcendence.* The Law of Transcendence can be stated as:

Every dichotomy is capable of being transcended by an overarching conceptualization that incorporates and unifies the dichotomy's polarities.

And what this means is that we can resolve every one of our dilemmas, our problems, our issues, by passing through a doorway of understanding into a new awareness where a transcending conceptualization shapes a different reality wherein our old pre-existing issues are dissolved.

Interchapter 14+

SAM: *Hold the presses!*

LEONARDO: *Now what?*

SAM: *This Law of Transcendence really is important. It needs special attention. I'm not sure how we can best go about doing that.*

LEONARDO: *We can flag it. Like putting up a big sign that says:*

> **Hey Reader!**
>
> **Pay Attention!**
>
> **This is Important!**
>
> **You Don't Want to Miss This!**

ALTHOR: *Hey! I like that! Do you have any more tricks like that to spring on our poor unsuspecting readers?*

LEONARDO: *Sure. Lot's of 'em. Want to see what it looks like upside down?*

SAM: *CUT THAT OUT!*

LEONARDO: *Althor, I think Sam wants us to play Straight Man to his Heavy.*

ALTHOR: *You think so? Okay, let's give it a shot. Sam, old friend, what's so important about this Law of Transcendence business that it's worth all this fuss?*

SAM: *Oh boy. I guess that's the best I can get from you guys by way of cooperation today. Okay. If that's your best offer, I'll take it.*

What's so important is that the Law of Transcendence very quickly became a primary principle around which I organized my life; particularly in my work as a psychotherapist. You might even say it became THE dominating principle.

ALTHOR: *You're being too abstract for me, Sam. It sounds like just words. Too high-fallutin' for us non-intellects.*

SAM: *Okay, Let me put it this way.*

Remember back in Chapter 4 when we talked about "mindscapes" and "the rivers of thought" that cut their own channels and guide how we think about things? Well, the Law of Transcendence has turned out to be One Great Big Mother of a river.

What I was suddenly seeing as a result of my one-and-only acid trip was that transcending dichotomies is what life is all about. Living, for all of us, is always a process of working out ways of reconciling the opposing forces that boil to the surface and cry out for attention. We give different names to this process, depending upon the context – Conflict Resolution, War, Sports, Work, Play, Love, Marriage, Politics, Religion, Humor, Psychotherapy – you name it! Wherever you see us struggling – whether it's inside our own heads or in society – we are working away as best we know how at the business of trying to resolve the dichotomies of our existence.

So all of us are grappling with our unresolved dichotomies all the time. Usually we deal with them by ignoring them in hopes they'll go away. Sometimes they do, sometimes we outgrow them – which often means that we've found ways to cover them over so they're out of sight. If we're lucky, they stick around and give us trouble until we wise up and identify them as "problems." Once we do that, we have a much better chance of really getting rid of them.

The Law of Transcendence suggests (or dictates, if it's <u>really</u> a law, but maybe it's still only a hypothesis) that the only genuine way to get rid of our problems – our unresolved dichotomies – is to transcend them, to reconcile them by lifting ourselves to a totally different understanding. Our new understanding must be one that allows the old arguments and polarities either to unify in a more comprehensive idea, or to dissolve as irrelevant.

And that's what living – and psychotherapy – is all about.

The really lovely part of this whole design is its simplicity and its power to release us into Joy. Each experience of transcendence releases us into a brand-

*spandy fresh new world where we can experience
ourselves as being reborn, if only temporarily. And
each transcendence is followed by the appearance of
new dichotomies, new challenges. And if we do our
work well, there is the promise of being constantly
renewed and re-challenged and re-invigorated.*

LEONARDO: *Send out the word! Ponce de Leon's Fountain
of Eternal Youth is alive and well, after all!*

SAM: *Why not? It's possible. It's certainly possible for each
of us as individual human beings.*

Chapter 15

And now, in the late summer of '68, we descend from the loftier realm of altered consciousness with its cosmic truths back down to the nitty-gritty "real world." In the days immediately following my blinding discovery of the Law of Transcendence, two circumstances drew me back to focus on the here and now of daily living. The first was my need to find a job and a new life apart from Odette. The second was a trip to New Mexico to attend the wedding of a dear friend that was to happen in early September.

Surprisingly, I had little difficulty with the first circumstance. I learned through the grapevine of an opening for someone with my qualifications at the University of California at Santa Cruz. A few phone calls, a few interviews and a few weeks later, I was offered a position as psychiatric social worker with the UCSC Student Health Center. My main responsibility would be to provide counseling to emotionally troubled students. There would also be an opportunity to do some teaching as an adjunct faculty instructor. It was made clear to me that I was being hired in the absence of the department head, a psychiatrist who was taking a sabbatical year in Europe, and that my appointment was conditioned on her eventual approval. Since she wouldn't be back to evaluate my performance until the following year, I would have a job for two years, at least, if I performed as expected.

So, just like that, I cake-walked into a dream job at one of the most prestigious and progressive universities, with probably the most beautiful new campus, in one of the most idyllic settings in the world. Just like that.

The second circumstance, that of the wedding in New Mexico, takes longer to tell and calls for some background history that I haven't provided yet. Why not? Because, as you may recall from way back there in Interchapter 2+, my artistic persona *Leonardo* decided (in his words) *to emphasize the significant connections between events across time, rather than present events chronologically.* *Leonardo*'s reasoning was that our minds don't work chronologically but by connecting events in our lives without regard to time. So, we – my personas and I – resort to flashbacks, and flashbacks inside of flashbacks, and flashforwards to link-up related events. I am selecting past happenings as I see them connecting with – and helping to make sense of – subsequent events. To put it another way, I am attempting to assemble as we go along essential elements of a grand dramatic mosaic – if I may so regard it.

So, with that loquacious preamble, I now deem it time to invite onto the pavilion of this performance those magnificent and worthy players, Beatrix, Douglas and James. And let us flash back from the autumn of 1968 to 1960 and the time when Odette and I had decided to set up housekeeping together:

Doug and Bea were married back then. They had just moved from Los Trancos Woods in the hills behind Stanford University to the Napa Valley, leaving behind their rustic and very liveable home. Which the two of them were kind enough to rent to Odette and me. Doug and Bea had met and fallen in love when both were students at Stanford and he played quarterback on the football team and got to throw a scoring pass in the Rose Bowl. I don't recall if it was a

game-winning touchdown, but it might have been. Doug was that
kind of a man: solid, purposeful, courageous in battle, a role model
for the rest of us struggling wannabes. Beatrix was Sir Douglas's
beautiful Lady – slender, graceful, and to the manor born. Well,
more truthfully, she was born in Hungary and I don't know if it was
in a manor. But as a child she used to roller-skate with her brother in
the corridors of Chicago's Edgewater Beach Hotel where her father
was the house physician. Actually, Bea and I enjoyed a childhood
connection of sorts. I lived a few blocks from the Edgewater for a
time in 1931 and it may even have been while she was inside roller-
skating. Naw, that's not possible. I can't imagine she was even born
yet.

Anyway – fast-forwarding from our respective childhoods back
up to 1960 – Doug had just acquired a half-interest in an automobile
agency in Napa and he and Bea bought a beautiful old ranch with a
6-acre lake in the front yard and barns for the horses out back. They
named the ranch *Rivendell* – "The Last Homely House in the West"
in J.R.R. Tolkien's trilogy, *Lord of the Rings.* How we all loved the
Ring books, and their precursor, *The Hobbit,* and how deeply immersed in their drama, and how caught up in the spell of their magic
the four of us adults and our children all became. Still are, I imagine.
But back there, we drew on Tolkien's mythical world to enrich and
enliven our own. Doug and Bea named their animals after Tolkien
characters. I remember that one of their Mallard ducks in the pond
was *Frodo*; and there was Doug's white stallion who might have
been *Gandalf's* horse *Shadowfax,* but I can't swear to it; and his
Weimeraner dog was *Strider.* Clearly, Doug was an *Aragorn* of
heroic proportion. Beatrix, though, was more *Goldberry, Tom Bom-
badil's lady,* than *Arwen Evenstar.* Odette was more the latter. And,
yes, I can see myself in that mythical re-enactment as one of the
Hobbits, *Sam Gamgee,* perhaps – the *Ringbearer's* loyal and trustworthy companion – although I have often failed to be as trustworthy as
he was. But then, there was always hope for tomorrow.

And basking in the nurturing warmth of our shared values and dreams, the four of us drew ever closer. We made numerous trips to Rivendell during that first year when Odette and I and our kids were living in Los Trancos Woods. In the following June, Odette and I were married at Rivendell and Doug and Bea stood up with us. The ceremony was performed by a recently-divorced reform rabbi who drove up from Palo Alto with his beautiful young mistress and the two of them paddled us newlyweds around the lake in a canoe. "Just like it's done in Israel," he told us. Our wedding was my deepest immersion in religious Judaism. Of course, there had been many immersions of the non-religious variety – two summers at Camp Jungvelt outside Toronto when I was 13 and 14; being a counselor at a YMHA (Young Men's Hebrew Association) Summer Day Camp in Montreal when I was 16 – but those are events in other stories whose time for re-telling still may come.

Around the time of our wedding, we all decided that Odette and I and our children should move to Rivendell. The large old ranch house was just big enough for all of us, and besides, we all felt the excitement of taking on the challenge of growing our families together. And it really worked. We lived together quite harmoniously for a year, thanks largely to long hours spent in open and often intense talk. I remember also long hours of shared reading, and doing joyful things like swimming in the lake, and riding horses, and roaming the 40 mysterious acres of land. That was a year during which I was commuting several times a week to the University of California at Berkeley where I was pursuing a master's degree in Journalism and a junior college teaching credential. It was also a year in which our daughter Teddie was born. And it was a year in which we all learned a great deal about nurturing our love for each other under not always easy circumstances.

Then, in the summer of '62, it was time for us to leave. With my brand new master's degree and teaching credential in hand, we packed the kids and our belongings into our old VW bus and headed south to the Mexico border and my first teaching job at Imperial Valley College in El Centro, California. On the day we arrived in El Centro it was an unbearable 120 degrees in the shade. A year later, we traded El Centro for another teaching job at Lower Columbia College in much cooler and wetter Longview, Washington, although by then we had adjusted to the heat and were loving the desert. The second year of teaching, in Longview, led us to Seattle and the University of Washington School of Social Work. And sometime during the El Centro and Longview years, Doug and Bea sold Rivendell and the auto agency and headed for a more leisurely lifestyle in San Miguel de Allende, a few hours drive northwest from Mexico City.

We all kept in touch. Odette flew down to spend time with them on one or two occasions. And, because immigration law required them to revisit the United States every six months, we would occasionally drive down to meet them in El Paso and spend a few days together camping in the mountains of New Mexico.

It was several years later – when our family was living in Ventura – that their marriage foundered. So did Doug. As I remember it, their marriage was already in trouble when Doug's sailboat was caught by a sudden storm off the Mexican coast and capsized. Doug washed up on shore, more dead than alive, still clinging to the wreckage of his sailboat. He was found unconscious by a group of Indians who nursed him back to health. When he recovered, he made his way back to San Miguel de Allende and found Beatrix deeply involved in a relationship with James. Doug and Bea divorced shortly thereafter and Doug came north on a pilgrimage of healing and recovery. He stayed with us in Ventura for a while and we all spent days and nights nurturing and caring and helping him re-structure a future.

And a little later, Odette and I met James on an occasion when he and Bea came to Ventura seeking understanding and acceptance.

Of course we gave it. Still, it was not easy for me to completely like James. He was clearly a complex man about whom there is much that can be said – and will be – but at the time, I could only see his surface prominences: success as author of a book that had earned a useful place in the literature of the counter culture; an impressive physicality; a dramatically easy way with people. He came across to me as larger than life – yet considerably obscured, and a mystery.

And now, in the waning days of the summer of '68, Bea and James were to be married in Taos, New Mexico.

Odette and I had planned to drive to the wedding together but the plans changed in the turmoil of our Esalen Summer. Odette and Mario decided that they would go to Taos together. I would be going – or perhaps not going – on my own. I had not made a firm decision as September rolled around, and I was on the verge of skipping the wedding altogether. Much as I loved Bea, I was anticipating awkwardness at my being there estranged from Odette who would be accompanied by her new partner.

Then, out of the blue, Odette telephoned to say that Mario would not be able to make the trip. Would I be a good friend and take her and Teddie to the wedding with me? So we arranged that I would pick them up in Morro Bay and the three of us would make the trip.

In fact, we had a rather pleasant time of it. I was able to manage my role as good friend to Odette largely because I was already accepting that we had too much shared history and respect for each other to completely disregard, now that our marriage was over. It helped that I was successfully neutralizing my sexual feelings for her. So our trip down was filled with circumscribed amicable talk, companionable parenting, and a minimum of discussion about her future with Mario.

The wedding was an humongous affair to which, it seemed, half of Taos – the counter-culture half – had been invited. It went on for days – music, food, laughter, dancing, colorfully-dressed people milling about or rapt in conversation, and a great variety of distractions. I remember a vivid outdoor wedding ceremony with a radiant Beatrix and a proud and loving James.

I remember pieces of the drive back to Morro Bay. Mostly I remember Odette's mounting apprehension. Mario, it seemed, was being torn. Odette had talked with him by telephone from Taos and he was being guarded about their future together. Nothing was decided but it was clear their relationship had run into troubled waters. I could feel Odette holding her breath most of the way home. I don't think I was holding mine. I think I was holding myself in neutral, in my loosely-involved, pretty-detached-from-it-all, mode.

Within a few minutes of our entering Mario's house, he was telling the two of us that he had given a lot of thought to everything that had been happening and he had made up his mind: His love for Odette was not of the sort that could lead to marriage. He loved us both and felt guilty for his role in the breakup of our marriage. He was involved in another relationship and felt conflicting loyalties and commitments all around. He had decided to end his relationship with Odette.

Humiliated and wordless, Odette turned and ran out of the house. By the time Mario and I set off to look for her, she was nowhere to be found. We searched everywhere. The cars were still parked, so she hadn't driven off. She was nowhere nearby. We turned to searching the vacant fields that surrounded the house, calling her name. We found her, at last, curled into a wailing, heaving ball of pain pouring her burden of agony and outrage onto the barely-yielding belly of Mother Earth. I motioned Mario away and knelt beside her. In time I put my arm around her shoulder and she allowed it to remain. I said, "Come. Come with me to Al and Pearl's. You can rest there. We can decide later what to do next."

And so we did.

Chapter 16

Those of you who are still couples and have succeeded in pulling your relationships back together after your hearts were broken on the rocks of your adventuring, know that it calls for a lot of forgiveness and great patience. Even then, forever after, your marriage is unalterably changed. Given time and devoted effort, it may even be changed for the better, but changed it will be nevertheless.

Odette and I decided, in the weeks that followed our return from Bea and James' wedding, to pick up what remained of our marriage and to go on together. How were we to do that? Slowly, carefully, and a piece at a time. Neither of us was ready to unreservedly re-commit to a life together forever. We were both too emotionally wounded. Minefields had to be avoided that might lead to the reopening of fresh wounds. But what we could offer each other to begin with were respect, caring, a certain amount of security and protection from needless hurt, a new start, and a commitment to not abandon each other.

So, just before I was due to report for work at my new job, we found a wonderful old house to rent on a bluff overlooking downtown Santa Cruz, the amusement park, the beach and Monterey Bay. The disintegration of the family that had been taking place in the spring and summer, was turning to consolidation in the fall. The family would come back together and hold, but it would be more dispersed. Odette, Teddie and I would now be our family in residence in Santa Cruz. Dean and Ian were ensconced for the school year in their own apartment in Ventura – with financial, medical and legal support systems in place. Dennis, who graduated from high school the previous June, was getting his start as an independent adult and already living with a young woman, Maria, in Pacific Grove. And our house would be large enough to accommodate everybody when we came together for family gatherings.

The university lay sprawled like clusters of shiny jewels in the wooded hills above Santa Cruz, each cluster one of the several colleges, each with its own community of students, faculty, academic emphasis, and distinctive architecture.

The University Health Center's small staff of counselors functioned on a decentralized plan with a counselor assigned to each of the various colleges. I was assigned to Crown College, a tidy Alpine village of residence halls, classrooms, offices, eating places and other facilities – all in brilliant white stucco offset with dark wood trim, and gathered among the redwoods. I would be dividing my hours between an office in Crown College and the Health Center, a refreshingly-hilly walk away. I was resuming my professional commitment to growth and healing in an environment that, clearly, the Gods were shining upon.

Experimentation with hallucinogens – specifically LSD, marijuana and hashish – was commonplace among the students at UCSC during the late sixties. This widespread experimentation frequently led to psychic trauma that stretched coping mechanisms to the breaking point. To put it in the vernacular of the time: a lot of folks were stumbling into bad trips during their drug experiences and subsequently were having a helluva time keeping their heads and their shit together. Mental health counselors were constantly having to address the drug-related issues of their clients. These days, of course, drug and alcohol related issues are old hat. By that, I mean, therapists have now been working with substance abuse issues for several decades. But back in the sixties it was all new and therapists were having to learn about hallucinogens – and the reactions of their clients to hallucinogens – as rapidly as they could manage.

In that regard, my earlier professional experiences and my newer learnings gleaned from my Esalen Summer and my acid trip served me and my student clients well at Santa Cruz. I knew experientially what students had experienced in their altered consciousness. I had walked the walk. I had been in their shoes. I could talk to them in a common tongue of shared experience. They could hear me and evaluate what I had to say to them. And together, we could work out ways by which they could deal with the anguish and pain of their unresolved dilemmas.

And that's what every bad trip involved: a painful unresolved dilemma. That is why Al Kraft had me prepare for my acid trip by establishing my resolve to not back away from any terror I might confront in altered consciousness. Bad trips – such as those I observed in my work with UCSC students – were the result of their being blindsided and overwhelmed by negative and painful experiences encountered in their drug-induced states. As the scholars at Esalen had explained: the drugs were acting as mind-releasing agents and were not themselves generating the hallucinatory experiences of their users. The minds of the users – released by the drug from their normal controls and constraints – did the generating.

The students I worked with who had taken hallucinogens were expecting to be carried away on wholly-pleasurable trips and were unprepared for the frightening visions their minds were generating.

Suddenly, they were confronting horrible nightmares from which they tried to run away and hide. But they couldn't. Once released from their hidey-holes in the subconscious, the nightmares refused to be stuffed back in for long. They were repeatedly springing back to life in the form of "flashbacks" screaming for attention.

It was in my work with the students at UCSC that I began consciously putting into practice my insights regarding what I am calling the Law of Transcendence. To refresh your memory, the Law recognizes that every problem can be stated in terms of a conflict between opposites, i.e., a dichotomy.

For example: If you've got problems with your mother-in-law, the problems can be stated as one or more dichotomies with your mother-in-law on one side of the argument and you on the other. And the Law states that every dichotomy – which means every dichotomy you can think of and all of those you haven't gotten around to thinking of – can be resolved by some overarching conceptualization within which the conflicting sides of the dichotomy either disappear or are reconciled. The new overarching conceptualization is transcendent – in the sense that it represents a higher order of thinking about the dichotomous situation.

In my work at UCSC, I focused more and more on helping students to identify and transcend the particular unresolved dichotomies that had flared up during their bad trips.

Obviously, if you're going to transcend a dichotomy, you first have to discover what it is. A client comes in with what therapists call *the identified problem*. He or she comes in complaining of a headache – that's *the identified problem*. The real problem – whatever is causing the headache – lies hidden somewhere underneath the identified problem.

Let's look again at the problems you're having with your mother-in-law:

You come to your therapist complaining, *I can't stand her!*

Your therapist asks, *How come?*

And you reply, *Because she's always meddling.*

Your therapist says, *What do you mean she's always meddling? Give me a for-instance?*

So you think of a *for-instance.*

What's going on, of course, is that you and your therapist are digging below the obvious to uncover underlying problems. And, in psychotherapy, there are invariably layers upon layers of underlying problems. That doesn't mean you have to dig down to China, but it does mean you and your therapist have to decide at what level you want to work toward a solution. Beneath your mother-in-law problem, if you dig deeply enough, you'll bump into *yourself* and you'll discover layers of unresolved stuff *within you*. In fact, the truth is: *you are always the problem!* – No matter what. Or, to put it more correctly: *your psychological problems are always rooted in your own thought processes.* Now, you don't necessarily have to dig all that deep to take care of your mother-in-law problem, but you could.

According to the Law of Transcendence, every one of our many layers of problems can be stated as dichotomies capable of being transcended. And the reason these layers of unresolved dichotomies still exist is that we never did transcend them. Instead of finding higher-order conceptualizations that would render the dichotomies inoperable, we perpetuated them by leaping onto the bandwagon of what we were told and assumed were the *right* sides and rejected the *wrong* sides. Except, when it comes to dichotomies, there are no right sides and wrong sides; only opposites capable of being transcended.

We are all running around with unresolved dichotomies inside our heads that we keep more or less under control with our nests of tidy assumptions based on our own peculiar notions of right and wrong.

I'm right and my mother-in-law is wrong.

My religion is closer to God than your religion.

My politics are better than your politics.

My values are better than your values.

My country is better than your country.

My kind of human being is more valuable than your kind of human being.

People are more valuable than animals.

It's right to kill those bastards because they'll do us in if we don't! And, besides, God's on our side!

History – like that being played out in Eastern Europe right now, and that played out during World War II, and that played out during the cultural and psychiatric revolution of the sixties – has a marvelous way of upending false assumptions and revealing the old outworn dichotomies underneath. But we don't have to wait for the epoch-making events of history to reveal and resolve our problems for us. We can do this work of self-discovery and transcendence ourselves, anytime we choose to put our attention and our energies to the task. Provided we have useful tools. At Santa Cruz – with the help of the wonderfully bright and creative students I was working with – we were shaping tools.

In retrospect, I would have to say that the most effective tool we were shaping together was an orientation that sees psychotherapy as a collaboration in learning. What we were doing – whether it was in individual counseling sessions or in group experiences or in the classroom – was working together to exchange useful information and figuring out how to use the information to resolve problems. That the problems were deeply personal didn't change the nature of the process. The same challenges and joys of learning were making the process work. And because the students were bright and eager, the process often illuminated and sparkled. I had known such sparkling, such illumination, in my work with a few patients in the hospital wards at Camarillo and, more frequently, in our weekend marathons. At Santa Cruz, it seemed at times that we were lighting up the sky.

So it was that in this idyllic setting and in this generative way my life at UCSC was proceeding on its pleasant course. So, too, were our deep personal wounds of the previous year healing and our marriage renewing. The school year drew to a close and, in early July of 1969, it was summer vacation time. Odette and Teddie and I were housesitting the Krafts' home in Menlo Park while Odette recuperated from an appendectomy performed at Stanford University Hospital some days before.

The phone rang. I picked it up, said "Hello," and I heard Doug's voice heavy with tragedy.

"I have very bad news so prepare yourself."

I took a deep breath.

"Ian had an accident. He's dead."

"Oh My God! .... How?"

"He was riding my motorcycle. Bringing it back to Big Sur from Monterey. The Highway Patrol says he was coming up a long grade near Garapata Creek. He was behind a slow-moving VW bus and went to pass. For some reason he lost control and swerved off the road and was thrown off. He was killed instantly. The officer says he broke his neck.

"They've taken him to a mortuary in Monterey."

Interchapter 16+

LEONARDO: *No! I don't know how to write about Ian's death. There's still so much pain. Every time I see a motorcycle, I see Ian losing his life in one brief crazy moment – him flying through the air and his world coming apart. I keep wondering what must have been going through his mind while he was hurtling through the air, just before he broke his neck. I have so much sadness for him. So much promise. So bright. Snuffed out at sixteen. Not even out of high school. How often I've grieved for what he might have accomplished as an adult.*

MINNIE: *I feel guilty. If we had held our family together as a unit, it might have been different for Ian. Maybe he would have been better prepared in some way.*

SAM: *I don't know, Minnie. I think Ian was doing what he needed to be doing and, until the moment of his death, he was doing it wholeheartedly and well. What more can we ask of him? To not get himself killed so we don't have to feel pain and torment because he's gone? So we don't have to re-live his death over and over? So we don't have to try to decipher the real meaning of his life and death for ourselves?*

MINNIE: *The real meaning! It's now twenty-two years since his death. Ian would be 38 had he lived. The real meaning is that neither Ian nor any of us can ever know Ian at 38. And we are forever left with our "What might have beens."*

LEONARDO: *I guess I'm left with sharp images of July, 1969:*

> *Odette's horrified grief-stricken face when I broke the news. ...*

> *Odette staying in the van with Teddie at the mortuary, saying she didn't want to see Ian broken and cold. ...*

> *Ian's body beneath a white sheet, peaceful and smelling of death on a stainless steel table waiting to be burned down to a shovelfull of bones and ash. ...*

> *The surprisingly large gathering of relatives and friends at the memorial service, all of us remembering Ian, and sorrowing, and celebrating his life . ...*

> *And much later, Odette and I wading into the surf off Garapata Creek with the canister of Ian's ashes. ...*

> *And Odette emptying the canister. ...*

> *What more do we have to say about the terrible loss of that shining young star?*

SAM: *Well, what Ian gave to me is two-fold: wonderful
memories of him when he was alive, on the one hand,
and the gift of experiencing the loss of one's child, on
the other. Nobody's death has had the impact upon me
that Ian's has had. Thanks to Ian, I know what it
means to lose a son; I know how never-ending the loss
of one's child is; I know the wave of sadness and
aching that sweeps over one again and again and
again – the wave that, so far as I can tell, goes on
forever, refusing to fade away and disappear until, at
last, we ourselves disappear.*

*I don't think any of us really knows what it's like for
another person to lose a child without having gone
through the experience ourselves. As a psychotherapist, I have Ian to thank for allowing me to know. But
for Ian, I am sure I would not be as well equipped to
understand and respond relevantly to my grieving
client friends.*

LEONARDO: *To me – the writer and artist – Ian is a contin-
ual reminder that we never know when time runs out
in this life. So, at least in part, I have Ian to thank for
my sense of urgency. Without him, this book might
never be finished. Of course, even with him, it may
never be finished because that may be the way the
cookie crumbles. But until this cookie crumbles, he
reminds me to keep working urgently.*

Chapter 17

Over the years, the shock and pain of Ian's death have subsided to deeply respectful memories of him alive and not infrequent resurgences of aching that, by now, I should have expected to almost-entirely disappear beneath a flat calm of acceptance but haven't. In the year following his death, our second at Santa Cruz, Ian was almost constantly with us – just around the corner of every moment, waiting to remind us again and again how much we longed for him to be alive, to be growing alongside us in time. Of course, the year unfolded its own scroll of events in accordance with its own mysterious patterns and rhythms, seemingly with little regard to the shocking loss of Ian's physical presence in our lives.

Bright among my memories is the ranch-style house that we bought. It sat on a large city lot with a small rustic barn in back that was vined over with Cecil Bruner roses. We did some remodeling to the inside of the barn and turned it into office space and a place for guests to sleep over. Odette came up with an idea for a large three-tiered planter for growing vegetables, and we built it along one edge of the back yard out of heavy redwood planks and filled it with rich loam hauled in from a mushroom farm, somewhere. The garden fulfilled all of our expectations and the veggies that we grew were plentiful and beautiful and delicious. And the back yard also contained rows of aged rose bushes over which I spent contemplative hours pruning with exquisite tenderness while trying to remember the rules governing rose bush pruning which I read over and over – apparently with the huge sieve-like portion of my mind that remembers almost nothing of what my eyes scan. But the rose bushes kept yielding their wonderful bursts of color, which led me to suppose that perhaps I knew more about the art of rose-growing than I credited myself with.

I will never forget the joy and satisfaction of living there. The house faced away from the street and opened onto the garden in back and the roses and the rose-covered wonderful old barn. Its priceless gift was that it gave us our own quiet, private, beautiful world. There, our lives were being slowly renewed. There, we could feel the grievous wounds healing again.

If memory serves me right, it was during the summer of '69 that Leiana came to live for a while in our barn with Paul, a classmate with whom she was exploring a relationship. The two of them were among the bright young undergraduate students enrolled in my class, *Introduction to Counseling Theory and Practice*. In addition to my sharing with them fundamentals of counseling, I was sending them off on weekly trips to Agnews State Hospital where they were assigned patients with whom they were to establish and maintain therapeutic relationships during the school term. Paul subsequently moved out of our lives, but Leiana joined our family and became an older sister to Teddie and a dear friend and daughter to Odette and me. Over the years, Leiana carved out a wonderfully scroll-like life for herself, very complex and intricate. It delights me to be still included among her dearest friends. As you will learn in due course, Leiana's path and our own have remained interwoven and supportive through both joyous and sad times.

In my memory of the Santa Cruz years, my work with students

stands out as the richest and most productive aspect of my existence. I invariably found interacting with them rewarding. Nor did I have difficulty relating to my professional peers and supervisors during my first year. But during my second year things changed.

I mentioned earlier that I had been hired in the absence of the psychiatrist who was to become my supervisor when she returned from her sabbatical year in Europe. It had been made clear that my continuing on at UCSC for more than two years would be subject to her approval. She returned on schedule in September, 1969, at the beginning of my second year. And by the time my contract was up for renewal for a third year, I had failed to win her endorsement.

It might have been that she had reasons for not approving of me that had little or nothing to do with me. She hadn't hired me and may have wanted someone more to her liking in my place. But aside from a possible agenda of her own, I can look back and see reasons that were operating within me that do much to explain why she and I didn't make it together.

A major one is that I have always felt less at ease with my supervisors and professional peers than with my clients and students. As a rule, I communicated easily and comfortably with clients and students, less comfortably with peers, and awkwardly with supervisors. With clients, I found little difficulty in identifying with them and with their experiences; I easily tuned into their worlds, spoke a common language, and shared parts of my knowledge that might be of use to them. More often than not, we found it easy to be on the same team. I felt myself making a constructive difference in their lives.

With my peers, and more particularly with my supervisors, I usually felt we were in different realities – strangers who barely spoke the same language. Often, I felt myself an outsider who couldn't fathom the intricacies of their language, or the subtleties of their rules of conduct, or the manner in which their thinking processes worked. So, often when I was called upon in supervisory sessions to talk about my work with my clients, the chasm between our worlds yawned wider and I would have difficulty in finding the words and concepts to bridge the gap.

It didn't help that my supervisor was a psychoanalytically-trained Freudian psychiatrist. Not only did we not establish personal rapport, I was also intimidated by what I regarded as the labyrinthine logic that Freudians use to generate their clinical understanding. It didn't help that in my work with clients I have always been intuitively and innovatively oriented. By that, I mean that I have always regarded my role as one in which I have a responsibility for being creative and constructive in how I respond. With each of my clients, I am exploring new territory, new life situations, and I am challenged to devise the most appropriate strategies by which they can move toward greater self-discovery and understanding. Back then, I couldn't explain myself and the work I was doing in a language that was not native to me: *Establishment Freudianese.* I didn't know how to do that.

Interchapter 17+

LEONARDO: *Help! I'm stuck.*

ALTHOR: *Not again! It seems like you get stuck at least once in every chapter. Can't you do anything by yourself? I thought you were a writer. Why do you keep calling on us to write for you if you're a writer?*

LEONARDO: *Why are you so defensive, all of a sudden? I thought you wanted to help out?*

ALTHOR: *Not me, old buddy! Remember, I'm the guy who said way back there in the Prologue that writing our autobiography was a big mistake.*

SAM: *Now slow down fellas – both of you. We all agreed to work together on this. Althor, if you're getting scared again, maybe we'd better pay attention to that. Is that what's troubling you?*

ALTHOR: *No, not really. It's just that I'm getting tired of Leonardo's calling on us to rescue him in practically every chapter. Can't he write one without getting himself stuck?*

LEONARDO: *Of course I can. I just think they go a lot better when we multilogue* **our way through the tricky spots.When we're undecided about what needs to happen next, I call us together to talk our way through it. And I have two very good reasons for doing that:*

First, I think the reader will appreciate being in on the process of writing this book. Frankly, I'm tired of reading books where the author seems to know everything and presents it all so smoothly that the reader gets seduced into believing the author really does. Well, maybe that's true for some authors. For me, if our writing is clear and authoritative, it's because we've worked our way through the confusion to clarity. I think that sharing with our reader some of the process of working our way through to clarity is an important part of what we're trying to do here.

The second reason is that ...well, damn, I've forgotten what my second reason was.

SAM: *Well, maybe you'll remember. But you said you called us together because you were stuck. What was that about?*

LEONARDO: *Oh, yes. Well, Chapter 17 feels choppy to me.*

ALTHOR: *Yeah, I don't like it very much, either. It's too melancholy for my taste – too much about loss and inadequacy. I don't think that's going to appeal to our readers very much.*

SAM: *Well, I think it's accurate reporting and that's our first obligation. I think it's consistent with how we experi-*

*enced that year following Ian's death. It just wasn't
an easy year. It was a year of grieving and of healing,
and it wasn't made easier by our supervisor's return
from her sabbatical to end our honeymoon at UCSC.*

LEONARDO: *Maybe I'm just a bit tired of trauma. Maybe
I'd like some easy-going happy stuff right about now.
I think our readers would, too.*

SAM: *Maybe they would. But we're committed to being as
true to our understanding of our personal history as
we can manage. And that means exposing some things
that we're not all that comfortable with.*

ALTHOR: *Why can't we just skip the uncomfortable stuff?*

SAM: *Because the only reason it's uncomfortable for us is
that we haven't fully worked our way through to
resolving it. The uncomfortable stuff, as you call it, is
really quite neutral. When we've fully resolved our
own issues around it, when we've transcended all the
dichotomies associated with it, we will no longer feel
the discomfort. And because this is a book about
working through human issues in the interests of
growing ourselves as healthy organisms, we don't
have the freedom to avoid our own areas of discomfort. We are here to tell it like it is for us. No more. No
less.*

ALTHOR: *You sound like you really understand all this, so I
have to believe you probably do. But I am finding all
this self-revealing pretty damn uncomfortable. I
prefer to not show our failings to the whole world. I
think folks will reject us if we let them see who we
really are behind the front we present to them.*

SAM: *What you're really saying, Althor, is that we still have work to do. We still have unresolved issues that are causing you pain. I think that's great! Think how dull our life would be if there were nothing left to work on?*

ALTHOR: *Oh Boy! Am I glad I'm making you happy!*

SAM: *Well, you really are. I find it exciting to be working away at discovering new things about 'How come people are who they are?' and 'What can we do to help them become the people they'd like to be?'*

ALTHOR: *Sam, you've just touched a nerve. You know, I don't think I understand yet, 'How come I am who I am?' I mean, How come I don't feel more secure? How come I still get scared in the world of people? How come I've had so much trouble with authority figures?*

SAM: *Yes, I know. There's still a lot we haven't explored – all the fascinating experiences of our adolescence in Montreal, and in the war-torn world of our young-manhood in England, and in the post-war world of Berkeley where we seemed, at last, to grasp some shaky handholds on the slippery slope of adult maturity.*

You know, Althor, it's taken a long time for us to become who we are. We've been – and still are – rather slow learners. Maybe that's not correct. Maybe it's more correct to say we've always been intrigued by how much there is to learn, and the learning just keeps going on and on.

ALTHOR: *Am I reading you correctly? – That my fears and feelings of inadequacy come from growing up in Montreal?*

SAM: *A lot of them, anyway. Certainly, it was during those sensitive years of adolescence that we struggled hardest to figure out how to respond to them. I think it was during that period that we discovered and fixed on our various strategies for managing our fears and feelings of inadequacy – or denying them, or working our way around them, or confronting them, or whatever. If you want to know 'How come you got to be who you are?' you need to explore who you were being back then.*

LEONARDO: *OK. Now I know what has to happen next. Before we move forward from the Santa Cruz years, we need to go back to our earlier years of growing up in Montreal.*

---

* *Multiloguing, n.*, and *multilogue, v.*, are words I have coined to denote the process wherein one's multiple selves or personas converse with one another.

Chapter 18

I was 13 and the 1933 Chicago World's Fair was about to re-open for its reprise performance in the early summer of 1934 when we abandoned Chicago and drove to Pickering, Ontario, not far from Toronto. There, our parents, Bernard and Emma, enrolled the three of us children – Evelyn, Hugo and me – for a month of summer camp while they continued on to Montreal to establish a new home. Dad – as General Organizer of the International Ladies Garment Workers Union – was being sent to Montreal to unionize the city's dressmaking industry.

I have some fond and some uncomfortable memories of Camp Jungvelt. The discomfort arose from my inability to speak or understand Yiddish, the camp's official language. On the other hand, I had no trouble understanding Joyish, the unofficial language. The counselors and other boys and girls were very friendly and we all sang and danced around campfires and swam and played games and ate a lot. And, all at once, I graduated into adolescence and fell madly in love for the first time since my Jerry Axelrod days back in the Modern School in Stelton, New Jersey. For the first time I was becoming acutely aware of how soft and marvelously-swelling girls' breasts are, and how gracefully their bodies curve outward from their waists to their hips and slope inward along their thighs, and how water rivulets down their smooth and shiny tan bodies after swimming, and how the water settles into iridescent droplets when they lie down in the sunshine. Oh, how I longed to be such a rivulet or droplet sliding slowly down a smooth warm neck where it mysteriously disappears into a Jantzen swim suit. Oh, the agonies of not knowing what to do with my sharp awakenings in adolescence.

Chave, the second great love of my life, spoke her name with a soft clearing of the throat. I remember black wavy hair and a husky musical voice and dark eyes in an oval lovely face. I remember magic, mystery and unknowable depths. I remember that her older sister was a professional actress who understudied Margo in the stage production of W*interset* starring Burgess Meredith. Isn't it odd what one remembers and forgets? I suppose I remember famous names – probably because they establish an implied proximity to greatness. *Aha!* I can hear an invisible audience say, *so he knows Ish Kabibble; he must be somebody!* I have to admit that even now, when I am certainly old enough to know better, it feels good to have at least a handful of *Ish Kabibbles* to scatter among the pages of this book.

My second great love burned for several years, fueled by a steady exchange of letters and my occasional sallyings forth on hitch-hiking trips between Montreal and Toronto, where Chave lived. Actually, it was the correspondence that provided the fuel. My trips to Toronto were dampening. There was this chasm between the passion of our letters and the awkwardness of our actual time together. Still, our letters fed the flames during those formative years of adolescence.

For our first two years in Montreal we lived in a three-bedroom apartment in a red brick, three-story apartment house on Lincoln Avenue just off Rue Guy about a dozen walkable blocks along Rue Sherbrooke from Montreal High School. The high school was a three-story, ivory-colored building laid out like a giant H that stood a block or two from McGill University. On my walks home from school in spring and autumn afternoons, I would pass the grounds and grey stone buildings of McGill and, further along Sherbrooke, the Museum of Fine Arts where I often went inside to lose myself in paintings of great battles, of heroic men, of pink, ivory and brown women, and of landscapes that drew me into their misty vastnesses.

The corridors connecting the two sides of the high school's giant H were cut through by a frontier that divided the high school in two: one half for boys and the other for girls. There were no visible signs or gates at the frontier but the rule against fraternizing with members of the opposite sex was total. I have no memory of ever sitting in the same classroom with a girl during my four years at the school, and only one of ever talking to a girl student – a brief fumbling evening phone call with a redhaired Goddess who's name lingered in my memory across many years but finally has dimmed into uncertainty. MacLean? Betty? In any case, I asked her for a date and she shattered me with her refusal.

In that first year, my eighth grade teacher was a Mr. King whom I remember as a kindly, tall, slender, black-mustached gentleman who also was retained by my parents to tutor me privately in French. I was already four or five years behind my classmates when I entered the 8th grade; they had been studying French – the native language of the majority of people living in Montreal and the province of Quebec – from the 3rd or 4th grade and many of them were already fluent.

The Sword of Damocles hanging over all our heads was the high school graduation requirement that we pass our final written and oral French examinations. So, during that first year, Mr. King would come to our home one evening a week to drill me in what felt like a vain effort to master *le Français*.

The only French examinations I ever passed during my four years were the very last – the final hurdles without the clearing of which I might still be lost somewhere in the bowels of the Montreal Protestant School System.

But more than his French lessons, Mr. King's most valuable gift to me was the passage from Shakespeare's *Hamlet* he wrote in my autograph book. The book has long since vanished but I still carry and honor the quotation as if it were a banner:

> *This above all; To thine own self be true:*
> *And it must follow, as the Night the Day,*
> *Thou canst not then be false to any man.*

I felt that Mr. King was seeing into my troubled soul and writing out the healing secret for me to follow. It took years of pondering before the truth of that quotation finally struck home.

My ninth grade teacher was named with Dickensian appropriateness, Mr. Bent. Stocky, balding with a light mustache, Mr. Bent was not physically stooped but psychologically I have my doubts. Some of my classmates ridiculed him because they detected a habit of his and made much of it in schoolboyish style: he kept one hand in his pocket and seemed to be scratching or fondling his genitals a lot. Perhaps he had a rash that screamed for attention. In any case, Mr. Bent was not admired as a positive role model by most of us. My own loathing for the man had little to do with his pocket manners. It had everything to do with the fact that he repeatedly chose me to read the part of *Shylocke the Jew* in our daily classroom recitations of *The Merchant of Venice*.

For the first time, I experienced myself as an object of anti-semitism in school. I remember one occasion where I was cornered by three or four of my classmates in the cloakroom where we parked our coats and hats each morning and retrieved them every afternoon. They taunted me for being a Christ killer, if memory serves me right, and were roughing me up. I suppose I fought back well enough because they didn't bother me again, but there was damage to my psyche. For many years after, I struggled with the painful ambivalence of neither wholly accepting myself as truly Jewish nor feeling entirely accepted as anything else.

It was also during my ninth grade experience that the school's headmaster, Mr. Sommerville, gave me a gift to rival Mr. King's. During one of my infrequent visits to his office, he forcibly drew my attention to the fact that I had been speaking to him while avoiding direct eye contact.

When you speak to me, I want you to look in my eyes, not at my feet or out the window! Do you understand?

I understood.

So far as I recall, it was my first conscious encounter with how much I was in dread of powerful authority figures in the adult world. It was also my first awareness of how I was translating my dread into socially-unacceptable behavior. And it was my first big lesson in the art of consciously shaping my own behavioral responses.

Conscious shaping of our own behaviors is a skill that seems important in managing and manipulating our way in the world. I practiced it with great dedication for many years and I guess it has been productive. But there is a difference between artfully-shaped behavior and authentic behavior – a difference that was epitomized in the two gifts of Mr. King and Mr. Sommerville.

Mr. King's gift – the words of Polonius to his son Laertes – argues for authenticity: *Be true to your inner self,* it seems to say. Mr. Sommerville's gift, on the other hand, seems to argue for artful

shaping: *Your outward behavior is the mark of your worth*, it seems
to say. But if our eyes are truly windows into our inner selves, then
am I not revealing my inner artifice for you to see when our eyes
meet, if indeed I am being false? So I have concluded that both Mr.
King and Mr. Sommerville were giving gifts from the same tree of
knowledge after all – gifts that have made it difficult and painful for
me to endure my own falsehoods. Their gifts might almost have
been enough had I not learned another thing in high school.

In fact, I probably learned more in my four years at Montreal
High than in any four-year period of schooling since. The quality of
teaching was very good and the curriculum, as I remember it, was
broad and basic. In the tenth grade we had to choose between two
learning tracks: one in math and the sciences, the other in Latin and
the liberal arts. I chose the math and science track. I wasn't interested in Latin – I was having enough trouble with French and wasn't
up to grappling with another foreign language. Although, I must say
that over the years I've missed not having studied Latin; I'm sure it
would have greatly improved my comprehension and competence
with both French and English. Nevertheless, my high schooling
provided a solid foundation: English literature – consisting of a
detailed study of a different Shakespeare play each term and extensive readings of selected English poets – Canadian and English History, Geography, Physics, Chemistry, Algebra, Geometry, Trigo-
nometry, and Physical Education. And, of course, ubiquitous French.

School started at 8:00 a.m. and ended at 4:00 p.m. with an hour
for lunch. Homework assignments kept me studying for another two
to four hours – much more in the days before final examinations.
For the most part, I felt myself challenged and exhilarated – both
from the excitement of learning and from anxiety associated with
fear of failure. Adding to the pressure was the knowledge that we
Jewish students had to pass our final high school examinations with
an average score of at least 75 percent to be accepted at McGill

University. As I recall, Gentile high school graduates were being admitted with scores of 60 or 65 percent.

Interchapter 18+

ALTHOR: *Okay! Now I can see where some of my anxieties and problems with authority figures come from. I guess that must have been before I was Althor – when I was being Albert and Arthur. Isn't that right?*

MOISHE: *Your question reminds me of a story: There's this woman who's asleep in her bed one night and a dark handsome mysterious stranger in a flowing black cape lined in scarlet sweeps through a pair of French doors into her bedroom and sweeps her up and carries her off in his arms and they ride away on his great black stallion to this great castle where he carries her into an ornate bedroom and lays her gently onto this luxurious bed. Then he stands beside the bed, gazing down on her for a very long time, until, at last, she asks,"What's going to happen now?" To which the dark handsome mysterious stranger replies, "Damned if I know! This is your dream."*

Chapter 19

Throughout my four years at Montreal High I was always the only Jew in my class, if not in the school. Nor were we living in a part of the city where Jewish families tended to congregate. The neighborhoods with large Jewish populations were, literally, on the other side of the mountain – Mount Royal, around which the city fanned itself out. There were two English-speaking high schools serving those neighborhoods: Baron Byng and Strathcona. Then, in 1936 when I was entering tenth grade, we moved from Lincoln Avenue in an English-speaking district to an apartment on St. Joseph Boulevard East in a French-speaking district but closer to a distinctly Jewish neighborhood. And, while I continued to attend Montreal High for the next two years, my cultural and social life underwent a profound and welcome change.

My memory still retains busy images of those years:

I remember the intimate sharing of innermost thoughts and dreams and plans with young men of my own age and orientation; the many hours with Lou Rapkin, Zangwill Godlovitch, Sid Phillips, and others whose names and faces have skidded off the pages of my memory. I remember the warm feeling of belonging.

I remember when the Spanish Civil War thrust itself into our consciousness. Zangwill, "Zangy" as we called him, wrote wonderfully heroic plays about Loyalist soldiers in battle against the Insurgent forces of Francisco Franco – which we acted out on the stage of the Young Men's Hebrew Association, the Jewish community's version of the YMCA.

I remember the summers our family lived in a rented cottage at Plage Laval – a small resort community on the Rivière des Mille Isles at St. Eustache, an hour drive from Montreal. I remember long hours of swimming, of sunning on the sandy beach, of rowing on the river, of fishing for bass, perch and sunfish. I remember balmy evenings dancing at the Kozy Korner to the music of a small dance band that, in memory, sounds like Glen Miller.

I remember the Saturday night parties during the school year that seemed to be passed from one girl's house to the next each week like an Olympic flame... the dancing in dimmed light to records playing... the fallings in love... the kissing... the quick-rising demands of sexual longing... the awkward fumbling with brassiere clasps and, occasionally, garter belts... the seemingly-impenetrable boundaries with their alarms and barriers that called for some mysterious passport not yet in my possession. How difficult it was to imagine that it would ever be.

I remember exhilarating weekend afternoons skiing the slopes of Mount Royal. I remember earning a place on the Montreal High water polo team, and of after-school games against teams from Westmount, West Hills, Strathcona and Baron Byng high schools.

I remember long satisfying walks home from school in green spring and golden autumn.

And I shall never forget that on just such a walk along a wooded path on Mount Royal, I stopped to rest at a park bench and an older man approached and sat down next to me and struck up a conversation. He put a hand on my leg and, as he talked, he slid it up my thigh and panic exploded in my brain freezing my responses between arousal and an equally powerful impulse to run. When he was unzipping my pants, I pushed him away and ran as fast as I could.

That experience so traumatized and sensitized me that, for years after, I could instantly read the subtlest signs of men expressing the slightest sexual interest in me. Perhaps in defense against my own latent homosexuality, I developed a homophobic armor which I held onto for years and which has not entirely disappeared to this day. It isn't that I disapprove of homosexuality; it's that I have a violent physiological and aesthetic response to thoughts of having my rectum violated by some man's invading penis. I have a powerful sense of knowing what it must be like for a woman to be raped.

In June of 1938 I graduated from Montreal High School with sufficient grades for admission to McGill University. Financing, on the other hand, was a problem. When I learned of a low-cost option of taking my first year of college courses through a special class at Baron Byng High School, I went for it. It turned out to be a good year both academically and emotionally. After four years as the only Jew in my class, I now found myself in a class where all 27 of us students were Jewish; only our eight instructors were Gentile. On the other hand, it was – once again – a class totally devoid of females.

By the end of the school year in June, 1939, Hitler was threatening the world and the gathering clouds of war were darkening the skies of Europe. For all mankind, the future was very uncertain. To bathe in freedom for what might be the last time, I took to the road for the summer and went hitch-hiking once again – this time on beyond Toronto to Chicago to visit old friends, and then on to Kansas City to visit my paternal grandmother and some of my father Misha's relatives, none of whom I had met before.

Somewhere around that time, my father and his family returned from his "tour of duty" as an American tool and die maker working for the Soviet revolution and settled in Redwood City, California. I remember meeting him for a brief visit in New York. What I really remember is our riding a subway together and his advising me in fatherly fashion to never go to a prostitute for sex – and my own shamed inability to share with him that I had tried it once, and that the whole affair's distasteful outcome had thrown me back into the clutching arms of an unsatisfying chastity.

Lutz, my older brother, had returned from Russia several years before. At the time of my grand tour, he was living in New York City and I visited with him for a few weeks before returning to Montreal. And then the world exploded into World War II.

I haven't said much about my kindly supportive Dad, Bernard, and my well-meaning, tenaciously-controlling mother during my Montreal years, but it was at this point that I wrested away from my mother control over the tiller of my life.

If it had been up to her, I would have followed a reasonable, straight and unbroken course to a predetermined and safe future: I would have gone at once to McGill University where I would in a few years become a doctor, or at least a lawyer or an accountant, marry a good Jewish girl, have babies, and make of my mother a proud matriarch.

As it was, I postponed enrolling at McGill for another year in favor of exploring what it would be like to work and earn the money to pay for college. So I got a job as a shipping clerk in a knitting mill and I became an expert at wrapping and labeling cartons of sweaters. For eight dollars a week. When I tired of that, after six months, I took my shipping clerk skills and got a job in a small factory where a score of nimble-fingered women assembled artificial flowers. For ten dollars a week. And so the year went by.

I don't recall what it cost for a year of study at McGill but I saved enough to pay my own way – but only because my parents continued to feed, house and clothe me. Still, it was my first major step onto my own chosen path that – hopefully, someday – would lead to independence.

When I entered McGill University's School of Engineering in the fall of 1940, the Battle of Britain was tearing up the skies over England and all of us young men at McGill were being enrolled in the University's reserve officer training corps.

Interchapter 19+

HAWK: *By God, Leonardo, I've been waiting for you to get to this point. This is where I really come into the picture. All at once, there I was in heavy boots and khaki uniform and we were marching briskly to the sound of bagpipes and drums. I remember being schooled in the martial arts, and the exhilarating sweep and snap of a British Imperial salute. I remember the Lee-Enfield rifles we were issued. I remember the proud ....*

LEONARDO: *For God's Sake, Hawk, cut that out! You're absolutely sickening with your London Illustrated News version of military life. You're nothing but a make-believe dress parade British colonel who can't accept the fact that the highest rank we would ever achieve in real life was buck sergeant in the United States Air Force. Get real!*

HAWK: *Sure, and I suppose you're really Leonardo da Vinci! Or is it Leo Tolstoy? Or Percy Bysshe Shelley? Or John Steinbeck? We're all of us actors. And if I want to play a stuffed-shirt colonel, or a heroic soldier of valor, that's my right. And who's to say that any one of the roles we choose for ourselves doesn't add to the whole of us? So don't give me any of your smart shit!*

MOISHE: *I love it! The artist and the soldier battling over their favorite versions of reality.*

"I'm more real than you are!"

"The hell you say, I'm realer than you are!"

Gee, fellas, I thought we all knew better than that.

How many times now have we heard Sam lecture us on the nature of personal reality. Sam, can we hear it one more time? Play it again, Sam.

SAM: *Okay.*

You must remember this,

A kiss is just a ...

MOISHE: *Ataboy, Sam. I love it. Now give us the lecture about reality.*

SAM: *How about a few short descriptive sentences:*

Personal reality is a strictly personal version of how things are for you. It may or may not have any particular relationship to anyone else's reality, or to what is commonly referred to as consensual reality, or to what is regarded as objective reality. We generate our personal realities in our heads and project them onto the mirror of our external worlds.

When we get them affirmed by other people's

personal realities, we lose sight of the fact that we generated them and start believing that they're bigger than that – that they're THE TRUTH.

When they don't seem to match other people's personal realities, we tend to think that either they're crazy or that we are.

MOISHE: [to Hawk and Leonardo] *See. You're both right. And if you fight about it, you're both crazy.*

Chapter 20

Hawk wasn't the only one of us who thrived during our year at McGill. It felt good to be back acquiring professional tools after a year off. And it felt good to feel myself growing up in a world that was now putting an extraordinary premium on being a young man.

It was an electric time. Hitler had overrun France and had pushed the British back across the English channel and seemed frighteningly invincible. We, the young, were being called upon. The future would open exciting new doors, no matter what path I chose or was chosen for me. We were being called upon to find roles for ourselves in a grand worldwide opera. That many roles – perhaps my own – would demand that we die early only added punctuating shivers and questions of personal will and courage. All of us were marching grandly onward.

At the personal level, the year was filling with events of lesser moment:

I found a friend at McGill – Martin Goldberg, a fellow engineering student, a peer with similar concerns and dreams and aspirations, a warm, caring, compassionate young man to share troubles with, to joke with, to grow with, to love.

I acquired some skill at the sport of fencing to add to my modest competence on skis and in water sports.

I fell in love at least one more time with another young woman named Sylvia. (I forgot to mention that at least half the young women I fell in love with were all named Sylvia.)

And I made a decision to move to California as soon as my school year at McGill was completed.

There were two considerations inducing me to move west. The first was that it was increasingly clear that I would probably be going into military service and that I would have to choose between my native country, the United States, and my adopted country, Canada. Many of my friends – like Zangy and Sid Phillips – were going into the Royal Canadian Air Force. I was looking at a probable – and not particularly heroic – future as a Royal Canadian Engineer if I continued at McGill. The war was catching up with all of us in my generation and I felt a pressure to choose.

The second consideration was that my brother Lutz had moved to San Francisco and was making good money as an electric welder in a shipyard and was inviting me to join him. I could share his San Francisco apartment and attend a nine-week welding school. That would give me a marketable skill and a union card that I could always rely on. Lutz assured me that – once I passed a routine welding test – I would have a job in the same shipyard with him, building destroyers for the U.S. Navy. And, I would be earning an incredible amount of money that – after my year of working for eight and ten dollars a week – would be a bonanza.

So, I would move to California.

I would defer my college education until after the war.

I would become an electric welder and work in the shipyards

with my brother while the world turned on its axis a bit more.

Who knew what Uncle Sam might decide to do with me after that.

Interchapter 20+

LEONARDO: *Hey, Gang. We've got to talk. There are decisions we need to make here and I want your input.*

VARIOUS VOICES: *Okay. ... Shoot! ... What's the problem?*

LEONARDO: *The problem is that I can't figure out where to end this particular flashback. We've got an awful lot of years and a great many exciting happenings that follow on the heels of leaving Montreal for San Francisco in 1941. We could write a whole book about the next 20 years – which would bring us up to the early 60's and the beginning of our odyssey into the realm of persona experience.*

But I really don't want to spend a lot of time writing about events that are only marginally relevant to the major themes and purposes of this book.

SAM: *So you're having trouble deciding what's really relevant from what's marginally relevant?*

LEONARDO: *Yes. I can't seem to back away from the material far enough to make sound distinctions between the two.*

SAM: *Perhaps you're operating on a false assumption.*
You're assuming there's a distinction to be made
between what's <u>really</u> relevant and what's <u>marginally</u>
relevant. I think there's a case to be made for the
assumption that everything that's happened to us
during those twenty years is equally relevant.

I'm sure we could find relevance between any event
in our life and any other event. It's easy to see every-
thing that's happened to us as all-of-a-piece, rather
than as being more or less attached by different
degrees of relevance.

But I'm passing over something you said, Leonardo,
that I'd like you to clarify. You said something about
not wanting to stray too far from the major themes
and purposes of our book. What do you see as the
major themes and purposes?

LEONARDO: *Damn, I should have known you'd catch that.*
Well, let me see... I'd list the major <u>themes</u> as,

First: the story of the history and development of
the Odyssey ways of working with one's personas;
and,

Second: the story of our personal history to the
extent that it helps to explain how we came to do what
we did.

Normally, the two themes need not be combined in
the same book. But for reasons that will emerge in due
course, we have come to the conclusion that the first
theme can only be effectively presented if it's told in

conjunction with the second.

> *As for the major <u>purposes</u> of this book, I see only one: to present the Odyssey System in understandable terms to any and all who may find it useful. That's the sum total of our mission. Whatever happens beyond that is out of our control and – so far as I'm concerned – irrelevant.*

SAM: *OK, that's succinctly put. So, to get back to your question of what to do about all the events of our life from 1941 to 1960, it seems to me that we have to decide which events, if any, we want to include because we think they help explain us to our readers.*

LAURA: *Sounds to me like you guys are going around and around and not getting anywhere.*

LEONARDO: *No, wait, Laura, I think we are. We're on the right track in linking our personal history with our development of the Odyssey System because there undeniably <u>is</u> a relationship between the two. We're also saying that it's the <u>linkage</u> that defines how much of our life story we will include here. If there's no linkage that we can establish between the two, then those parts of our life story get left out.*

LAURA: *That's just silly. Our life history isn't made up of a piece of this and a piece of that, it's all one flowing stream, it's <u>all</u> of it. If you break it down into this piece and that piece – if you break it down into little segments and try to establish linkage between each segment and our development of the Odyssey System – you're playing a meaningless game. Sam was right when he said it's <u>all</u> relevant. I think we have to* *decide what segments of our life story we* <u>want</u> *to include because we feel* <u>that</u> *segment says things about who we are better than some other segment. But in the end, I don't think it really matters. No matter what we say about ourselves, the story of who we are is being told. And any attentive reader will see who we are through her own senses and her own eyes.*

LEONARDO: *Okay, Laura, I hear you. So – if it really doesn't matter all that much which segments get included and which get left out, I vote for taking us back up to 1970 and getting on with the very complex story that still remains to be told.*

VARIOUS VOICES: *Okay ... I agree ... Let's do it ... Let's get on with it.*

Chapter 21

At the time we moved to Willamette, Oregon, in 1970, I had never held a job for more than two years, aside from my service time during WWII when I had no other option I cared to exercise.

So it was that when I accepted a position as psychiatric social worker with Willamette Mental Health, it was with a firm intention of breaking my short-term-jobs habit. I believed that remaining with one organization for a longer period of time, say for 10 years or more, could teach me a lot that I had failed to learn by virtue of never remaining in one spot long enough. I came to Willamette with the feeling that up to that time I had been running away – from something, from myself perhaps, from a fear of becoming mired in meaningless, mundane routine. I know I feared the dull life. I was used to drama and excitement. But, by the time we left Santa Cruz, I was drained and limp from too much drama and looking forward to years of tranquility. Still, I didn't know if I would be able to handle tranquility for long. Perhaps I couldn't cure myself of my addiction to the out-of-the-ordinary. Perhaps I could never settle down. But I was determined to give it my best shot.

In this regard, the first seven years at Willamette Mental Health were the easiest. Each year beyond the first two were testimonials to my ability to remain in one job. I was proving myself an apt adapter.

I was being approved of. I was climbing the ladder of bureaucratic success, earning expectable advances in position and responsibility with each passing year. There were many times during those years when I found myself basking in the security that comes with the belief that one is no longer in danger. It is precisely in those times that I am most apt to rock the boat, to test limits, to court the exciting pulsations of peril.

The heart of the matter has always lain in my own ambivalence toward orthodoxy – my own longing for acceptance and acclaim by the establishment juxtaposed by my rebellion against those of its customs and rules which I considered to be lifeless or unreasonably constraining. On the one hand, I was the establishment's loyal citizen doing my best to carry out my responsibilities and obligations. On the other, I was the revolutionary, the dissident, seeing *Life* in resistance and change, and *Death* in submission to the oppressive forces of the established order. So long as I clung to these conflicting sets of demands, I would be struggling to satisfy them both as well as I could contrive.

My own style of contriving involved occasionally surrendering to an irresistible urge to explore new tunnels beyond which there appeared to be glimmerings of light. One of the lovely feelings that accompanies surrendering to irresistible urges is the totality of surrender. One is blissfully helpless – no responsibility or guilt or blame; one is simply doing what cannot be helped. Where else, how else can one experience such total freedom to be – and do – whatever one must?

Of course, such surrendering cannot be long sustained so long as the underlying conflicts remain unresolved. In time, the ambivalences reactivate and topple one's awareness from the needlepoint of bliss. Still – the lure of blissful surrender to the siren song of one's dreams and fantasies stretches one's will to hang-in with the ordinary. Sometimes to the breaking point. There come times when it seems more than the soul can bear to not give way.

I am speaking here of gravitational forces that were shaping the form and posture of those years. Sometimes I was aware of them and grappled with them at conscious levels. At other times they did their thing while I ignored or denied their existence. But gravity manifests, regardless. And the shape of events always reflects the inherent forces that create them.

Looking back on those first seven years at Willamette, I see three drama-filled scenarios – sequences of events – that dominated the landscape of our lives and were clearly responses to the gravitational forces of which I speak.

The first scenario involved our entering into a Grand Alliance with Beatrix and James, whose wedding in Taos, New Mexico, we had attended three years before. Now it was mid-1971. Since our arrival in Willamette, Odette and Teddie and I had been renting a house in town while we considered what and where to buy. We were checking out small acreages within commute distance when Beatrix and James dropped in on the last leg of an around-the-world tour enroute to their home in Mexico.

We have money to invest, they said. *Why not find a ranch that we can buy and the two of you can live on it and manage it.*

What forces propelled us into such a Grand Alliance? For me it was longing – longing for loving friendship, for the recurrent dream of extended family, for communion, for the feel of walking the land, for the pride of ownership, for the soul-work of a contractual relationship with nature, for the thrill and excitement of venturing beyond the ordinary, for a grander vision, for a more complex drama.

So Odette and I researched the market and found a 100-acre ranch for sale with ranch house in good repair, barns, fenced fields, trees, and a year-round stream and pond. Beatrix paid cash in August. Odette, Teddie and I moved into the ranch house in September. The arrangement was that Odette and I would manage the ranch, live in the house, for which we would pay rent to Beatrix, and we would do what we could to have the ranch help pay it's own way. Because we also wanted to build a home of our own, it was agreed that Odette and I would go ahead and build our house with our own money on a portion of the ranch to be deeded to us in exchange for our services as ranch managers.

So much for the bones of the contractual relationship between us. The flesh and blood and spirit of the Alliance went far beyond the bones. For the next two years we were all bonded together by ties of kinship, love and well-meaning. Letters full of regard and reassurance chronicling the latest happenings on the ranch and in our lives flowed between Willamette and San Miguel de Allende. The letters spoke in winter of harvesting Christmas trees and birthing lambs and repairing burst water pipes; in spring, of pruning fruit trees and rototilling and planting our garden and clearing the creek of debris; in summer, of late afternoon walks through aromatic pastures and cool wooded acres and the tastes and smells of fresh-picked beans and carrots and tomatoes and peppers and cabbage and lettuce and herbs that never failed to reincarnate my country childhood; and in autumn, of mowing fields and mending fences. And in all seasons, of the visitations of friendly neighbors and the sharing of food and drink and comforts and visions.

During those two years, we gradually grew our house on a

wooded hill overlooking a gentle valley that cut through the ranch. We recruited a small collection of friends to help us build our house and work the ranch in exchange for room and board and a modest wage and a share of a communal dream.

Each January, Odette and Teddie and I flew to Guadalajara where we rendezvoused with Beatrix and James and assorted children and drove in two packed cars to Manzanillo on Mexico's Pacific shore. There – for a whole month in each of the two years – we swam and scuba'd in life-filled green waters and baked in the hot sun and scampered across hot beach sand and ate exciting food and drank more than was prudent. We danced and talked and strolled village squares in warm evening hours and wandered through colorful shops and ate marvelous strange foods and languished for hours engulfed in sounds of Spanish conversations and Mexican Mariachi music. And there were some days when we attended to business and reviewed the past and planned our future.

Then – in the spring of '73, as our new house was nearing completion – the fabric of our Grand Alliance tore asunder amid searing screams of pain and outrage. Whatever the internal forces at work that brought about the disaffection, the salient external facts were that Beatrix and James declared they had never agreed to deeding us the land on which we had been building our house and, further, they questioned our handling of the financial accounts of the ranch over the two previous years. Within a few months, the foundation of trust and common purpose undergirding the Alliance disintegrated into a legal and accounting struggle that sucked and drained us – and our marriage.

It was a struggle from which Odette distanced herself. Odette valued her long friendship with Beatrix. I believe Odette saw the breakdown of the Alliance as a betrayal perpetrated by James and as an ego-driven pissing match between James and me, and that Beatrix and she were being pulled apart more by loyalty to husbands than by basic differences between them. Perhaps she also saw the struggle as unworthy of a major share of her attention and as a useless waste. Whatever the reasons, she was clearly unwilling to cast herself on the funeral pyre of another dream consumed. I remember her saying more than once, *Let's walk away from it and get on with our lives.*

But for reasons of pride and manhood and inward raging against insult and injustice, I could not follow her. I stayed and fought and channeled my rage and – in the end – came across a letter that James had written to the attorney in charge of the ranch's legal affairs. He had written the letter in December of '71, shortly after the Grand Alliance was formed. In it, he described in detail the arrangements to which we all had agreed. James had provided Odette and me with a copy of the letter at the time but it had buried itself in a file somewhere and had disappeared from sight and memory. When I unearthed it again – more than two years later – there, in clear unmistakable language, the truth shone forth:

They (referring to Odette and myself) *are acting as managers and as such are entitled to recompense which will be a deed, free and clear ...to the land upon which they build their house.*

Ahh, the wondrous satisfaction of righteous victory over calumny and deceit!

A big part of me – *Hawk,* no doubt – still looks upon the reappearance of James's long-lost letter as an act performed by a benevolent God who could not forbear granting victory to a just and noble cause. And with no legal leg to stand on, James and Beatrix, through our respective lawyers, worked out an arrangement that was agreeable to all. But great and lasting damage had been done.

The second dramatic scenario that shaped the landscape of those years is one for which I can find no one to blame but myself – and those gravitational forces of which I spoke earlier. This second scenario unfurled in the spring of '73, during those very months when the Grand Alliance was coming apart. Its impact – added to that of the crumbling Alliance – further burdened Odette's and my marriage with an unbearable weight.

To put it bluntly, I fell into an affair with Imelda, one of my clients.

Imelda and I had been working together for several months as therapist and client. At what point we sensed each other's availability and were drawn into sexual fantasies, I don't know. Perhaps we had been sending messages to each other more openly than I remember. In any case, there came a session in my office when sexual feelings were sparking and ricocheting around the room and we undertook the risk of talking about our feelings for each other. Then, there she was, languishing on the floor and challenging me to come make love to her. I remember a confusion of intense desire and apprehension, the pull of an unknown and dangerous course. I felt my manhood being challenged to follow through and to be there for her as she was being for me. I felt great longing to know, to invade and join and explore this body, this woman, this deep and mysterious world.

Imelda and I became lovers. We went through a formality of terminating our relationship as therapist and client and, in the days that followed, we met in her apartment when we could manage and visited and talked and made love.

No doubt it was meeting needs in each of us.

Our relationship as lovers went on for several weeks. She appeared to me to be flourishing. My own feelings of guilt and conflict were dragging me like dirty water swirling down a drain to where I felt I must have professional help. So I reached out to a fellow therapist who was also a close friend. Her counsel was clear: Clarify my ethical responsibilities to my clients. Shut down my affair with Imelda at once. Should Imelda wish help from another therapist, she would make herself available.

When Odette learned about the affair, her response was fierce and decisive:

She raged at me for betraying her and our marriage.

She confronted Imelda and warned her to not see me again.

Then she left for California, taking Teddie with her.

Interchapter 21+

ALTHOR: *You FELL into an affair with one of your clients?*
Just like that? That's it?

SAM: *Don't be naive, Althor. You were there. You don't have*
to pretend like you weren't.

ALTHOR: *I know I was there and I wish to hell I hadn't been.*
But I think saying, "we just fell into an affair" sounds
irresponsible. Like, we didn't really do it – it's just
something that happened to us while we were waiting
for a streetcar.

SAM: *Okay, you're making a very good point. Of course*
we're responsible. And, of course, there's no escaping
total responsibility for every last shred of our behav-
ior. Nevertheless, we fell into the affair in the sense
that we were drawn by forces we either didn't under-
stand or were unwilling or unable resist.

ALTHOR: *The gravitational forces again?*

SAM: *Yes.*

ALTHOR: *Well it seems to me like we didn't fall into the affair, we leaped.*

SAM: *Okay. You're right again. There was a point in time at which we made a conscious decision to commit to a course of action. A decision was made to take the leap. And your point, Althor, is very well taken. It is a lot easier to deny responsibility and blame what happened on gravitational forces over which we had no control. And a point that I want to make is that one thing we can do – even at this late date – is to get clearer on exactly what those gravitational forces were.*

LAURA: *I know one of them. I know that I chose to become involved with Imelda. I am a sensual being. My antennae are always testing the atmosphere for opportunities to relate sensitively and with feeling. For me that's the essence of sensuality.*

ALTHOR: *But how about the sex? And with a client? Where does that fit in?*

LAURA: *For me, the physical sex is incidental. Sexual fantasies and sexual feelings nourish and enrich sensuality. Sometimes physical sex and sensuality join in a rapture that merges them. That can be nice when it happens. But usually the sex kills it. In comes the sex and out goes the sensuality. Particularly when you, Althor, and your guilt show up. As for sex with a client, ask Sam, he's the therapist here.*

SAM: *Well – our more recent work with the Odyssey System has led us to a whole new appreciation and understanding of the therapist-client sex issue. Hindsight can be very illuminating. But back there, I think we were being pulled by a commitment to experiment and stretch the rules. That's what therapists operating on the cutting edge were doing. And there's another force that was operating – although I'm not sure how much weight to give it. It seemed apparent to me that some of my therapist role models had affairs with clients at one time or another – so I have to ask: "How great was my need to emulate my California mentors?"*

ALTHOR: *Or to use them as an excuse.*

SAM: *Yes.*

LEONARDO: *I know another one of those gravitational forces: Getting even with Odette for her affair with Mario.*

HAWK: *And there's my need to be manly and heroic and courageous in the face of danger. Don't underestimate my fear and hatred of cowardice when the gauntlet has been thrown down.*

ALTHOR: *I know another one. I'm not sure who's doing it, but someone is always rocking the boat. One of us is always challenging the way things are and trying to upset the apple cart. It's like one of us is always trying to destroy us. Sam, you're the therapist. Which one of us does that? Or is it one of our fellow-personas we haven't uncovered yet?*

SAM: *It isn't just one of us, Althor. The Odyssey System has taught us that any one of us personas has the power to upset the apple cart if we get hurt or scared or angry enough. That's why it's so important to keep talking to each other and taking care of each other and working together. We're all legitimate parts of Vic. We all need to be recognized. We all need to be appreciated and respected for who each of us is and what we can contribute. We all need to love. We all have great power . And it's really up to all of us to see to it that our power is used for good rather than evil – however we define those concepts.*

ALTHOR: *So we're all potential saboteurs.*

SAM: *That's right. But it's important to remember that even when it looks like we're bent on self-destruction, we're doing the best we know how in the service of the organism. We may not know enough – and if we knew more we might do it differently – but we always do the best we can.*

Chapter 22

So once again, in the early summer of '73, our marriage came apart. Odette left with Teddie for the less chaotic, more supportive environment of tried-and-true friends in California. There, she did whatever she had to do to recover her emotional center and redirect her life. I remained in Willamette, carrying on, sorting myself out and grappling as best I could with the legal and emotional shambles all of us had strewn onto the floor of our lives. I moved into a rented apartment in town, a two-bedroom affair, just in case Odette decided to come back. There were weeks, months, when it seemed that that wasn't going to happen. The damage had been massive, the wounds profound. How many times can one glue a broken vessel back together and expect it to hold water? How many betrayals of trust, how many infidelities can a marriage survive?

But, in the fall, this second scenario that unfolded during those first years in Willamette drew to a reconciliatory close. Odette returned and we picked up the pieces. She demanded and I agreed to a marital contract permitting of no extramarital hanky-panky. We both committed to providing a family and home for Teddie, at least for the duration of her school years. She was 11. Graduation from high school was six years into the future. Enough time, it seemed, to grow together the quality marriage we both yearned for.

So, on the heels of the second scenario – my affair with Imelda – Odette and I began unfurling the third dramatic sequence of events that was to shape the landscape of our lives: we undertook a re-commitment to working together as a husband-wife therapy team in private practice. This would be in addition to my full-time job at Willamette Mental Health, and it was to be the first time since our marathon-weekend days in Santa Barbara that the two of us would be working together professionally. With regard to the future of the Odyssey System, working together would give us opportunities to experiment with practical applications of our shared multiple personality theory.

The centerpiece of our private practice was to be marital counseling with couples. In preparation for this, we decided to expand our repertoire of skills by travelling to southern California for a month of intense training as sex therapists. By spring of 1974 we had rented a downtown suite of offices, refurbished it to our taste, listed ourselves in the yellow pages and opened our doors for business. For the next several years, the couples and individual adults came, and Odette and I helped them reclaim their relationships and their lives as well as we knew how.

Odette was a warm, knowledgeable and skilled facilitator to whom our clients, both men and women, responded with trust and movement. She was also a dedicated and avid learner who devoted big blocks of her time to reading, thinking, writing and growing. And among the books she came across in her readings were the two volumes of *The Psychology of Personal Constructs* by an all-but-forgotten American psychologist, George A. Kelly, Ph.D. [1]

I want to make an effort here to put all this in terms of the Odyssey System and its development. By "all this," I'm referring to various elements of the learning curve that Odette and I were on. Specifically, our work with clients included creating experiments in which clients developed and became familiar with their own personas and then learned how to give them life and form and voice. With our help and direction, personas learned to talk and cry their way into and through their pain, learned how to work through problems together, and learned to give themselves the freedom to change and grow.

Kelly's psychology of personal constructs provided us with a theoretical model that lent structure to our experimenting. A professor and clinical psychologist at Ohio State University, Kelly started out intending to create a handbook of clinical procedures for his students and ended up twenty years later with "an extensive exploration into a strange new land of personality theory and clinical practice."[2] As a consequence, *The Psychology of Personal Constructs* is both a theoretical model that explains how our thinking processes operate, and a manual of instruction for psychotherapists.

Of particular relevance to Odette's and my interest in helping people work with their personas, Kelly also provides a model for understanding how and why each of us develops our own unique personas, or sub-personalities. Further, his work helps to explain why and how our personas – and ourselves – are enabled to change and grow.

What is a construct? Kelly defines a construct as: *a way in which some things are construed as being alike and yet different from others.*

A construct is basically any pair of opposites you care to name. *Black/white* is a construct. The construct *black/white* allows us to divide our world up into things that are black and things that are white. *Mom/Dad, democracy/dictatorship, rich/poor, love/hate, war /peace,* are also constructs.

A construct is any dichotomous or polarized way of thinking and perceiving. Constructs are ways of understanding based on perceived similarities and differences. They are the basic units of thought that we use in all of our mental processing – the molecules that make up the substance of understanding that fills our minds.

Our collections of constructs are our personal reference catalogues of differences and samenesses by which we determine what's going on and make guesses about what's going to happen next.

The way in which we organize our constructs has a lot to do with how we think and behave. While we may use constructs singly at times (*This is white and that is black*) our thought processes usually involve numbers of constructs working in combination with each other (*Of the two, I prefer white because black reminds me of nighttime when I can't see and scary things can leap out and attack me, so I'm afraid of the dark,* and so forth.)

The particular way in which we connect our constructs into a *system* of constructs determines and shapes our style of thinking about the events that draw our attention. Most importantly, our own particular *construction system* is an organized affair with a relatively few dominant constructs directing things at the core and bunches of relatively less powerful constructs working away at the surface.

Kelly refers to our dominant constructs as *Core constructs.* These are the ones that generate our fundamental assumptions about the nature of things; these are the ones that we can identify as the ingredients of our value system.

Man is good and well meaning by nature.

People whose skin color is different from mine are not to be trusted.

There is a God and He sits in judgment.

Men are superior to women.

I have only this one life to live.

Our core constructs are the ones we have to examine and revise if we are going to make fundamental changes in the way we think and behave. And, because many of them were formulated and learned early in life, they have slid beneath the surface of our awareness and have solidified into firmly-rooted assumptions – notions or ideas that we take for granted as true without ever taking them out and examining them to see if they still hold water. These are the ones that the Odyssey System is most concerned about, for they are the keys that will unlock our ability to make significant changes in our lives.

Kelly's *Psychology of Personal Constructs* is aptly named. While we all draw our supply of constructs from shared pools of knowledge, our individual construction systems are unique and highly personal in their detail. Your own system of constructs is like your own set of fingerprints – similar to but not exactly like any other fingerprints in the whole world. Our personal construction systems are the glasses through which we see and examine the events happening in our worlds. Consequently, they form the matrix, the directing pattern for all of our thinking and behavior.

It is this notion – that our personal system of constructs leads us to our particular understanding of the nature of things – that constitutes the basic premise of Kelly's personality theory. In his words, the *Fundamental Postulate* of his psychology is: *Each person's processes* (thinking, feeling, behaving, etc.) *are psychologically channelized by the ways in which he anticipates events*. We use our constructs to distinguish and interpret events occurring within our awareness, to predict future events, and to decide what to do about them.

Kelly elaborated his fundamental postulate by generating eleven logical extensions, or *corollaries*, that expand our understanding of personal constructs, how they operate, and what we can do with them. [See Appendix for Kelly's *Summary of Assumptive Structure: Fundamental postulate and its corollaries*.]

For example: his *Individuality Corollary* states: *Persons differ from each other in their construction of events*. What this means is that no two of us see a given event in identical ways. You make your sense of what's happening, I make mine, she makes hers, he makes his, and they are all *necessarily* different. Our perceptions and interpretations are different because our construction systems – the glasses through which we see events – differ from each other.

While all of Kelly's corollaries give us valuable information, some of them are particularly helpful in explaining the phenomenon of sub-personalities or personas. For example, the *Fragmentation Corollary* states that *a person may successively employ a variety of construction subsystems which are inferentially incompatible with each other*. Translation:

First of all, our personal system of constructs is not static. When Kelly says, *a person may successively employ a variety of subsystems,* he's saying we have a built-in capacity to generate new subsystems of constructs. He is also implying that we may not, for whatever reasons, take advantage of this capacity.

Secondly, Kelly is saying that our subsystems *are inferentially incompatible,* or markedly different from each other. The importance of this for the Odyssey System is that personas make sense as manifestations of these subsystems. Each of our personas can be understood as the living embodiment of aspects of ourselves whose values, perceptions, ideas, feelings and behaviors flow from a particular subsystem of constructs. If our subsystems are incompatible or markedly different from each other, as Kelly says, then the personas who speak for each of our subsystems will be markedly different from each other. And our experience tells us that this is so.

During those years of our working together – roughly from 1974 to 1979 – Odette and I, with the help of Kelly's writings and the experiences of our clients, accomplished much in the direction of growing what has since evolved as the Odyssey System. We were gaining increasing confidence and assurance that persona work provides a different and practical approach to unraveling the tangled webs of human behavior. We were creating useful strategies by which our clients could apply persona principles to themselves and their partners. We were becoming increasingly skilled as teachers of how to nurture and use personas as problem solvers. We were intensifying through experimentation and experience our belief that persona theory provides practical keys to personal transformation.

In many ways, these were our best years. We had been growing together as a family. As we had done earlier in Santa Barbara, Odette and I developed a strong circle of friends, a number of whom we had first come to know as clients. We established a couples support group that carried on for several years in which we functioned usually as participants and occasionally as facilitators. Teddie, in her high school years, was blossoming into a sensitive and beautiful young woman with some passion for literature and the theater. In the summer following her junior year, she expanded her horizons by traveling with classmates and their French language teacher to France for a month of Paris and Nice and all the in-between countryside that EuroRail skims over.

In most years there were month-long vacations for the three of us.

One summer it was Hawaii, where we camped on lush mountainsides and travelled narrow winding roads through drenching rain and languorous heat, rendezvousing by pre-arrangement with Leiana – our extended family daughter from our Santa Cruz days – on her ancestral island of Maui; driving before dawn up the long climb to the top of Haleakala to catch the sun lifting above the opposite rim of the volcano's crater and bursting upon its vast moonscape at our feet; meeting Leiana's friendly island family at bustling luaus where strangely exotic foods were abundant and excellent – except for poi, the taste of which I simply can't stand.

Another autumn, we combined separate and together vacations that took Odette to a Claude Monet exhibit in St. Louis and me to a nostalgic reunion of Steltonites in New Jersey where encrusted cobwebs were scraped from childhood memories, and acquaintances were renewed with childhood friends both remembered and long forgotten. Odette and Teddie and I came together in New York where we wallowed in as much theater and good food and stimulating conversation as we could manage in five or six days; then down to Washington D.C. to bathe our senses in the new East Wing of the National Gallery and the Smithsonian.

Teddie had plans of her own for the few weeks before school reclaimed her, so after Washington, Odette and I saw her off for home at Newark airport. Then Odette went to Boston for more art gallerying and I drove north through the autumn colors of upstate New York to Montreal, the one place that I still identified as *home*.

It was my first visit back since 1946. I spent the first two days revisiting as many of the old settings of my teenage years as I could find. McGill University campus appeared not to have changed much in my eyes, but nearby Montreal High School – awesome in its ivory magnificence during the 30's of my youth – was now a discolored and rundown inner-city school. The rest of Montreal appeared to have grown way beyond my memory of it.

It wasn't until I had taken the time to become re-acquainted with the city that I made any effort to contact old friends. I found my former classmate at McGill, Martin, who was now a civil engineer and a refurbisher of abandoned but structurally sound old buildings. We met in his latest acquisition, an impressive very old apartment building to which he was administering rebirth. He and I spent the better part of a day trying to re-connect but the currents of our lives had swept us far apart.

Then, a day or so later, Odette came by train from Boston and I remember meeting her at Bonaventure Station amid echoes of past arrivals and departures from years long gone. For a few days, I was her tour guide, introducing her to the sights and splendors of the city that, by now, had begun to reclaim some familiarity.

Then it was over. I have no memory of our return trip to Willamette.

Another autumn, we houseboated the waters and shoreline of Shuswap Lake in British Columbia. That was the most peaceful and restful vacation of my memory. Just enough challenge in navigating the sometime-unpredictable winds and tides, and in finding the coming evening's shoreline sanctuary, to keep moderately alert; lots of absolute quiet, broken only by murmurs of wind, splashings of rain and occasional callings of birds; long stretches of rarely broken peace and serenity.

Odette and I were enchanted by the sudden unexpected absence of turmoil in our lives. And we were enchanted even more by an old, seemingly abandoned, estate-like house and grounds on a remote shoreline. We walked the grounds, peered in windows and found a for sale sign with the name of an agent in Vancouver, B.C. Odette said, very seriously,

Let's buy it! Let's move here! Let's get away from it all!

I believed I knew what she was saying: that we needed a fresh start; that only that might allow us to preserve our marriage. I don't know if we could have managed it. Through my Capricornian glasses it appeared at the time too much of an undertaking to bring about. Perhaps I couldn't bring myself to want it enough. In any case, I still can't help but think that things would have turned out much differently if we had.

Chapter 23

The house on Shuswap Lake may have been our last chance. Shuswap Lake happened in the autumn of '80. In my mind it marks the final event in our attempts to create our dream house together.

In the last two chapters I have written of three scenarios of unfolding events whose gravitational forces were directing the course of our lives during those Willamette years of the 70's, or thereabouts. I say, "or thereabouts" because not all scenarios have their beginnings and endings clearly marked. The punctuation is always arbitrary and artificial. Beginnings are preceded by preconditioning sequences of events without which an identified beginning could not have occurred. Endings – the truly memorable ones at least – have aftershocks that catch us unawares long after the curtains have been drawn, jolting us with bewildering reminders that all is not done .

Of course there were additional scenarios also playing out in our lives during those years. Every life, more certainly every marriage, is a many-staged affair with now this play, now another one in progress, either being made visible or transpiring behind the scenes.

A fourth scenario centered on Odette's and my ambition to create our dream house. It had been influencing our thoughts and actions from the beginning, surfacing in our first purchased home in Santa Cruz. Then it sprang to life anew in the early seventies in the days of the Grand Alliance. With an architect's help, our own small house had taken form on our own wooded hillside. Oh, the dreams we had spun of what living there would be like. What pleasure and satisfaction flowed as we carried and sawed and raised and hammered and shingled. How much love flowed through all that creative energy and effort. How satisfying it was to be living out our dream.

It all crumbled into shards with the shattering of the Grand Alliance. We never got to live in our house, even for a night. When the long legal battle ended and we had won title to our homestead, the thought of living there was more than Odette would put up with. I might have considered doing so, out of love for the land and unwillingness to abandon the dream, but it was clearly not to be. And so our dream, along with much that it stood for in our marriage, lay broken.

Still, all was not yet lost and the dream resurrected Phoenix-like several years later in the form of a hillside half-acre with seven mature white oaks in Willamette. We bought the land with money earned from the sale of our hard-won portion of the ranch. Once again, we retained an architect to turn our visions into our dream house and, after many months our laborings flowered once more into architect's blueprints. But when the contractors' bids came in, the lowest was way beyond our pocketbook. So, we all went back to the drawing board and, for more months, anguishing revisions sapped our enthusiasm and growing doubt gnawed holes in our hope and determination. Again the contractors' bids came in much too high. I don't recall the number of times we tried and failed, but each failure fed a foreboding and painful message: our dreams, it seemed, were unrealistic and unbuildable in the world in which we were doing our best to live.

A fifth scenario was a subtle distancing in the direction our two lives were taking. Odette – highly skilled in growing and nurturing an extensive network of personal relationships – was connecting with more and more people I never met who seemed to be living intellectually-exciting and productive lives in far-away places I never got to visit. A voracious learner with a driving hunger to explore fresh pools of knowledge, Odette was, I felt, growing beyond me. I saw her going off to exotic centers of creative activity, mixing with great minds, finding her place in an alive, stimulating world. In the late seventies and early eighties – particularly after Teddie went off to college in Colorado – Odette was quite free to travel and spend her time according to her own liking. Certainly, I encouraged her stretching to fulfill her potential. Certainly, I learned from her as she enthusiastically shared her expanding horizons. Nevertheless, I saw myself locked into a more prosaic and shallower world where I remained tethered to a job that limited my freedom to explore as I wished. Increasingly, I felt the gap between our worlds widening.

At what point does one conclude that the widening gap was more than just a disparity of opportunity? For me, it was when Odette mentioned – quite casually, as I recall – that one of her newfound scholarly friends had characterized me as being gifted with a second rate mind. The scalding brand left its mark. Perhaps her friend was right. Certainly I am aware of limitations. Who knows how deeply they are rooted or where they come from? The particular scoop of genes doled out to me from my gene pool? Too few vitamins? Too many? And since I have a tendency to brood over real or imagined inadequacies, the brand of a second rate mind burned into my self-confidence. Even more painful was the clearly implied message: I was not acceptable in the realms to which Odette was gaining access.

There were additional scenarios pulling behavioral strings as well. And for a sixth scenario, I have only to return to the beginning of this book where sixth scenario passages leap off the page:

...I began to take my own impending retirement seriously when I turned 59. That was in January 1980. The most subtle and far-reaching change in my thinking at that time was that I surrendered to the idea that I had better hold on to my job because it was too late for me to make a change.

... Now, the security of job seniority and a vested interest in a retirement system anchored me. I felt trapped by the logic of survival and determined to stick it out as well as I could for the two-plus years that separated me from early retirement.

I am reminded of the poster that lived on the inside of my office door during those times: a desperate kitty dangling grimly from the branch of a tree, the caption underneath urging the poor kitty to "Hang in there, Baby!" The kitty was my talisman, my charm, whose single purpose was to carry me through the dragging remainder of my days at Willamette Mental Health.

But back to Chapter 1 for more sixth scenario themes:

...At a deeper level, I can see several long-held beliefs that fueled my dissatisfactions with my job. The most evident to me is that I never believed and often didn't feel myself to be a committed authentic member of the mainstream.

... I always believed myself to be different and special, and I

determined to have my uniqueness perceived and acclaimed.

... I loved being of benefit to those with whom I worked and my job allowed me to do a lot of that. And here I can see operating another of my deeply held beliefs, namely, that my basic purpose in this life is to be socially useful to the best of my ability. But perhaps this belief amounts to little more than an excuse to indulge my overriding passion. I am correct in speaking of passion here rather than belief. I believe in the essential goodness of people. I believe in their infinite wisdom and power to heal themselves. I believe that human potential is unlimited. Those are all beliefs. But I love people. I love relating to people with honesty and caring and the absence of authoritarian judgment. And I love to be instrumental in another person's opening up to their own flowering. Those are passions of mine beyond belief.

And while those passions served me and a good many of my clients well – so far as I was able to tell from their feedback and evident progress – they also led me into deep waters that, in the swirling currents of all the scenarios being played out in those days, came very close to engulfing me beyond saving.

The dangerously deep waters of which I am speaking are those through which I was sailing the craft of my psychotherapeutic art. The exercise of one's art is rarely a simple matter and, if one is to understand it, one must be prepared to address complexity. Of course, in a sense, all is complexity and for the most part we ignore or acknowledge or are intrigued by its convolutions and its un-knowns, perhaps its unknowables. Usually, we don't push very hard to unravel and understand. A simple explanation will do, thank you. But in the search for understanding with which the art of psycho-therapy is engaged, unraveling complexity is the mechanism by which understanding is achieved.

Understanding my relationships with the scores, perhaps hun-

dreds of clients with whom I worked at Willamette Mental Health in
the late 70's and early 80's, calls for some understanding of how I
was practicing the art of psychotherapy in those days. Toward that
end, I can share with you pieces of how I saw myself operating as a
mental health practitioner in those times.

One piece had to do with what was usually going on inside of
me as I related to my clients. There is a deliberate shifting of my
attention back and forth – now attending to their words and feelings
and body language, now scanning my own thoughts and feelings
and memories that are being triggered. It amounts to a fairly constant monitoring of the flow of information being generated by both
the client and my own senses. And my intent in all this monitoring is
threefold: first, to formulate a meaningful understanding of my
client's world as she experiences it; second, to identify specific
roadblocks in the way of her growth and aspirations; and third, to
formulate clear statements of problems for which workable solutions can be generated during the course of therapy.

A second piece focuses on communication. As a rule, therapists and clients rarely start out speaking the same language. Words
and phrases mean different things at different times to different
folks. Personal languages vary, depending upon a host of factors
having to do with personal histories. I'm comfortable with multi-
syllabled words that have a scholarly or literary flavor, but I also
have to feel comfortable speaking in other idioms if I'm going to
communicate clearly with those who aren't comfortable with a
language that is natural for me. And there are always the unspoken
words and emotions of which I, as your therapist, must be mindful
or risk misreading you entirely. It boils down to the fact that therapists and clients must relate to each other in the same communica-
tive modes. Where communication fails, communication needs to
be repaired. Clarifying communication constituted a major focus of
my work with clients.

A third piece has to do with empathy and the kind of loving Carl Rogers called unconditional positive regard. I long ago came to believe that love is a natural consequence of allowing oneself to open up to it. The compassionate heart is always there, a state of grace waiting behind barriers we erect to protect ourselves. As The Beatles proclaimed for the rest of humanity to hear, *All you need is Love*. As a psychotherapist, I have always looked upon my capacity to open myself to love as a tool for establishing rapport with my clients, for accepting them without judgment. Not that I formed no judgments, but I always felt I also needed to see them through uncritical eyes.

My ability to see with uncritical eyes has resulted in my never having met a client in whom I could find nothing lovable. All that was required of me to feel a connection with any client I ever had was to let go of my own internal barriers. I could always find qualities I could identify with by shifting my focus and sliding past my own prejudices. And sliding past my own barriers allowed me a greater sense of knowing my clients, of walking with them some distance along their paths, of gathering valuable information to help me collaborate with them in their growing as they wished.

There were two more pieces to the artistic puzzle: One was my driving interest in deciphering and solving the particular riddle of each new client and life situation. I had faith that no two people, no two human tapestries were ever identical. I accepted that each client offered a fresh challenge for both my powers of understanding and my healing skills. I saw myself as a detective solving deep personal mysteries, each one different and more intriguing than the last.

And going along with my interest in solving personal puzzles was the last piece: my willingness, perhaps my compulsion, to experiment. I had no thought of using my clients as guinea pigs, no sense that I was operating *on* them. I saw myself as collaborating *with* them. Each of my clients and I constituted a research team devoted to generating workable solutions to the problems plaguing the client's life at the time. I brought my knowledge, my skills, my hunches and my intuition to the research effort; my clients brought their experiences, their pain, their intelligence, their motivation to grow and their willingness to participate. Between us, we braved what was always for the client and sometimes for me, the unknown.

Chapter 24

Elaine and Gilda were two of the clients whose opening up to their respective flowerings was a professional concern of mine during the late 70's and early 80's. Elaine and Gilda had much in common with each other: both were in their mid-thirties, both gifted with an intelligence burnished to brightness at the best of East Coast universities, both struggling against circumstances that alternately angered and depressed them terribly. In all the years of our working together, I never failed to experience either of them as women of stimulating and challenging complexity.

I speak of Elaine and Gilda as if they were a unit; they were not. They were strangers to each other when Elaine first became my client at Willamette Mental Health in February, 1977. My memory is that she was seeking help for severe depression that occasionally led her to consider suicide as a way out. Unhappiness in her marriage and marginal success in her chosen career were primary concerns of hers, and there were also unresolved father-daughter/mother-daughter issues that had torn the fabric of her self-esteem. During the remainder of 1977, I helped Elaine extricate herself from despair and make some decisions about her own future. By December, she felt strong enough to make it on her own and therapy was terminated.

Six months later, in July of '78, Elaine contacted me again. She was struggling through a separation from her husband and was feeling in need of guidance and support but did not want to return to the mental health clinic. Would I agree to see her in my private practice? I would and, because money was a problem for her, I would not charge for my services. So, for the next year and nine months, Elaine and I met regularly – usually weekly but with periodic gaps – during which she established a life of her own, found work that more closely matched her abilities, and quenched her artistic thirst with piano lessons from a concert pianist. Expectedly, Elaine was growing. Also expectedly, our relationship grew and changed.

Aside from the bond of commitment to growth that Elaine and I shared, there was another bond that connected: the bond of Jewishness. I was drawn to Elaine, as I'm sure she was drawn to me, by all the tentacles of familiarity and family reaching out to us from the shared history of generations of European Jewry. As we worked together over the years, I came to see familiar aspects of myself in her wit, her quick mind, her sadness, her pain, her courage, her laughter. Elaine became my sister, my spiritual companion, my friend, long before she became my lover.

That happened sometime around mid-1980, probably not much before Shuswap Lake. Once it did, I knew it was only a matter of time before my marriage had to end. And by then, Gilda was also playing a more prominent role in my life.

There were similarities of pattern in my relationships with Elaine and Gilda, the principal one being that both began as traditional therapist-client relationships and, over time, transformed into more involving personal ones. Gilda became my client at Willamette Mental Health in December of '78, following the beginning of

Elaine's therapy by almost two years. It was during 1980, the year of gradual tearing apart of Odette's and my marriage, that I began allowing myself to respond to emotional and sexual stirrings awakening in my sessions with Gilda. The boundaries between therapist and client were blurring once again as I struggled with my own feelings, now playing out my professional role honestly and well, now giving way to expressions of my own turmoil and need that had no professionally-appropriate place there.

There was a small park next door to the clinic and, if weather and client situations warranted, my clients and I occasionally spent therapy sessions strolling around the park as we talked. Gilda and I took to spending our sessions in the park whenever weather permitted, and the less-formal setting encouraged a more informal relationship between us. Gradually, I shared more of myself with Gilda – the goings on in my life, my thoughts, my feelings. Occasionally, thoughts and feelings were clearly sexual. I remember one time when she was wearing a white T-shirt across which little colored rabbits were scampering. *Neat bunnies!* I remarked, and, of course, I was admiring more than the rabbits. And there was a later time when she confided that she had resumed sexual relations with a former lover, to which I responded, somewhat mournfully, I thought, *I could wish it had been me.* Clearly, I was becoming more deeply involved, and Gilda was responding out of needs of her own.

Gilda was a talented and skillful writer who was hoping to some day strike it rich as an author of romance novels. Between immobilizing episodes of depression, she worked away at her manuscript-in-process and also wrote extensively in a personal journal. Over time, she came to share with me more and more of her journal in which she chronicled much about her therapy and her thoughts and feelings toward me. And, in time, there were telephone calls between us that crossed the boundaries of intimacy appropriate between therapist and client. Expectedly, my nervousness and discomfort at our situation grew as our relationship moved along its increasingly irregular path. Slipping away was my sense of control over our situation and my own feelings.

My anxiety was, in part, an expression of my own ambivalence with regard to the distribution of power in Gilda's and my relationship. Orthodox psychotherapy distributes power and control unevenly between therapist and client. The therapist is officially in charge, the assumption being that he or she is better qualified to use it wisely. My own inclination was to empower my clients as much as possible in the belief that therapeutic power works best when it is shared equally. This belief led me to support Gilda in her struggles to assume mastery of her own life. I was empowering her to the best of my ability. But as our relationship moved toward greater intimacy I also felt at risk. In my paranoid moments I feared the consequences if she should ever decide to use her power to harm me. But I was committed to trusting that such would not happen.

Complicating matters further, Gilda and Elaine happened to meet socially at some point during that tumultuous year and became close friends. I found myself in an unexpected and twisted situation in which each of them would confide information about their newfound friendship and I, bound by my commitment to protect their respective rights to confidentiality, pretended to not know the friend of whom each of them spoke. I know I felt endangered by their relationship, for by then, Elaine and I were lovers and Gilda and I were drawing closer. My own discomfort mounted in the weeks that followed as I learned that they were talking to each other about their respective therapies and their respective therapists without their realizing that it was me to whom they were both alluding. In time, the realization came to them.

Toward the end of 1980, my situation had become unbearable and I was searching for some reasonable way out of the morass of problems I had created: I still had to endure two years of service before I could take an early retirement from Willamette Mental

Health; I was about to have my 60th birthday and "Life's final years" were staring me in the face; my marriage was hanging by a thread, and – while I was not revealing to Odette or to anyone else that I was being unfaithful – I was haunted by the knowledge that I had failed to honor the pledge of sexual fidelity I made to Odette when we reconciled back in the Fall of '73. Moreover, it looked to me as if I was incapable, for whatever reasons, of honoring such a pledge and Odette was unswerving in her insistence upon one.

The bottom line was that I was feeling that Odette and I had caused each other too much pain for too long a time and I wanted an end to that. I concluded that the only reasonable and perhaps honorable way out of the morass had to begin with steps to end our marriage. By the end of the year, Odette and I agreed that we would separate and we spent painful weeks explaining our decision to all of our friends, many of whom had been regarding us as a model marriage.

Perhaps it's only a technicality, but Gilda and I didn't consummate our sexual longing for each other until March of '81. By then, Odette and I had separated and she and I had moved her and a vanload of belongings to her own new apartment in Boulder, Colorado.

A few weeks later, Elaine asked me if I was sexually involved with Gilda and I responded truthfully, immediately upon which, without saying another word, she turned her back and walked out of my life. I have always admired that in her; her response was clean, neat and, I thought, entirely appropriate. A fitting way to deal with all relationships that no longer serve one's growthful needs.

So, with still more than a year to go to retirement, I felt my life simplifying and coming under my control once again. Yes, Gilda and I were continuing our sexually active relationship but we quickly got me back on a more ethically-correct track by graduating her to the status of ex-client. Now, at least on paper, I was no longer having sex with one of my clients. In time, I hoped, my indiscretions would be buried and forever lost from sight under a growing pile of professionally correct behaviors. And now I could begin thinking about and planning for the years that lay beyond Willamette Mental Health and formal retirement.

Interchapter 24+

ALTHOR: *Oh, what tangled webs we weave, when first we practice to deceive!*

HAWK: *That's true enough. But you've got to admit that the more we practiced, the better practitioner of deception we became.*

ALTHOR: *No! I don't agree with that. It may seem that we became more practiced but, as I see it, we only got ourselves in deeper and deeper until, in the end, it all had to blow apart.*

MINNIE: *That's because we could never entirely square it with our conscience. We've always managed to suffer from guilt, just like Mama said.*

SAM: *Well, that's true enough. But there's more than just the consequences of guilt feelings involved here; there are consequences of having made the choices we made, regardless of whether we were feeling guilty or not. We made choices and they worked out well or badly and we paid the price. That's true for everyone – for all of us who were players.*

MINNIE: *But we weren't all equal players, Sam. You – and maybe I should be saying 'we' – were in the role of therapist, so far as Imelda, Elaine and Gilda were concerned; each of them was in the role of client, no matter what the fine points of the relationship may have been; so, the playing field was not even. We had special responsibilities, special restrictions on what was permissible behavior in our relationships with them. I don't think we ever thought otherwise. If we had, we wouldn't have felt guilt at all.*

SAM: *Well, I agree with that, Minnie, but to some extent you're looking at yesterday through today's eyes. Back there in the sixties, seventies and early eighties, the behavioral dos and don'ts for therapists were less clearly defined, and certainly less-clearly monitored.*

I don't mean to hide behind the generalization, "Everybody did it and therefore I'm no more guilty than the next therapist." That is not what I'm saying, nor would it serve as suitable justification.

But I think that back then, we were each finding our own behavioral path in our work with our clients. Back then there was greater freedom to experiment with different kinds of relationships between therapists and their clients.

Today there may be a clearer understanding of dos and don'ts of behavior. Certainly there is a greater openness and awareness about the extent to which inappropriate sex plays a part in relationships between professionals and their clients. It's not limited to mental health professionals and their clients; you can hardly open a newspaper without reading about some lawyer or priest or doctor or dentist or whatever professional being charged with having violated his – usually, but sometimes her – code of conduct. And that usually means sex.

I'm saying that professional conduct is much more scrutinized today and has far more dangerous consequences for professionals than back then.

MINNIE: *I think that's good. Too many clients, most of them women, have been victimized by professionals taking unfair advantage.*

SAM: *You're right, Minnie. But I'm also concerned about the rage phenomenon that distorts and blames way out of proportion. Over-reaction and extremism at either end of the professional/client balancing act is toppling. I'm not sure the imbalances of the past are being corrected by the weight of today's fingers on the scales. The best I can say is that we're probably moving in a right direction and that tomorrow, perhaps, we'll come even closer. You see, I happen to think the real culprit in professional-client relations is not sex but dehumanization.*

ALTHOR: *What do you mean, "dehumanization"?*

SAM: *Well, maybe depersonalization is a better word.*

ALTHOR: *Come on! No hiding behind fuzzy six-syllable words! Spell it out.*

SAM: *Okay. Let me give you an example:*

Bureaucracies – public and private agencies that

are charged with providing social services, like mental health, like children's services, like medical clinics, like hospitals – are being driven primarily by consid- erations relating to the bottom line. Agencies, and the professionals who work for them, are drowning in a sea of paper work and computer printouts that have reduced everyone – professionals and their clients alike – to categories and ciphers.

People aren't being served anymore; categories are being served; numbers are being served. Or not served, depending upon whether the category has been mandated somewhere in the sea of paper spewed up by the bureaucracy in the desperate throes of its own drowning. This drowning monster of bureaucracy no longer is responsive to human needs, either those of its professional staffs or of the clients they are supposed to be serving. All are prisoners of the drowning system. Human needs and appropriate responses to them are, as we used to say, sucking hind tit.

MINNIE: *Very colorful. But I really don't see how any of that justifies professionals taking sexual advantage of their clients.*

SAM: *No, of course not. I'm seeing dehumanization and inappropriate sexual behavior by professionals as separate issues. Of course, there can be an interaction between the two issues that perhaps warrants some discussion. I'm thinking of the distinction between a sexual act that is dehumanizing in the way it's carried out and one that is not. Rape is dehumanizing. An affair of the heart that is based on mutual understand- ing and that culminates in agreed-upon sexual union*

between consenting adults, is not. Whether or not a
sexual union of the latter sort, or any sort, between a
professional and his client can qualify as appropriate,
remains a murky issue, as far I can see.

ALTHOR: *My God! You mean you're still not convinced that*
any sex between therapist and client is destructive?

SAM: *Oh yes, I'm convinced. I'm convinced that as a practi-*
cal matter the odds against its working out to the
benefit and growth of everyone involved are over-
whelming. But, in theory, I still have doubts about its
not being able to work out. In theory, it's simply
another problem situation for which there ought to be
a variety of solutions; one shouldn't have to be locked
into an iron-clad "no" that pertains in every case.
There have to be folks and situations for whom a
"yes" ought to be possible. At least in theory.

ALTHOR: *You and your theories scare me. I'm never sure*
where you're going to lead us next. You're not safe.

SAM: *Well, perhaps not. I admit I have a higher regard for*
being correct than for being safe. Searching for
workable solutions to problems is exciting and very
satisfying, but you're right, it isn't always safe.

Chapter 25

To challenge life or to languish is the choice confronting all us senior citizens on each of our remaining days. For me, in my final year before retirement, it was a choice filled with great personal pain, doubt and fear. I mourned the losses of my marriage, Odette's presence, and all that we had created together – and I doubted and feared what lay ahead of me. With the gyrocompass of marriage gone, and the structure of job about to go, I was feeling rudderless, without a clear sense of purpose. Single old men die quickly, alone and lonely, often by their own hand, or of too much alcohol, which is the same thing. I had a vision, a premonition, of falling by the wayside within a few years, helpless and useless. Clearly, I was at another major turning point, going through critical transition.

I was confronting the choice of challenging life or languishing.

I recognized that what I would be needing most, after retirement, was a period of time in a supportive environment to consider anew and evaluate the future course of my life. And what better environment for making major transitions had I ever found than academia? At times of radical change, I had often turned to centers of learning for intellectual and spiritual sustenance and a path. Graduate study, degree programs, Esalen, all were crucibles in which I had forged the next venture, the next chapter of living. Why not now?

I had always felt the lack of a Ph.D., always felt I had sold myself short by not challenging the highest rung on the academic ladder. Was it no longer possible? Was it too much to undertake in my sixties? Was I too old? Was my mind no longer up to it, no longer viable and resilient enough for the intellectual and academic challenge? And if I was bright enough, did I have the will and stamina to make it all the way to a doctorate, the reward for completing a three-to-seven year academic obstacle course? I couldn't know, of course, but I could give it a try.

I didn't spend a great deal of time choosing a course of study in which to pursue a Ph.D. One in the helping professions would take advantage of my years of experience, and I judged that I would need every advantage I could muster. Moreover, while considering my options, I rather quickly bumped into myself as I confronted an obvious paradox:

On the one hand, I considered myself something of an expert in helping people through their various crises. I had read and studied much in the field of adult transitions and I had helped hundreds of clients negotiate their mid-life crises, their dissatisfactions with life, their marital disharmonies, dissolutions, disengagings and re-engagings.

On the other hand, I myself was now undergoing my own transition into a time of life I really knew little about – the time beyond the kicking-in of social security; the time of the sunset years; the time of late adulthood.

So I resolved to focus my graduate studies on learning as much as I could about navigating the unknown waters beyond which lay the so-called golden years. In this way, I thought, perhaps I can save myself. If I couldn't do that, I would certainly be of no possible use to anyone else.

In the months before retirement, I was fortunate in connecting with Dr. Mary Jane Wall who interviewed me and then encouraged me to apply for admission to the doctoral program offered by the Counseling Department of the School of Education at Oregon State University. Mary Jane was a wonderfully-feisty and motherly professor about my own age with a keen interest in the mental health aspects of aging. She also had her own set of Esalen experiences and a New-Age belief system rather similar to my own. I'm sure her support helped ease my way into the doctoral program scheduled for the fall of 1982. Once that happened, I could see my future path unfolding.

I was officially launched onto my future path on July 1, 1982, the first day of my long-awaited retirement. Retirement is such a strange word to apply to the launching of a new life. The word is inappropriate when one chooses Challenge rather than Languish; it refers more to that which is being left behind – a job, a position, a career – than to what lies ahead; it's a word of renunciation, of withdrawal from the field; it's a word that holds much negative power – an innocent-appearing, virus-laden word that can drain optimism and energy at a time when one needs them most. I much prefer *retooling* to *retirement*. It more accurately describes the transition one has to make in a society where productive usefulness is assumed to end at 65, or 62, or whenever one retires.

July turned out to be a busy month in which I seemed to be transitioning on a wholesale scale. In addition to my being released from Willamette Mental Health and a life of *having* to go to work every day, Odette and I – after a year-and-a-half of amicable separation – were ending our marriage in a disappointingly-acrimonious divorce. And, on the heels of that, Gilda and I brought our relationship out of the closet and rented a house together.

There's nothing quite like the feeling of sweeping everything away and starting out fresh.

There is also nothing quite like going back to school in one's later years. It was scary at first because I was forcing myself to confront a lot of unknowns that in my imagination were frightening. The biggest unknown had to do with my fear that, through aging, I had lost the necessary vitality of mind required of a graduate degree program. Since I had never heard of anyone in their sixties undertaking and completing a Ph.D. program, I assumed that I was somewhat of a rarity. I suspected that the admissions screening committee were saying, in effect, *Oh, what the hell! Yes, he's way over age but let's let him in anyway. He probably won't make it, but he's an experienced clinician and, while he's here, he'll prove useful as a teaching assistant to students in our master's program.* But once I gained acceptance, pursuing the doctorate became a test of my resilience and my determination to stay young in mind and heart.

With its emphasis on late-adult transitions, my studies were forcing me to examine and re-frame many of my own assumptions and attitudes about aging. I had always assumed that aging is an unrelenting negative force that signals the onset of all the deteriorations that degrade one in that grey dismal band of time between the vitality of middle age and the grave. I had always assumed it to be a time of *diminishing*: diminishing attractiveness, energy, intelligence, power, control, health, potency, interest, and, of course, ability to learn. The best that I could say of aging was that some of us manage to postpone it longer than others, and that some of us are luckier than others in the degree to which it afflicts us. But I assumed it to be more like a fatal disease. You might get to spend your afternoons languishing in a deck chair on the lawn being warmed by sunshine, but you are losing your hold on life and slipping away.

What I discovered instead, much to my great relief, was that, like all the other transitions I had gone through, this one, too, opens up into an unlimited panorama of possibility. I discovered that seniorhood presents us with a fresh new stage. Given a modicum of health and means and motivation and guidance, seniorhood offers opportunities for new growth, new learning, new experience. It is, for those who can regard it as such, a fountain of youthfulness wherein we can rediscover and reclaim aspects of ourselves we thought were lost, and lives to live we thought were gone forever. Aging need not translate into inevitable shrinking and loss. It can also translate into becoming, at last, one's fullest and best expression of God-given potential.

I think that all of us who undertake the transition to seniorhood need to enroll in a doctoral program of one sort or another. I don't mean *doctoral program* literally; I mean it as a metaphor for *a next stage of learning*. Whether we've acquired much formal education or little, we seniors have amassed under our belts sixty or more years of learning, and we have trod the long hard roads of experience that yield up the kind of reflective knowledge that we often refer to as *wisdom*. You and I, and the rest of our generation, are the population from whom wisdom can flow like fresh springs out of the hard rocks and rolling hills of our personal histories. All it takes is a vision, a will to make it happen and some follow through. So, before your time runs out, take some of it to re-focus and re-examine where you have come to in your life. Stretch yourself to chart and plan fresh futures. Immerse yourself in programs of new learning and skill-building that can bring your new futures into your daily life. Doing these things can revitalize you and uncover the wellspring of wisdom that is surely beckoning among the hidden vaults of your awareness. And, of course, you would not be alone for there are increasing numbers of us seniors who are doing just that.

Chapter 26

By the fall of 1983 I had completed all my course requirements for a Ph.D. with a grade point average of 3.84, the equivalent of an A-minus. Not too shoddy for a budding senior of 62-and-three-quarters. Now all that remained was the completion of my dissertation and I could finally let my mother know it would be okay to call me *Doctor*. But the challenge of the dissertation was to keep me busy for another year and, while I labored to come up with a final product that would satisfy the five members of my dissertation committee, my life was also proceeding along several other paths.

Gilda and I moved our relationship along on one of them. We shared a small rented house together for a year during which our relationship migrated from intimate-and-sexual to friendly-and-supportive. When the year's lease was up, we rented separate apartments in the same complex and continued our friendship. Gilda was pursuing her career path as a writer of romance novels and, while she labored to write and sell her first novel, she supported herself by providing typing and editing services to graduate students struggling with their term papers. Perhaps because romance novels were never my cup of tea, I suspected that Gilda was not playing to her strongest suit in attempting to crash that lucrative market. Still I did what I could to be supportive. I respected her writing and editing skills and, when it came time for me to write my dissertation, I contracted with her for word processing and editing assistance. In this way, our relationship was altering over time from therapist and client, to lovers, to friends and collaborators.

Then, in the fall of '84, I was fortunate in landing a 10-month house-sitting arrangement that plumped me down in an estate-like setting on the beach at Otter Rock on the Central Oregon Coast. For years, whenever I could manage, I had been driving my VW bus to the coast to walk the beaches. I love the world of ocean and sand and birds wheeling against a background of incessant rumble and thunder of rolling crashing waves. I walk beaches to meditate, to regain my soul, to rediscover myself, to wonder, to contemplate my origins, to rejoin all things in nature from which I feel apart. I walk beaches for sensual nourishment, for links to sanity, for balance, for inner peace. And now I would be walking the beaches whenever the hunger called. The ocean would become my constant companion and her presence would make writing the dissertation much easier.

In addition to my doctoral program and my dissertation, there was another path, another agenda that I had been following. I had never abandoned the dream of continuing to develop the Odyssey System to a point where I could justify devoting my professional future to it. In my thinking, that would be warranted when several conditions had been met:

1. *The system itself would have been elaborated to a reasonable degree of completion or wholeness through clinical use.*

2. *The system would have been tested by the experiences of enough clients to assure me of its safe and productive usefulness.*

3. *I could demonstrate that the system is in fact teachable and that its widespread use is feasible.*

Once these conditions were satisfied, I could then proceed to write a book about it.

I saw advantages in pursuing both the doctorate and the more complete development of the Odyssey System concurrently. A book about the Odyssey System authored by Victor Bogart, *Ph.D.*, or *Dr. Victor Bogart*, would probably be regarded as more credible than one written by Victor Bogart, *M.S.W.* And because at my age time is of the essence, working on both agendas concurrently would allow me to write the book sooner rather than later.

So it was that during the years of my doctoral studies, I also maintained my private practice as a laboratory devoted to the further elaboration of the Odyssey System. It was during this period that *journeying*, the system's second way of working with one's personas, evolved, thanks largely to the experimental willingness of a long-term client, Stan.

To refresh your memory about how the Odyssey System works, it's based on our ability to identify, name and manifest at will our various role players or aspects of our personality. It further requires that these personas of ours learn how to talk to each other and to work together to arrive at mutually-acceptable decisions concerning whatever problems we want to resolve. This is the nuts and bolts of the persona system's first way of working, for which I coined the term *multiloguing*.

Journeying is the second way of working, and it grew quite logically out my years of experience with the first way. I had come to asking myself questions about the limits of working with one's personas:

How deeply in one's consciousness are one's personas to be found?

Are they operative only at surface and near-surface levels of awareness?

Or can they persist in deeper voyaging into one's unconscious processes?

And if traveling with one's personas into deeper levels is possible, to what kinds of uses can such traveling be put?

And so on and so forth.

It was as a consequence of my sharing these questions with Stan – after our having worked together for years during which he mastered the tools of multiloguing – that we decided to explore these unknown territories together. Let Stan describe his journeying experiences in his own words: [1]

> *I started doing these journeys because I had a lot of experience meditating. I had been meditating for 15 years by the time I started working with Vic. The first journey that I went on – that was amazing! We tried to set the stage before and it never worked. He tried to get me to do some visualization and I was having a lot of trouble. He tried to wind me down into these states and I wasn't going. So finally I said, "Let me do it my way." So I sat back and meditated for ten minutes and I came back to this half-awake state. I had essentially calmed my mind down and then came back up to a point where I could respond. So I was kind of dipping down into a transcendent state and moving back out to where I sense everybody is still alive and I'm still here.*
>
> *Vic recommended we just see what's there, and that*

*kind of characterizes the way I do my journeys. I take
about ten minutes and meditate and then "try not to try."
That's the biggest thing: Don't try. See what you can see.
Now beforehand, Vic talks about how we'll always pick up
where we left off in the previous journey. If you try to do
that it's difficult. At least it is for me. So what we do is, we
just preview the last journey before I start to meditate. And
then, when I just see what's there, it takes off. It works.*

So I'll meditate... come up... and then: "I see green."

*What I do is, I speak with just the minutest effort to
communicate. I try not to disturb myself much. Just the
smallest amount of disturbance I can get and still get the
words out. In one instance it was "Green." That's all I
saw, Green! And so I didn't worry about it, I just sat there
and let Vic know I saw green ... That's heavy duty stuff! ...
and the tape's still running and I'm worrying that, "Jeez,
it's costing me a fortune to sit here and say, 'Green'." But
you just have to trust the process and say, "It doesn't
matter."*

*So then, as I sat there, I didn't try to make anything
happen. I was just looking, and all of a sudden I was aware
that there was green overhead and green ... Oh! I was in a
forest. I let Vic know there was a forest in here. And then,
slowly but surely, Ah, yes! I can see the trees, and there's a
pond. And then I became aware that there's another
"somebody" there. I was aware that it was a woman there.
That was before I was aware of who I was – before I
figured out which persona I happened to be who was doing
the narrating. And when I discovered, "Oh yes, this is
Mark.. Mark here, and there's a woman here." Then it
started rolling.*

The initial startup is difficult to get going because you're trying to pull yourself out of this state and then fall back in, trying not to disturb yourself. And then slowly you wander down into it to where it's not as difficult to narrate anymore. Up to that point, it's all kind of hazy stuff. There's no clear distinction of what's going on. But then it becomes more and more clear, until – when I get involved, like five minutes into it – it's as though I'm watching a movie. It's clear. I see the people. I see the trees. I hear the music, if there's music. I'm living in this movie.

I characterize it as being an alternate reality for me, it's so real for me. For instance, I may be standing around talking at my work and I may speak of something that happened in my journey as if it really did happen because it's that real in my experience. It's part of my reality now. Vic can read the transcript over and I can go right back. I can feel the emotions. I see the action.

I took a creative writing class and it was a kick because I could write out some of these journeys and they were great. It was cheating but it worked. It worked because I knew what I was feeling. Everything was there. Everything was there for me.

That Stan was able to journey into a strange new world operating at a deeper level of consciousness and return with near-total recall of everything that happened there – including a detailed memory of his feelings – struck me as remarkable in itself.

His journeying seemed to fall into a class of experience somewhat similar to, yet different from, an acid trip. From Stan's descriptions, journeys seemed more ordered and sequential than most acid trips and certainly most dreams; more like living out a film script of one's own devising, the locale for which was another world and another time.

And no drugs of any kind were involved.

Moreover, Stan was journeying virtually on his own. For the most part, I served as therapeutic watchdog and secretary. During the journey, I would record in longhand the periodic progress reports mumbled by Stan's narrating persona whenever he surfaced. When the silence between surfacings became too long – *i.e.,* when I suspected that Stan's narrating persona was forgetting his obligation to report – I would ask him gently, *Can you tell me what's happening now?* He always did.

Between journeys, I also served as Stan's fellow-searcher after the meanings of his journeys. They obviously held messages of importance for him. For me, the real adventure was in seeking out plausible meanings contained in the messages and then finding ways to put them to practical use. I saw Stan's journeys as tools to be used in his drive to make his life more fulfilling and effective. I also saw them as potentially of great use to a lot of folks, in addition to Stan.

Stan took his first journey sometime during 1982. Over the next three years he journeyed on some 35 occasions. For the most part, each journey continued the story that had been unfolding in the previous ones, like chapters in a book that Stan was writing from the deeper levels of his awareness. Occasionally, he would find himself on a journey that broke the sequence, that stood on its own, so to speak. When that occurred, he was able to "get back on track" in the following journey.

While Stan's journeys were remarkable in their own right, they also raised a great many questions which I felt needed reasonable answers, such as:

Is journeying a skill that can also be learned by other normally healthy folks?

What kinds of folks might benefit from journeying?

What kinds of risks are involved in its use?

What kinds of safeguards are needed to ensure that journeying will be reasonably safe?

Questions such as these popped up continuously and I could hardly wait to get at the answers.

Chapter 27

My dissertation[1] was completed and approved by the powers in charge of such things on October 24, 1984 – a shade over two years from the time I started my doctoral work. While I would have to wait until the following June's graduation ceremony to receive the diploma, for all practical purposes I had scaled and cleared the last of OSU's academic hurdles to my coveted Ph.D. Now I could turn all of my attention to further work on the Odyssey System and, at the same time, begin to write the book.

The book, as I saw it, would explain the Odyssey System and how to use it to two audiences of readers: a general audience of adult readers interested in discovering new ways to help themselves grow, and professional mental health workers who wished to expand their healing repertoires. The outline for the book was quite simple: it would consist of two parts, the first dealing with *multiloguing* and the second with *journeying*. Each of the two parts would contain a lot of case-history material drawn from tape recordings of actual sessions. Names and other identifying information of clients would be altered to protect rights to privacy and case material would be used only where clients signed release forms granting permission to use their recordings.

In the fall of '84, there was still much developmental work to be done with the Odyssey System, particularly with regard to acquiring a more complete understanding of journeying. But since I would begin the book by writing the first part on multiloguing, about which I felt a high level of confidence, I decided to push ahead with writing Part 1 while I continued to expand my experience and confidence level with journeying. I hoped that by the time I finished Part 1, I would be ready to write Part 2. In the months that followed, the writing proceeded smoothly, all things considered, and – as was the case with my dissertation – Gilda's editing and word processing skills were of considerable help.

By the fall of '85, my idyllic house-sitting arrangement at Otter Rock had run its pre-ordained course and I was house-sharing another beautiful home within walking distance of my beloved ocean at Little Whale Cove, a peaceful, private residential resort just south of the colorful fishing village of Depoe Bay. That is a part of Oregon Coast preferred by whale watchers who come in droves to catch sight of the California Greys as they migrate twice each year between Alaska and Mexico. There is a rocky point at Little Whale Cove where the coast juts out into the ocean and the whales often come within yards of the shore.

Miles of walks and bicycle paths wind through Little Whale Cove. My favorite walk was from my home at the northern end, out to the rocky point to check for whales and seals, then along the shore watching for the occasional low-flying squadron of Pelicans and a particular pair of red-legged Oyster Catchers that dwelt among the rocks, then on to the quiet, beautiful lagoon at the southern end from which the resort drew its name, and then home by any one of several paths. The walk took about an hour – unless I brought along pen and paper in which case I might be gone for up to half a day. I have always loved writing in natural environments.

In addition to writing the book, I was keeping busy with other

Odyssey-oriented activities. Two in particular were instrumental in adding to what I already knew about the system: my part-time counseling practice in which I continued to specialize in an Odyssey System approach to working with clients; and a series of workshops I conducted to introduce the system to small groups of interested people.

My private practice provided an arena in which growing numbers were learning to work with their personas using multiloguing, and some of the more experienced ones were opting for more advanced work – learning, as Stan had, to benefit from their personas' journeying in inner worlds of their own making.

The workshops were held in a variety of comfortable settings and usually drew between 12 and 20 health professionals and interested others. They were demonstrating that small groups of people with varied educations and backgrounds could acquire – in the span of a weekend workshop – a persona-based understanding of human functioning; could generate an array of their own personas; and could learn basic multiloguing skills.

This pattern of continuing to grow the Odyssey System through writing the book, working with clients and conducting workshops, provided the format for my professional life from the fall of '84 to sometime in '87. There were, of course, myriad other happenings transpiring in my life, but the organizing principle of these years was my determination to bring the Odyssey System to the attention of a wider audience. I had come to believe that working with one's personas offers huge advantages for those who are committed to shaping and controlling their own lives. But belief is one thing and bringing belief to manifest reality is another. It was – it still is – my life's dominant interest.

I was not entirely alone in working toward this end. Helping me in those years was a small group of enthusiasts who shared the Odyssey vision. Alice, a fellow social worker, co-therapist and friend of many years, had become skilled in the Odyssey system and she and I shared a private practice and worked together as co-presenters of our Odyssey workshops. Jim, my favorite psychiatrist and a supportive friend, enriched the workshops with his Jungian explanations of why and how the persona system worked. Stan shared his personal experiences. Gilda helped with brochures and newsletters. And I was seeing a collaboration of like-minded people working together to manifest a useful reality. We were a team and I was doing a good job as the team leader. Or so I thought.

In this way, we moved forward toward the day when the book would be finished and published. In the meantime, it was hard work all around and finances were proving to be a problem. The workshops were not paying their way and I was floundering in my struggle to meet all of my business and personal expenses. As was my habit in money matters, I was taking the optimistic "trust in God" (or whomever) view. I assumed that somehow "things" would work out. When the book was published there would probably be enough money coming in to take care of everything. In the meantime, I managed financial affairs with a month-by-month, hand-to-mouth, don't-waste-too-much-energy-dwelling-on-it approach. And I borrowed from Peter to pay Paul.

More accurately, I borrowed from Stan to pay Gilda. I was paying Gilda $12 an hour and her wages were one of the costs of bringing the book manuscript to completion and publication. Both Stan and Gilda believed in the value of the Odyssey system and were strongly committed to our collaborative effort. Moreover, Stan was willing to invest some of his savings toward that end and I took the view that borrowing from Stan with a commitment to pay him back with interest was a reasonable short-term solution to a pressing need for money. That was in the fall of '86.

I finished writing Part 1 of the book in early '87. Gilda was instrumental in putting together a dozen photo-copied versions of the manuscript in pocket-book size for use in our workshops. It felt good to have something tangible in hand to hold and admire. It wasn't all that useful as a book: the type was too small to read comfortably. But the cover was a bright Chinese Red and there, in small typed letters, one could read:

ODYSSEY THERAPY

A Practical System for Personal Exploration,

Problem Solving, and Growth

by

Victor Bogart, Ph.D., RCSW

By July of '87 I was well along with writing Part 2 and we were drawing still closer to the dream of bringing the Odyssey System to market. And then, the structure on which the dream was being carried crumbled, like a house of cards.

But in slow motion.

Chapter 28

July 27, 1987

Dear Vic:

...I would appreciate it if you would not call
on me to do things for you any longer. It's true
that I always need the money, but it's more
important for me now to get mentally healthy,
and I can't do that if I'm still into interacting with you at this time. One of the major
reasons that I have returned to therapy is to
take an honest, probing look at my relationship
with you, with all its permutations, and I
definitely need to have space to make this
assessment without your influence.

Much of what I feel is rage — having to do with
recognition of your inappropriate behavior
toward me when I was your client, and the realization that, one way or another, I have been so
dependent on you emotionally and financially,
and so bound up in your system of rationalization and justification for such behavior that I
ended up supporting you in behaving inappropri-
ately with yet another client — Stan. And I'm
seeing a long pattern of inappropriate behavior
in your interactions with clients that, rather

than helping those clients grow, stalls them in patterns of dependence and dishonesty. With Imelda, Elaine, and me, the inappropriate behaviors were your sexual relationships with each of us. With Stan...the inappropriate behavior revolved around borrowing money from clients or previous clients.

This kind of behavior is unethical in a therapist, according to any consensual standards I know of, and your rationalization that these are simply healthy 'nontraditional' relationships just doesn't hold up under examination. Clients should not be required to meet their therapists' needs for sexual gratification or money. Clients come to you for help in solving their problems, not yours, and you get paid for your services; to expect endless and boundless gratitude is inappropriate. In my case, because of the extensive and complex relationship we've developed, it has taken me over six years to even begin to separate from you.

In our last conversation on this matter, you asserted that you gave your clients "challenges to grow", rationalizing that Stan had somehow been helped to separate from you by loaning you money ... Perhaps you believe that the lengthy period of time that I've spent depending on you served the same purpose. I don't. Not any longer. And I believe you are deceiving yourself when you make those assertions. And, furthermore, I believe you are doing yourself harm in the process.

In any case, I need to sort all of this out, and I need to replace rage with reason before I can deal with you. ...

One thing I would appreciate is some help with the therapy bill...as I am dealing to a large

```
extent with difficulties proceeding from my
relationship with you. ...
```

```
Yours,
```

```
Gilda.
```

My response to Gilda's letter was an explosion in my brain and a horrified cry of terror. I read the letter over and over, each time catching hold of some accusation that had previously escaped my attention. I found myself repeating time and again, *My God, I didn't think this would ever happen.*

For the next several days, I squirmed and sweated, building on the enormity of it all. But for all my squirming and sweating, the hard fact was incontrovertible. Gilda and I had become sexually involved while she was still my client.

But we were very much in love and were in process of terminating therapy when it happened, a defensive voice cried over and over, but the voice sounded hollow and had a wailing quality of which I felt ashamed. And the hard fact remained.

But it happened a long time ago, more than seven years, the voice persisted. But the fact remained.

And the voice stilled for a while before rising up again to argue mitigating circumstance after mitigating circumstance. And still the fact remained. Much as I squirmed and struggled, the fact remained, and I screamed against the sharp hook lodged solidly just above my Adam's Apple.

In time, the outbursts of denial and pain and rage subsided and gave way to engulfing helplessness and resignation. And, as I dangled and waited for my life to shatter in ridicule and disgrace, I felt the cold steel edge of the incontrovertible judgment: *There is never a justification for going to bed with your client! Ever!*

In ensuing weeks and months my terror slowly subsided to a constant apprehensive ache of foreboding. I feared it was the beginning of the end, even as I hoped that Gilda and I would be able to reach a satisfactory agreement by which I would provide financial help for her therapy and she would provide assurance that I would not be blown out of the water professionally. In compliance with Gilda's demand that there be no personal contact between us, our negotiations were carried out entirely by exchanges of letters. Lengthy detailed position statements and explanations, accompanied by carefully worded proposals, went back and forth, each proposal falling short, each counter-proposal responding to the perceived shortcomings of the previous one.

September 22, 1987

Dear Vic:

...I'm also going to be using your name as a reference while I look for editing work. Please let me know if this is not okay or if our personal tangles are going to influence your reference.

With regard to our relationship, I appreciate your respecting my continuing need for distance. I'd also like your help with my therapy, as I mentioned before. There are a couple of reasons that I think this is reasonable:

- I know of a client in a similar situation whose lawyer worked out such an arrangement with the therapist with whom she (the client) had been sexually involved;

- it seems appropriate, because some of what I'm having to deal with is the excessive dependency I developed on you — in large part because you moved to attach me closer to you in therapy rather than teaching me to separate from you, which is part of the responsibility of the therapist, as I understand it.

Regarding the latter, the results were perhaps more damaging in my case because that was the very issue I needed you as a therapist to help me resolve... You've often commented on how seductive you thought I was as a client. Actually, when I look over my journal entries from that time, there are many early episodes that indicate you were behaving quite seductively well before I even allowed myself to consider those feelings. Because I've been depending on you for so long, I bought your rationalization that it was somehow my fault. How long did I stay in therapy with you simply because I didn't know how to separate from you, and you didn't want to teach me how? Ditto with Stan?

In the case of the previously mentioned client, her lawyer arranged with the 'offending' therapist to cover the costs of therapy and (I think) then some damages. This is not what I'm suggesting. ...I'm also not interested in punishing anyone, and I don't want to get into any legal hassles — that's not at all how I'm thinking, if you're worried about that. ...

Gilda.

P.S. If you want to read about the kinds of problems you feed into with clients like Stan and me, a good starting book is Co-dependence by Anne Wilson Schaef. ...

And a week later, during which I agonized my way through to a reasoned reply, I wrote:

September 29

Dear Gilda:

I am writing with the sincere hope we can be
responsive to each other's needs at this time
and do whatever is necessary to honor and respect all that happened in the course of our
long multi-faceted relationship.

First: I have no problem with your using me as a
reference. As you know, I hold your editing and
writing skills in very high regard and I wish
very strongly for your personal success, as I
always have. I do not intend that "our personal
tangles" will influence my judgment regarding
your professional competence or my sincere
valuing of your many qualities.

Second: I will continue to respect your need for
personal distance between us for however long
that need exists for you. I also acknowledge the
legitimacy of your feelings, and I accept that I
bear some responsibility for behaving in ways
that contributed to them. I want to do whatever
it may be in my power to do to assist you in
working through to a better place for you and,
hopefully for our relationship. And I invite
your suggestions for helping me grow, such as
your recommended readings.

Third: I do want to help toward the costs of
your therapy.

Fourth: I also have fears and apprehensions that
I need help with from you. I know that you said
it is not your intention to punish me or to get
into legal hassles but I do have to deal with my
fear. I do need to feel safe from potential

```
threat, real or imagined, of a legal action that
would surely destroy my professional life and
would have far-reaching repercussions for every-
one touched by it.

I would like to see us deal with our respective
needs, feelings and concerns in a way that does
not violate the sensibilities of either of us. I
think it would be helpful if we ask a mutual
friend we both feel safe with...to act as a go-
between (and intermediary if we should feel we
need one) to enable us to reach an agreement we
can both feel good about... Can you let me know
if this approach is acceptable to you. ...

Please know that I have as a goal that we both
come through this difficult time salvaging
whatever may be healthy and good in our rela-
tionship and at least making possible a produc-
tive enduring friendship in the future.

Vic
```

As each of my responses went forth, I would allow myself a
resurgence of hope for a non-lethal outcome. With each of Gilda's
responses, hope would flounder in a wave of despair. Rising hope
and sinking despair cycled wheel-like in unending parade across the
bleak landscape of weeks that stretched to months.

What barrier stood in the way of mutually-acceptable agreement? I was amenable to helping financially with Gilda's therapy to
the best of my ability, and doing whatever else I could accept as
reasonable, but I wanted, in exchange, Gilda's commitment to refrain from punitive legal action that I felt would destroy me professionally. I have no doubt we each did our best to resolve the
situation, but we were seeing it from different vantage points and
what seemed fair and reasonable to one, seemed unfair and unrea-
sonable to the other. Gilda had come to regard herself as abused

victim and me as abusing victimizer. Paradoxically, I was experiencing myself as victim with my personal and professional future being held hostage. From her vantage point, relinquishing her legal right to prosecute me would perpetuate her victimization. From mine, not insisting on legal protection would be professional suicide. At the same time, I was trying to hold onto the perception of the two of us as well-meaning people living out the consequences of our adult choices and behaviors.

But as Gilda and I responded to each other's letters over the months that followed, the dreaded handwriting on the wall refused to go away.

Chapter 29

As our negotiations dragged through the rest of '87 and the spring and summer of the following year, other events were eroding my hope of survival:

A firm of lawyers I consulted sketched a very grim picture indeed. They predicted that Gilda would sue for malpractice, that I was in deep doodoo, and for a $5,000 retainer they would go to work to bail me out.

About the same time, my insurance carrier advised me that my professional liability policy would not cover any portion of my legal fees. While I had always carried liability insurance, the company with whom I was insured in 1981 – when Gilda and I were sexually involved – had since gone out of business. My current policy was of no help in my existing situation.

The walls of my professional practice came tumbling down with amazing swiftness. Not overnight, but in a matter of weeks the stream of clients coming to me for help was drying up. I was sinking further into debt. It was becoming apparent to me that reports of Gilda's troubles with me were making their way through the mental health network and I was rapidly becoming a professional outcast.

And socially, I found myself withdrawing more and more into my shell, avoiding eye contact, narrowing my unguarded world to those few close friends who knew all about my problems with Gilda and whose commitment to our relationship had not withered.

On the more positive side, there still existed that small circle of friends who remained loving and loyal.

And with the help of my personas and Jim, my friend and favorite psychiatrist, I began the painful work of digging into the sordid tangle of my life.

ALTHOR: *I don't like what's happening and it just keeps going on. I don't see an end to it. It just keeps getting worse.*

JIM: *What does?*

ALTHOR: *Everything!*

JIM: *Be more specific, Althor.*

ALTHOR: *Oh, God!*

[Althor glares at his psychiatrist and then responds resignedly]

Well, for one thing, the way I'm feeling more and more alone and isolated. I'm feeling more and more that I'm persona-non-grata here. I can't tell how much it's something that I'm doing to myself and how much of it is what others are doing to me. I bumped into Dan Obersdorfer in the checkout line at Safeway yesterday. [He turns to Jim and explains that

Obersdorfer is a university professor, then continues]
*Dan has always been very friendly and we've done a
lot of work together. Well, yesterday he was very
quick to say he was in a hurry and couldn't stop to
talk and he rushed out before I had a chance to say
"Boo!" I think he was embarrassed and lying in his
teeth.*

*It's very clear that Gilda has made a point of letting
people know about her complaint against me but I
don't know how far that has gone. I have the feeling
it's like a slick of oil and it's spreading very quickly
and there's nobody interested in cleaning it up.*

SAM: *That's an appropriate metaphor and I think that's
probably an accurate reading. It does hurt and I feel
that too. Probably more than any of you, I'm the one
who sees psychotherapy as a learning process. To the
extent that we are good facilitators of our client's
learning and growing, we are good psychotherapists.*

ALTHOR: *Sam, you're too fucking rational for me! You're
talking like you can close your eyes and walk away
from the shame and pain of having our world collapse
around our heads but, goddam it all, I can't! I've got
to live with this shit! We've got everything we own
tied up in this, along with our dreams for a comfortable and productive next twenty years. It's all crashing down because seven years ago we didn't know
enough to stay out of this kind of trouble. Well, SHIT!*
[Althor screams and storms up out of his chair and
rages around the room.]

And, in between Althor's agonized wails, the negotiations with Gilda, and my struggling for sense and survival, I doggedly continued work on Part 2 of the Odyssey book. In the summer of '88, I completed the first draft of the entire book and started peddling the manuscript to potential agents and publishers.

Then, in September, the next seemingly inevitable blow struck.

```
September 13, 1988

Dear Vic:

It's time for me to let you know that I've
reported our sexual relationship in therapy to
the State Board of Clinical Social Workers. They
should be notifying you soon.

I did this for these reasons:

1. As you began to offer more money in our
   negotiating process last spring, I began to
   feel as if I were somewhere in the gray area
   of blackmail and I did not want to be there.

2. You clearly did not understand the dimensions
   of your exploitive behavior or the degree to
   which you manipulate to suit your own ends in
   therapeutic situations, and I didn't feel
   ethically that I could enable you further, no
   matter how much money you were offering.

3. I've been damaged and I need to do something
   about it. The more I learn about this problem
   — sexual exploitation of clients by thera-
   pists — the more I realize the damage is
   profound. After I sent in the complaint to
   the Board, I read a book called Sexual Inti-
   macy Between Therapist and Patient by Pope
   and Bouhoutsos. I recommend you read it. All
   the lines and excuses are in there, including
```

the fantasy that we were "in love".

Among other things, I'll note that I've had many more suicidal thoughts and impulses since therapy with you than I did before. I had not linked the two until I read this book.

4. I don't want to lose any more therapists over this issue, so I'm taking care of it now.

5. It became clear to me, after our failed effort at negotiating an agreement, that your professed concern for my well-being was more manipulation. Had you been genuinely interested in helping me, you would have continued to offer the help. That you did not was eloquent indeed.

Thus far, I'm doing this without benefit of therapist, advocate, or legal counsel, though I've filed copies of my complaint report to the Board and copies of our letters with the Center Against Rape and Domestic Violence as well as with a few friends to ensure that they don't disappear mysteriously.

I've told (four names withheld) because they're my friends. Further, if someone asks me who the therapist was who "sexually abused" me, I tell them. Some people have been surprised, to say the least.

Frankly, I doubt this will have much effect on your practice or your career. If you get more than a slap on the wrist, I'll be surprised — partly because it's been so long since you were my therapist and people tend to think that after a while, I should have figured it out, a smart woman like me, right? Also because there's probably a certain tendency on the part of the

Board to protect a fellow therapist. Also because you are a master manipulator and I know
you will be well able to ingratiate yourself
with whatever powers that be to make things
easier on yourself.

One of the side effects of this situation is
that I am feeling quite fearful about my safety,
so I would appreciate it if you would keep your
distance — by which I mean to say, no calls, no
visits, no efforts to plead your case with me.
"X" (name withheld) has suggested that you might
try to buy me in some way. Please don't. If I
have to get a court injunction to keep you away
from me and to keep you from contacting me, I
will, and I 'spect that will raise some eyebrows
in (the district attorney's) office.

I don't think you'd do anything to endanger me,
but if you have such thoughts, please know that
too many people know about this situation —
including the Center Against Rape and Domestic
Violence — and if something untoward should
happen to me, an awful lot of people would know
that it was you who committed the untowardity.

Do I sound paranoid? Yup, I do. Another one of
the aftereffects. Pope and Bouhoutsos contend
that "sexually abused" clients suffer from post-
traumatic stress disorder — like Vietnam vets
and rape victims — and that they have flashbacks, guilt, feelings of isolation, feelings of
emptiness, etc. To give you an example of the
flashback syndrome, I can still remember exactly
how your face looked the second time we had sex
together. Furthermore, I can remember the time I
told you that I had ended my five-year celibacy
with someone: I can remember the way you leaned
against the building (we had been out walking
for our session), the wistful look on your face,
and the words you said: "I could wish it had

been me." In both situations, I was still your client.

Like I said — flashbacks.

If you're going to trot out the notion that we were "in love", or that you were somehow challenging me to grow, I refer you to Pope and Bouhoutsos, particularly Chapter 1. Or perhaps "X's" comment might be apt: "How come," she asked, "these guys don't ever want to challenge old, ugly women to grow?"

If I sound angry and hurting, I am. The more I learn, the more I grieve and rage, and the more I have to confront the degree to which I'm damaged, the more I despair of ever being whole again.

— Gilda.

Interchapter 29+

[From a multiloguing session among my personas in the wake of Gilda's filing a formal complaint against me with the state board of clinical social workers]

ALTHOR: *It isn't so much that our hopes and dreams are shattering; our world has come apart before and we've always managed to come through it and build a new life. What I find really devastating is that I feel our time has run out. I have a real dread that we're too old to make it through this time. I find myself thinking we don't have many years left. Here we are, about to be in our seventies, and we're losing everything. We're discredited professionally; everything we own will be gone; we're losing our friends and people who have loved us; we'll not only be up a creek without a paddle, we won't have a canoe or a compass or a tent or anything. Even if we had a compass, where is there for us to go, and what is there left for us to do?*

I'm terrified that this time we're going to die. I just feel so awfully sad about that. After a lifetime of

*struggling to have our life mean something really
significant, to end up like this. It just drains all hope
out of me. I don't think I want to go on anymore.*

SAM: *Oh, it isn't quite as bad as you're painting it, Althor.
There will still be worthwhile things to do when all of
this dark time in our lives is over. The problem, as I
see it, is that we don't have a clear path that will take
us to our future. So long as we kept to the small world
of our private practice, we could go along assuming
that, perhaps someday, it might lead somewhere that
would constitute an even more meaningful future.
There was even a hope that we might someday transform into a shining star for all the world to praise and
wonder at. Your biggest sadness, Althor, is over the
loss of that hope; and now you despair of our life ever
again having positive meaning. Well, that is certainly
a likely possibility.*

*I have to believe that this path which Gilda has
decided we need to be on, is the correct path for us to
be taking if we are to find our way out of the darkness
and into the light of another time. I have to believe
that this devastation is happening because we are all
willing it to happen in order for us to grow. I have
debated within myself whether it is happening because
we have a pathological need to self-destruct, or
because we have a need to create new life. Perhaps
they are the same and the debate is meaningless.*

*But the real crisis lies not in what happens or
doesn't happen out of the Gilda affair, but in our will
to go on. We are experiencing a crisis of faith. The
old is crumbling away and there is no promise yet of
anything to replace it. We are facing a void that may*

very well be our death. That can be either terrifying or reassuring, depending on whether you believe or don't believe in a glorious future of some kind. I have to go on believing. But there's only one of me. The rest of you can outvote me and have us join all the other lemmings of our generation in their resignation to untimely and fruitless death.

Chapter 30

And now in the world at large, it is already early October and Willamette enjoys an idyllic Indian Summer stretched, it seems, by a diminishing ozone layer that has been playing havoc with the rest of the world. Elsewhere, on the heels of drought-stricken harvests and burning forest lands, hurricanes and tornadoes rampage, villages and towns are being levelled, cruise ships are being swept away with all hands lost, and nuclear wastes continue to pile up in mismanaged and unmanageable mountains. In Willamette, the nights are unusually clear, the days are unusually sunny, the vine maples shade from dusty greens to golden yellows to wine reds as they always do in October, and a characteristic aura of well-being and of change happening in slow motion continues.

I, however, am living in another world, a world in which time is unhinged and dark clouds shut out the light and friends and acquaintances distance themselves with remarkable swiftness. A few come, in understandable awkwardness, to express their sadness, or their anger, or to assure me of their continuing loyalty as friends while apologizing for withdrawing from further professional association. As one succinctly puts it, "I've thought long and hard on this one and I've just had to separate my feelings of friendship for you from our professional relationship. I've decided I need to be squeaky clean in this town if I'm to continue as a therapist."

And that was that.

It had seemed that this year, the long Indian Summer might never end and that Oregon's dwindling snow pack and reservoirs might finally dry up and disappear, but the rains have come at last amid great sighs of relief. By Thanksgiving Day, the rivers and reservoirs are once more seasonally high against their banks and crowds of skiers are reveling on the slopes of the snowpacked Cascades nearby. It has been raining steadily for the past month now, and for those Oregonians who fail to find joy in the subtle nuances of light and contrast that mark the rainy season, the world is turning grey and the annual contagion of depression is beginning to set in.

Now it is November, and another month has dragged by since Gilda's letter and, in contrast to the burgeoning creeks and rivers, my days are emptying of their old familiar routines. Days once filled with clients and useful purpose are drained and stagnant. Hours once alive with challenge are giving way to long spells of staring unseeing into some fogged-over middle distance. Short lists of chores and long periods of brooding expand to fill the emptiness left by the diminishing flow of productive work. More and more, I am withdrawn into a waiting mode – waiting for the state board to review my lengthy and detailed responses to the allegations and assertions in Gilda's formal complaint; waiting for the board to issue its verdict; waiting to make up my mind as to what to do next.

I am considering the option of not waiting, of throwing belongings into my van and taking off and not turning back. There is a world out there I could explore and dozens of things I could do. But thus far, inertia, despondency, and a riveting, morbid curiosity as to what will happen next, keep me from moving beyond the thought. Later I will review my options and, who knows, perhaps an exciting new path will reveal itself. For now, there is nothing of substance beyond the grey shroud of my waiting.

George Bush has been elected president and the fact totally fails to move me. I can't tell if it's because Bush and Dukakis both strike me as victims of the superficiality that this nation persistently demands in its political diet, or if it's because of my own preoccupation. Almost-total preoccupation is certainly monopolizing my attention. I wallow in despair for only so long before the alarm bells go off, reminding me: *I must move!* If only to preserve some vestige of dignity and hope.

Jim, my friend and psychiatrist, says I need to experience the depth of my sorrow and despair; that I must come to a psychological death and the end of all hope if I am to rise, like Lazarus, from the dead. Well, I guess I'm not a Lazarus. In the midst of my drowning I struggle to the surface and reach once more for a life preserver. *Don't drown!* I scream at myself and reach again for something, anything, to hold onto. But whatever life preserver I find in daytime slips away in the night and come morning I'm drowning in despair again.

What is the source of my despair? A combination of loss and fear that I may not recover.

What have I lost? The ability to practice my profession, at least in this community. A reputation as an honorable and trustworthy man. A sense of belonging. Face. Material things like money, house, income. Mostly I have lost a 25-year bet that I would be able to work my way through my own fallibilities and limitations that impose upon me an unwelcome level of mediocrity. Further, that I could do it by working in this profession, and by remaining in this community. In fact, I thought I had been doing a good job of accomplishing just that. The despair flows from the harsh reality that the world out there is suddenly saying in unmistakable words, *No way, Buster!*

And after twenty years of reasonable success and apparent headway.

As for the fear that I may not recover? Certainly, I do not expect to recover what is gone for me here in Willamette. Nor do I want to. Let them stew in their own juices and let them dwell deeply on the meanings of their own responses to my stoning. The fear that I may not recover is the fear that – at 68 – I face my future with irreparably diminished resources. I question that I could muster and sustain the physical energy, the emotional resilience, the intellectual vigor, the optimistic spirit, that going on to a new and productive life would demand of me. *Once more into the breach, dear friends!* is the cry I hear from Olivier's *Henry V* inside my head. But I am too engrossed in my feebleness to respond. And if such a revival were possible, what is there for me to do?

And now it is December and my days are filling with ever more devastation. My collapsed practice no longer pays the bills and the option of holding on for a turn in fortune falls away like the last of the brown leaves on the wintering oak in my yard. So I surrender to the inevitable and put out the word that I will terminate my practice at the end of the year. Occasionally, someone calls asking for an appointment. I tell them I am no longer in practice and refer them elsewhere with a strange acceptance of a kind of death.

Yet, here and there, patches of tiny fresh green shoots appear, promising new life. The practical requirements of maintaining the house and grounds for quick sale keep me from drowning in listless immobility. Pulling the weeds that flourish beneath the rhododendrons and among the red bricks of the walkways, cutting away the rotting undergrowth and dead brown fronds from the green ferns, bring some relief from my helpless despair.

But nothing halts the steady deterioration of the life I had come to know. Once-zestful exuberance has collapsed to moody intro-spection. Optimism, once flowing with bubbling vigor, lies dammed in stagnant pools, festering in the dry shallows of my mind, exuding a stench of decay and death.

It is the inevitability of death that traps me into little games of, *Why not now?* And, on occasion, I stare into the black waters of my own dying and dangle a hesitant toe to feel the palpability of the option. And where at first I pulled back in shock, now I stare into the darkness and consider various answers to the question, *Is this the time?*

It is the last Tuesday in December and I have settled into the "Patient" chair and Jim's concerned soft voice asks, for the ump-teenth time in our client-therapist relationship, *How are you doing?*

Well, I think I'm beginning to see a little light at the end of the tunnel.

Tell me about it.

Well, for one thing, I find that I'm thinking a little more posi-tively about the future. I still have no clear idea of what I want to do or where I want to go, but I'm not feeling quite as hopeless. I can see that if I can find a path that has some meaning for me, I could be Okay.

What sort of path might have some meaning for you?

I'm really not sure. I feel it's going to take time for me to sort that out. I'm clearer on what I don't want than on what I do. I don't want to go on working as a psychotherapist, even if that remains an option. I feel through with that. I don't want to remain here. I'm finished with this chapter in my life and I want to leave it behind as

*soon as I can get unstuck from the business of selling the house and
tying up loose ends.*

Jim sips his coffee, pondering.

*So, you've finished your business here and are ready to move
on – but you just haven't figured out where. Have you been thinking
about your future in terms of what you need at this point in your life
to grow yourself?*

*That's a good question. I don't think I've been that clear about
it. I've been just trying to find enough reasons to go on living. I'm
still shaky on that. I am not all that confident I can start a whole new
life at my age. "Old dogs" and all that sort of thing. I guess I'm not
having much faith in my resilience. When I was younger I didn't
have this kind of trouble. I believed in a future – well, at least
enough to push on into the unknown and run a lot of risks. Now, I
feel that, win, lose, or draw, I'm at an end point. And I think,
'Doesn't this mean that it's time for me to let go of the struggle?'*

What kind of an answer do you come up with?

*The answer that I come up with is that I don't trust the answer I
come up with!*

We both laugh and refill our coffee cups before Jim picks up
the conversation.

*OK. What I'm hearing is that you're debating whether you
should withdraw from life on grounds that it's too painful and
you've stopped growing, or whether you should try going on. What
I'm hearing is that you've bought the assumption that there's a limit
to your growth that's tied to your age, and that maybe – just maybe,
but you're really not sure – 68 is the end of the line for you.*

Jim pauses and sips his coffee before he continues.

As we both know, suicide forecloses on other options. What is not quite so obvious is that buying the assumption that you've reached a limit to your growth has the same effect as blowing your brains out. Only it's a slower death.

Jim pauses again. Staring past my shoulder and off into the distance somewhere, he murmurs,

On the other hand, there's always the possibility that you'll stop believing in limits.

Now it is 1989 and a new year. Somewhere up ahead there is going to be a hearing before the state board in Salem. For now, I am doing my best to put it out of my mind.

On January 10, the clockwork of my life strikes 68, and my psychological pendulum begins a slow swing away from preoccupations with ignominious death. With the closing down of my private practice, I am free to turn away from Willamette forever. For me, it has become a city of hair-triggers waiting around every corner to fire off explosions of painful memories and paranoid anxieties. I had chosen to "hang in there," as my poster kitty had encouraged, for too long. Perhaps if I had had 20-20 foresight years ago, I might have escaped back to a more lenient and forgiving California. Now, it is too late for any kind of escape. But I can still turn my back on Willamette and start seeking a new life.

Now, for the first time, I begin to accept that it is time for me to retire. I intend that my retirement will mean the freedom to follow a new and different creative path leading to further growth. But what

path?

In the months that follow, I do a whole lot of driving up and down the West Coast and a whole lot of walking – activities that always provide me with long hours for pondering and processing. I find temporary homes for a few weeks or a few months on San Juan Island in the Straits of Juan de Fuca; in Seattle; in Oakland. And I walk. Preferably along shorelines and lakesides and riversides where the birds wheel and hover and dive, and the waves crash and the ripples murmur. And I explore other paths, as well. I buy art supplies and take a short class in charcoal sketching. I take a small part as a member of the jury in the stage play, *Inherit the Wind*, and another as "Father" in *Little Women*. I start writing a novel – heavily autobiographical – about the trials and challenges of late-adulthood. And I begin exploring a new application for the Odyssey System.

I had abandoned my attempt of the previous summer to publish my Odyssey manuscript when my professional world crumbled. Although the official verdict of the state board lay somewhere in the future, I saw myself as totally discredited professionally. Going down, as well, would be all the work I had done on Odyssey. That, I felt, was the greatest loss of all. My profession, my peers, the world would not have the opportunity to explore and evaluate its worth. But in the early months of this new year, I could discern another application for Odyssey that was not restricted in its use to the mental health establishment. I had given my book manuscript the title, *Odyssey Therapy*. But Odyssey is more than a therapy for use by mental health practitioners in their treatment of the mentally-ill; it is also a system for use by the mentally-well.

It started with a call from a former client in my private practice who had moved on professionally to a management position of considerable responsibility with a large industrial firm in the San

Francisco Bay Area. He had been using persona work successfully in making personal and career choices and was wanting guidance in exploring its use in solving management problems, as well. Would I help? So I signed on as a management consultant and we began looking together at possible uses for the Odyssey System in business and industry. With that as a beginning, I soon found a scattering of other management-type clients in the San Juans and in Seattle. My travels up and down the coast were becoming a pleasant mix of business and pleasure. I could begin to see the future taking shape.

Chapter 31

The time is somewhere around 10 a.m. on July 11, 1989. The public hearing has been going on for an hour in a large auditorium off the main corridor of the State Transportation Building in Salem, Oregon. The auditorium has a stage at one end overlooking rows of seats arranged on two sides of a center aisle, enough seats for perhaps four hundred. There are about twenty people in the audience. I have no idea who they are. I sit at a table below the stage with a microphone and a three-inch high stack of records and documents I brought in with me. Gilda and Stan sit in the first row of seats slightly behind me to my right. I have turned to look at them as each of them offers statements to place in evidence, but our eyes never meet.

On the stage, behind a curved high judicial bench sit five or six – I can't remember exactly – members of the Oregon State Board of Clinical Social Workers. They have been sitting in silent judgment since the hearing started. Speaking for them are a Hearing Officer and a Prosecuting Attorney. Not one of the silent judges will have said a word by the end of the hearing. Years later, I still find myself wondering what thoughts were going through their minds.

Back there – around 10 a.m. on July 11, 1989 – the trial seems to be winding down to its preordained conclusion. Preordained, because the purpose of the hearing – which was to consider the revocation of my clinical social worker's certificate of registration – is no longer at issue. It was due to a technicality. I had failed to renew my certificate earlier in the year and, just prior to the hearing, I was drawn aside by the Prosecuting Attorney and informed that my certificate had now permanently lapsed. I no longer had a certificate to revoke. So, the hearing was sort of a non-event. The Prosecuting Attorney had offered me the option of having it called off, but I declined. How can one know what happened at one's trial if the trial doesn't happen?

HEARING OFFICER: *Thank you Ms. Gormé. Dr. Bogart, did you wish to make any response?*

DR. BOGART: *I wish I had a transcript of what Gilda just said because there are many statements in there that I really do not agree with.*

HO: *Well, I would agree that a lot of her testimony was speculation.*

DR. B: *I think what I'd rather... oh dear... I've prepared a statement, uh, to read to the Board, and perhaps I'd better just do that... I'm really unsettled with regard to all of the things that Gilda has just represented about me...*

HO: *You may respond, if you wish.*

DR. B: *Gilda's characterizations of me as a therapist who manipulated, who abused, who's totally incompetent to practice as a therapist, who is incapable of remorse or feeling sorry or whatever – I mean all of these characterizations of me are what Gilda believes. They do not coincide with my own perceptions of me. They do not coincide with the perceptions of me of hundreds of clients, of peers, of people that I've worked with professionally.*

I did not come today to try to defend my reputation or my competence as a therapist. The mistakes that I made with Gilda happened in 1981, that's eight years ago or seven years ago. You can quibble about whether it's seven or eight. I made great errors. It was not appropriate for me to have had sex with Gilda. Since then I have had no sexual involvement with any clients whatsoever. And the implication that I have not learned from my experiences is totally incorrect.

I am a man who is committed to learning, who is committed to growing. And when I left Willamette Mental Health in 1982, I re-committed my life to growing and to learning and went on to the doctoral program to become an even more effective human being, as well as therapist.

I do not know of anyone else who characterizes me as unfit as a therapist. I did not subpoena people to come here and testify in my behalf, because I felt that all of the evidence that has been submitted to you in written documentation and tapes is sufficient so that you can come to your own judgment about my competence, or whatever. ...

As I speak, as I defend myself, as I make my points, it all seems so futile. Who am I talking to? Who am I defending myself against? To whom am I appealing for some fragment of my self-respect, my character, my name? No one here seems to be listening. The thumbs of the judges are already turned down and the lions are let loose. There is nothing left but to endure, hopefully with some courage.

> Dr. B: *If I may, I would like to read this statement into the record and then give you a copy of it.*

> HO: *You may.*

> DR. B: *Statement to the Board, Registered Clinical Social Workers:*

> *I've expressed to you already in my written testimony that I am fully aware that I have violated ethical standards which I had an obligation to uphold at all times. I have acknowledged in my written testimony that with respect to the allegations against me, while my version of what took place between Gilda and me differs in detail from her version, we did become sexually involved and that it was a violation of my ethical responsibility to have done so.*

> *I have not come here today to deny these facts. I have already acknowledged in my written responses, the extent to which I am guilty. In my own mind it doesn't really matter whether my version of the facts or Gilda's version is believed – both versions constitute violations of proscribed ethical behavior.*

> *It also doesn't matter whether Gilda entered into our relationship as a fully informed consenting mature adult, nor whether we both did our best to support each other materially and emotionally for the next half -dozen years. I am guilty of unethical conduct and I fully deserve to be punished.*

*Well, I'm here today to inform you of the extent to which I
have already been punished for my transgressions.*

I go on to repeat the sad litany of the punishing losses I have
been experiencing since receiving Gilda's first letter two years
before, almost to the day. But of course, there is nothing I might say
that would change the course of events.

HO: *Okay. Before we get to questions, could you hand me
your written statement and we'll enter it as Exhibit 6.*

Thank you, Doctor.

*We'll enter the written statement just read by Dr.
Bogart as Exhibit No. 6. Okay, Mr. (Prosecuting
Attorney), did you wish to ask Dr. Bogart any ques-
tions?*

PROSECUTING ATTORNEY: *No questions.*

HO: *Any further evidence for the record?*

PA: *No. I'd like to make a comment.*

HO: *Certainly.*

PA: (Addresses Dr. B) *We started off this hearing basically
saying that the end net-effect was going to be declaring the loss of your registration due to the lapse
status, and that really is the bottom line. You are no
longer registered or, I believe, pending our Hearing
Officer's ruling, you will no longer be a registered
clinical social worker in the state of Oregon.*

*However, I think that there are other issues that
were cleared here as well, and I think it was probably*

healthy for everyone concerned that those issues were raised and dealt with. The issues that we're talking about can be summarized as just involving a dual relationship situation. The line wasn't drawn.

DR. B: *That is correct.*

PA: *And I'd like to say that I don't believe that even your victims – and I'll call them that – think that you are a terrible person or a bad person or a person without worth. And I do believe that you probably have accomplished a lot of good in your practice, but I will sit here and tell you that, but for the technicality of the lapsed nature of your registration, I would be arguing very strongly to revoke your license without any possibility of reinstatement – not to punish you and not to vindicate your victims – but to protect the consumers of therapy from RCSW's in this state. Because what I heard in this hearing, frankly, was a pattern of behavior that involved a long period of time and more than one client that was not willful on your part, that was not intended to hurt, that was probably intended with the best of intentions, but that was injurious and that was contrary to what we try to do here.*

It is my recommendation to future Boards that may or may not review a re-application from Dr. Bogart, that it should be summarily denied. And I'd just like to close by again saying that this is a consumer protection act that I am proposing to the Board regarding future reconsideration. And that this does not imply that there was any degree of maliciousness or willfulness or intent to hurt anyone. I don't believe that's the case. That's all that I have to say.

HO: *Dr. Bogart, did you wish to make any closing remarks.*

DR. B: *Well, it really doesn't have any bearing with regard to me because I'm no longer an issue for you – I mean, clearly you've come to a decision. But I would suggest to you that your decision is not the most productive one you could make in behalf of the profession. I suggest that no matter what errors therapists commit, it is possible to learn from them. It is possible for therapists to use that experience, not only to help themselves, but to help other therapists and to help their clients. It is possible for therapists to learn and grow from their mistakes and to use their new knowledge to help the profession.*

   That's all I have to say.

HO: *Thank you Dr. Bogart. With that then, we'll close the hearing. I'll be submitting a proposed Order to yourself, Doctor, and to the Board.*

   Nothing further?

   Then the hearing is closed.

I gather up my stack of papers and documents, turn my back on the stage and its players and, looking neither right nor left, retrace my steps along the center aisle, out through the door to the fresh Oregon air outside and whatever futures might await.

Chapter 32

The wounds each of us suffers are monstrous. They are also the most important teachers we can ever know. We are the fortunate ones for whom so much of life is given over to healing. Healing is learning time. Reflecting time. A time for the dawning of new understanding, and new appreciation for the rare gift of the shockingly unexpected. For me, the Salem hearing left a monstrous wound. And I have been fortunate that in the 18 months between it and the undertaking of this book, I reflected much and have come to understand much that had not been all that clear.

My newer understandings have led me to the conviction that the Odyssey System is particularly relevant to the dilemmas facing the profession from which I have been cast out. Further, that the Odyssey System makes available to a broad segment of the general public tools of merit and easy access that provide rich opportunities for self-enrichment and growth. My newer understandings have led me to the conviction that I have no moral choice but to bring the Odyssey System to your attention so that you may do with it what you will.

One of my newer understandings is that the Odyssey System addresses the biggest problem concerning sex between therapist and client, a problem that is rarely addressed. It has to do with the distribution of power between therapist and client and its consequences. It has to do with the way orthodox psychotherapy – or counseling, if you prefer that term – is structured.

Traditional psychotherapy sets up therapist and client in a relationship that runs along the lines of traditional doctor-patient relationships. The underlying assumptions are that the doctor, by virtue of years of professional training and experience, has the answers to the patient's problems, is the fount of wisdom from which the patient is to draw sustenance, and is the holder of most of the keys of power and authority.

What do such assumptions have to do with the issue of sex in therapy? They seduce both therapists and their clients into perpetuating the power-oriented relationships that gave rise to the very problems from which the clients – and often their therapists – have been trying to escape. In such an environment of unequal power and responsibility, both therapist and client are subject to being seduced by the unfinished music of their respective histories, trapped into resonating like taut strings to the familiar keenings of the past. For both of them, therapy risks becoming a mélange of all things past and present seeking expression. In such a charged environment, given the intimacy of the therapeutic relationship, sexual feelings can become flames that consume both therapist and client, diverting energy from the proper task of solving client problems.

Does it surprise that sex happens in therapy? *The New York Times,* in an article published on December 20, 1990 ("New guidelines issued on Patient-Therapist Sex"), reported that in a national survey of 1,320 clinical psychologists, half of them said they had treated patients who had had sexual relations with a previous therapist. And that's only the tip of an iceberg whose actual dimensions are not known. What is known is that all therapists and all clients are human beings endowed with emotions and sexual feelings that can and do surface in the intimacy of therapist-client relationships. The environment in which such feelings surface very much influences what happens next.

What makes Odyssey's approach fundamentally different from traditional psychotherapy is that its structure redresses the imbalance of power and responsibility that tends to infantilize the therapist-client relationship. Odyssey's structure leads both therapist and client to refer all of the client's questions and feelings back to the inner circle of the client's personas. It is they, not the therapist, who are empowered to work through to the particular solutions that will liberate the client from her bondage.

By empowering the client's personas – and the client's sense of wholeness – Odyssey's structure does not entrap therapist and client in a fruitless *folie-a-deux* searching for liberation from the webs of feelings and desires that can entangle them both. Unresolved personal issues and feelings are always referred back where they belong – onto the intra-psychic stage where one's personas can play them out to uncover their historical antecedents and find their true meanings. In an Odyssey context, sexual feelings of client for therapist and therapist for client can be seen and respected for what they are: projections of unresolved personal movies onto the nearest available screen – the form and presence of the therapeutic partner.

"Well," one might ask, "if that's true, how come the Odyssey System didn't help to protect against sexual involvement in your relationships with Imelda, Gilda and Elaine?"

The answer is that it was never given a chance; the Odyssey System approach was never utilized in their therapies. I can't know how much difference it would have made if it had been, but I do believe it would have given us an alternative – and less entrapping – therapeutic scenario with which to work.

Afterword

Summer, 1992

LEONARDO: *Hey, guys, that's it! We're finished! We've done it!*

At which point the multitude of personas erupts in boisterous shouting and dancing about, amid which, the following multilogue can be heard:

LAURA: *Fantastic. Let's go to the seashore and hang out for a year.*

ALTHOR: *Sounds great to me. Let's pack and split. Hey, what the hell, maybe we don't even need to pack!*

SAM: *Slow down guys. We're not all that finished. We've got another book to get out. But that shouldn't take too long. And then we can go to the seashore and hang out.*

ALTHOR: *How long?*

SAM: *Maybe six months. Most of it's written already. We just need to revise it and bring it up to date.*

ALTHOR: *Let's put it off – do it later.*

SAM: *I think we're committed to getting the Odyssey System out in a book that tells folks how they can use it – pretty much like the book we finished in '88 and didn't publish. A lot has happened in the past four years. There have been some exciting developments and we need to bring it up to date.*

But now, I want us to reflect on this book, the one we've just finished. I want to know what you're thinking and feeling. Particularly you, Althor; you were the one of us who had the strongest reservations about going ahead with it.

ALTHOR: *Well, I'm surprised at how I feel. I'm still concerned about what people will think. I want people to like me but I'm less anxious about that than I was. I'm much more prepared to accept that a lot of them, maybe almost all of them, won't. That's okay now. I can handle that and maybe grow with it. Before, I didn't feel I could – I just wanted to withdraw and hide out. I feel better now because we did an honest job with the book. We did our best. I think that's important.*

LEONARDO: *For me, writing this book has taught me how much I still have to learn about writing. I don't think it's a particularly good book, technically or artistically. I think it's an honest book – as honest as we could make it anyway – and it has a lot of drama. It doesn't back away from difficult material. I guess I think it's a better movie than it is a book.*

LAURA: *I learned from our writing the book, too. One of the things I learned is that I'm a very incomplete persona. I'm more of a caricature of a woman than a woman. I represent some feminine aspects of Vic, but a woman I'm not, as Moishe would say. Maybe in a next life somewhere.*

MINNIE: *And I've learned that I'm the support staff without which no book gets written. I'm the homemaker, the nurturer, the cook, the mother, and I love all of those roles, otherwise I wouldn't do it. I'm necessary and needed and nothing would get done if it weren't for me. So I'm important. And so are you Laura. You shouldn't be discounting yourself.*

HAWK: *I've learned that it's never too late for courage. Here we are, or at least Vic is, plowing ahead with courage and determination at the age of 71 as if he were indifferent to the aging process. This is a tale of courage. It may also be a tale of stupidity and weakness and conceit and all those human foibles, but it is a tale of a courageous quest and I like that. That's my bag. I feel good about that.*

SAM: *I've learned a lot also. And I have all the women in my world to thank for so much of what I've learned – Gilda, Elaine, Imelda, Odette – especially Odette.*

MOISHE: *I haven't told you this before, Sam, but Gilda's calling you to account and the whole Salem business was the best thing that could possibly have happened to you.*

SAM: *Moishe, I have to agree with you. It has allowed me to move to a next higher level of understanding out of which it has become much easier for me to be a more authentic me. I no longer have to pretend about anything. I am – we are – Vic is – free, at last.*

MOISHE: *Well, I suppose you think that just because I'm the closest thing you have to a transcendent persona, that I don't have anything to learn because I know it all already. Well, I've got a surprise for you. Even God is learning. That's why He has so many of us running around the universe learning things. Why do you think He has us doing all this learning? It's so He can learn more of whatever it is He's interested in finding out. Oh, excuse me, it's She, not He. Well, it's really They, or We, but who's counting.*

Anyway, what I wanted to say is that I've learned from this book-writing business, too. I've learned that all of you are taking life much too seriously. If you don't lighten up, you'll never get to live to a hundred and twenty – which I've recently learned is what your biological system is capable of, if you can figure out a way to keep it going that long. So, I say: Forget about the books for a while. Let's go to the seashore first. We've got fifty more years to write the books.

Mazeltov and Shalom!

Notes
and
Appendix

Notes

Chapter 4

1. Thigpen, C. H., & Cleckley, H. M. *Three Faces of Eve.* Kingport, Tenn: Kingport Press, 1957.

2. Bateson, G., Jackson, D. D., Haley, J., & Weakland, J. H. Toward a theory of schizophrenia. *Behavioral Science,* Vol. 1, No. 4, 1956.

3. Satir, V. *Conjoint Family Therapy.* Palo Alto, Calif.: Science and Behavior Books, 1964.

Chapter 5

1. Yablonsky, L. *The Tunnel Back.* New York: The Macmillan Company, 1965.

2. Moreno, J. L. *We shall Survive: A New Approach to the Problems of Human Interaction.* Washington, D.C.: Nervous and Mental Disease Publishing Co. 1934.

Chapter 7

1. For more information, see:
Kempler, W. Experiential family therapy. *International Journal of Group Psychotherapy,* 1965, 15(1), 57-71.
– The experiential therapeutic encounter. *Psychotherapy: Theory, Research & Practice,* 1967, 4(4), 166-172.
– Experiential psychotherapy with families. *Family Process,* 1968, 7(1), 88-99.

– The therapist's merchandise. *Voices: The Art & Science of Psychotherapy*, 1969-70, 5(4), 57-60.

2. From: Last stanza of "In Distrust of Merits." Reprinted with permission of Macmillan Publishing Company from COLLECTED POEMS OF MARI-ANNE MOORE. Copyright 1944, and renewed 1972 by Marianne Moore.

> *Hate-hardened heart, O heart of iron,*
> *iron is iron till it is rust.*
> *There never was a war that was not*
> *inward; I must*
> *fight till I have conquered in myself what*
> *causes war, but I would not believe it.*
> *I inwardly did nothing.*
> *O Iscariot-like crime!*
> *Beauty is everlasting*
> *and dust is for a time.*

Chapter 8

1. Stoller, F. H. The Long Weekend. *Psychology Today*, 1967, 1(7), 28-33.

2. Bach, G. R. The Marathon group: Intensive practice of intimate interaction. *Psychological Reports*, 1966, 18, 995-1005.
   – Marathon Group Dynamics: I. Some functions of the professional group facilitator. *Psychological Reports*, 1967, 20(3, Pt. 1), 995-999.

Chapter 9

1. Murphy, M. Esalen: Where it's at. *Psychology Today*, 1967, 1(7), 34-39.

2. Perls, F., Hefferline, R.F., & Goodman, P. *Gestalt Therapy*. New York: Dell Publishing Company, 1951.
   Perls, F. S. *Ego, Hunger and Aggression*. San Francisco: Orbit Graphic Arts, 1966
   – *Gestalt Therapy Verbatim*. Lafayette, California: Real People Press, 1969.
   – *In and Out the Garbage Pail*. Lafayette, California: Real People Press, 1969.

Chapter 10

1. Rimmer, R. *The Harrad Experiment*. New York: Bantam Books, 1967.

Interchapter 10+

1. Leonardo was wrong. The line comes from a poem by Delmore Schwartz titled, "All Clowns Are Masked and All Personae." See: *What Is To Be Given*, a book of selected poems by Delmore Schwartz published by Carcanet New Press Ltd., Manchester, England (1976).

Chapter 12

1. A year later, Fritz Perls drew on his poem to introduce and to provide the title for his next book, *In and Out the Garbage Pail* (1969). The complete poem reads:

> In and out the garbage pail
> Put I my creation,
> Be it lively, be it stale,
> Sadness or elation.
>
> Joy and sorrow as I had
> Will be re-inspected;
> Feeling sane and being mad,
> Taken or rejected.
>
> Junk and chaos, come to halt!
> 'Stead of wild confusion,
> Form a meaningful gestalt
> At my life's conclusion.

Chapter 15

1. Tolkien, J.R.R. *The Lord of the Rings.* New York: Ballantyne Books, 1965.

   -- *The Hobbit.* New York: Houghton Mifflin, 1966.

Chapter 22

1. Kelly, G.A. *The Psychology of Personal Constructs: A theory of personality.* (2 vols.) New York: W. W. Norton & Company, 1955.

2. *Ibid.*, Fillmore Sanford in Editor's Introduction, Volume 1.

Chapter 26

1. Excerpt from a taped workshop presentation (1987).

Chapter 27

1. Bogart, V. (1984). A study of relationships between selected factors associated with retirement and measures of dyadic quality. *Dissertation Abstracts International*, Vol. 46, Number 5, 1985. (University Microfilms International No. 8514817.)

Appendix

[Transcript of remarks by Julian Silverman, Claudio Naranjo, John Perry, Kasimierz Dabrowski, and Stanislav Grof at a session of the month-long Esalen series, *Value of the Psychotic Experience*, held in July, 1968.]

Julian Silverman:

I'd like to start by just reading from the brochure which presents The Value of The Psychotic Experience in terms of a revolutionary quote:

"Recent developments in psychological, physiological and anthropological research on altered states of consciousness indicate the need for a revision of psychiatric and philosophical conceptions in this area. This month-long series of seminars and workshops is concerned with an appraisal and re-evaluation of these conceptions. In the course of these sessions a model will be developed which (1) considers the positive, integrative, problem-solving features of altered states, and, (2) systematically recasts it in major aspects of modern day 'mental illness'."

[Silverman sets the brochure aside and begins a recapitulation of the workshops that were held during the past three weeks.]

We began with a series on the sense and nonsense of psychosis. We talked about an increasing number of researches and clinical impressions appearing in psychiatric literature which indicates that a radical reformulation is necessary of our understanding of the psychotic and psychosis. These were some of these issues in the first weekend.

*We went on to an elaboration of the notion of "the mind journey,"
the entry into a different realm of consciousness associated with psychotic
experience. In the workshop presented by Dr. Perry, we examined in
detail some of the aspects of the mind journey.*

*In the weekend just completed, Dr. Dabrowski presented his work
on "positive disintegration." In his workshop, a personality theory was
elaborated which would integrate a concept of positive disintegration in
such a way as to present a model of personality development and growth
in terms of disintegration.*

*Tonight, we are beginning a weekend seminar entitled, "Perspec-
tives in psychosis" in which our aim is to bring together people from
different areas of the world who share a particular interest, which is: this
revolution in psychiatry, this need for a radical reformulation which
recasts the notion of mental illness in a way that allows for a substantive
growth aspect to psychosis.*

*What I'd like to do tonight is to introduce the various members of
this panel who will tell you where they're at. Then, during the course of
this weekend, we'll meet and discuss various critical issues in relation to
this reformulation of the value of psychotic experience. Both positive and
negative.*

*The revolution in psychiatry is part of a larger revolution which is
going on in the culture. It's not restricted to the notion of sanity and
insanity. It seems to be creeping into various aspects of culture. It's
represented by such disparate kinds of writers, such as McLewin,
Buckminster Fuller, the architect, the kind of Eastern philosophical
resurrections that have been presented by Alan Watts and others.*

*There are a lot of things going on which we're going to try to tap
into in relation to this very nuclear issue of constructive aspects of taking
the mind journey; of blowing your mind; of gathering inspiration in the
shamanistic primitive notion of "going somewhere else" to problem solve,
to reorientate oneself to one's world when all other things fail at the
problem-solving mode; when you're no longer in control.*

*The members of this panel have approached this problem of the
value of psychotic experience from various perspectives. What we'll do
tonight is let them tell you where they're at. They are, Doctors Claudio*

Naranjo, John Perry, Kasimierz Dabrowski, and Stanislav Grof.

Claudio Naranjo:

My own interest in psychosis, more specifically in schizophrenia, is probably the least clinical of the presenters here. It's been several years since I've done work in a psychiatric ward; that was part of my medical training. But mostly my interest at present is a speculative one from other angles.

One of my areas of concern and teaching has been psychology of art and therefore I am interested in the process of the use of symbols as a means of expression. And I see in schizophrenia the universal and paradoxical process in which we use symbols, not only to convey distress, but also to substitute the reality we want to convey.

The schizophrenic is a person who is very proficient in making models of the world, and he can be more in touch with certain concepts of reality than we ordinarily are. At the same time, it is legitimate to say that the mirror in which he sees his world, allows him to look at things we don't look at, at all, because we would probably be paralyzed. And this mirror is the mirror of symbolic representation, of symbolic language, of metaphoric language, of poetic language, through which he can afford to look at truths that we would probably not bear. And he doesn't, quite. Therefore, he's not at ease, not even with this symbolic language, and every act in schizophrenia, as I see it from this point of view, is a contradiction of <u>wanting to say</u>, and at the same time <u>wanting not to say;</u> wanting to say, but always staying one step removed and ready to step out of the picture: "No, I didn't mean it! It's just a symbol."

A very rich field of inquiry is that of the difference between the successful use of symbols by which the artist conveys reality, and this half-way form of expression that is schizophrenia; which is a promise of potential, and yet is a measure of failure in that he does not come fully across.

That's one aspect of my personal interest in the matter.

Another is related to my interest in psychotherapy in general and, specifically, the use of psychedelic drugs in psychotherapy. This has had an impact on me, like on many others, in stressing the importance of the disintegrative aspects in any human change. If we want to get rid of something, if it's really to fall off, it has to break before we can achieve any aim. We have to shed old personalities, old identifications, old forms and leave them behind, like a snake shedding its skin.

Thirdly, in terms of this introduction, a third field of interest to me is the connection between schizophrenia and the shamanistic experience. There's a very close relationship, as I see it, not only between the schizophrenic process and the personal process – the critical period of the vision which the medicine man undergoes in primitive cultures – but also between the schizophrenic process and much of what we consider typical of the primitive, in quotes, mentality in which, metaphorically speaking, the myth maker believes his myth. As the schizophrenic does. Because the myth is at-one-with the Truth speaking through it.

We tend to disassociate ourselves and to interpret myths from a safer distance. We say,"Well, the literal interpretation of the myth is one thing, but the content is another." And we believe that this more sophisticated approach is more true. And it both is, and, not. Because what we're doing is only translating into another language, translating into a different set of symbols – verbal symbols – the visual pictorial symbols of the myth. So, in some ways, the real myth makers – and the schizophrenic is a natural myth maker, like the primeval myth makers whom we see not only in the shaman but in the general population of primitive cultures most of whom are creative artists – these real myth makers are more closely identified with the symbolic medium of their cultures.

I have been drawn more and more into my interest in shamanism through my interest in some drugs that I think hold a great promise for our contemporary world in terms of what they can do to facilitate change processes. We can borrow from shamanism, not only these tools which are the psycho-catalysts, but also their extremely sophisticated notion of how to use these particular tools in terms of the world to which they guide.

John Perry:

My interest in this topic originates in my work as a Jungian analyst in private practice in San Francisco. Along with this, I've spent a good many years putting in part time in the county health service in San Francisco, and other places, working with psychotic patients, trying to see some way in which analyst's and therapist's knowledge of the experience that the schizophrenic is going through can apply to the therapeutic process. At the same time I've been teaching and supervising psychiatric residents.

I must say, over the years, I've found it a bit distressing to watch the kind of thought and development that becomes eventually the prevailing mode of psychiatry. It seems to be going in the direction that is the typical American thing – that is, in the direction of the pragmatic, the practical, that which consumes the least amount of time, the least expense for the most people. And while there is a great deal of effective therapy that comes out of this – in terms of getting people back home, getting them back into their active life again – the fact remains that the individual patient really gets overlooked.

Not only that, but the resident who is in training gets very little chance – as I used to twenty years ago – to sit down with the individual patient who is psychotic and go deeply into the patient's experience. Each year, I sense that the residents have less and less room in their thinking for depth psychology, for any kind of understanding of what goes on in what we would call "the unconscious," the "depth of the emotional processes." Their emphasis is entirely on the interpersonal, on group work, on family, on therapy, mostly on the level of manifest feelings and manifest interactions.

I don't mean to devalue that because, again, it is the area where the practical, pragmatic things do have to get done. However, I think it overlooks the fact that the schizophrenic patient is in a different place when he comes into the hospital. I found that when he is in the throes of his disturbance, the patient doesn't connect with that area at all. It's alien to him. He's rather unwilling to get into that part of the work right away. He's preoccupied with other matters. The best analogy I can think of is to say he's living in a myth. It could be a beautiful myth when it's assembled together. But in hearing it, it comes in wisps and fragments; so that you have a whole myth that's broken up into fragmental parts revolving around kaleidoscopically in odd patterns.

It sounds like nonsense if you take it purely at that phenomenal level of just hearing the fragments as if they have no sequence. What I found was, that if you listen to enough patients, and to the flow of concern – the flow of preoccupation that's there – you do find recurrent motifs. So that the stray, odd, bizarre fragments do fall into place in a recognizable set way. There is vaguely some sort of process going on.

I think it's important to get in touch with this process, to get the patients back in touch with the real concerns of their emotional life, back into their relationships with family and friends. But the motivation to do that, as a matter of fact, is not there. At that point they're a little alien from the group on the ward. The patient's emotions are down at this level of the mythological expressions, the symbolic expressions that Claudio is talking about. Emotions and images are part and parcel of the schizophrenic patient's affect.

Emotion and image are counterparts of each other; and the avenue to the emotional life of the schizophrenic, I think, is through all these images. You can communicate with the patient on that level – which is exactly the thing psychiatric residents are told not to do.

"Keep away from that irrational stuff. Have nothing to do with it. Don't encourage it. Don't lead the patient down that path. He can't go out in the world like that. Just talk about everyday things: talk about pressing concerns, tomorrow's breakfast. Keep with reality" (so-called).

Which is fine, except the affect is not there. And if you do manage to bully the patient into that level of reality, you are very apt to get a patient who consents, all right, to be there, but they arrive there without the affect; and they live in a kind of pale, grey world, very likely, if they're so lucky.

I'm operating on the assumption that if you do follow the imagery and the symbol, the patient does have the possibility to see where the affects are, and where the grinding issues are in his life.

What this sounds like, roughly, is that the patient is going through an agonizing experience with his world collapsing, his having died, rocked back, so to speak, to the beginning of time and his own beginnings. And there he is thrown in the midst of a confusing, bewildering and very threatening clash of opposites: a world of order and disorder; a world of his culture and that of an opposite, alien, enemy culture; a world of confused and threatening sexual identities, and new kinds of erotic, emotional, boiling-up feelings he has no idea what to do with, but which somehow feel enriching and good. The whole thing is like a roller coaster emotionally, if you connect with that level of experience.

I think the confusing thing about schizophrenic withdrawal is that it seems to be as if the affects are quite inappropriate, scattered and just off somewhere else – that they're repressed, so to speak. And I think quite the other way: that through this avenue of connection with the patient, the affects are very very much there but buried and concealed in this odd, unusual poem that's very hard to understand unless one can learn to think metaphorically, poetically, or symbolically.

Let me add one bit to that – another interest that's grown out of this: It's time to throw light on some of the comparative symbolism that does come into play at this level of psychotic process. And I find to my great surprise that the kind of process that the schizophrenic patient is going through, in this direct emotional turbulent way, does have parallels in very archaic ritual practice. I've been turning up the most ancient written forms of myth and ritual which give the appearance of corresponding very closely, indeed, to this process.

And that makes me feel that there's a renewal process that came into being about five thousand years ago that was concretized in governmental civic forums, communal forums, participated in by the entire community. And what stands out in it, is the establishment of a cosmic center: a center of potency, a center of creativity, of vitality, of life-givingness. And this center seems to be the thing that I keep finding again and again with schizophrenic patients. That the journey of the mind is a journey to that very potent, numinous center which they seem to identify with a great deal, in which they die, in which they can be born. I have a feeling that the study of that center is going to throw a great deal of light on the schizophrenic process so we can come to understand what it is and how it works.

Kasimierz Dabrowski:

After many years of experience with schizophrenics as a psychiatrist in Poland, I am coming to the conclusion that most psychotics – about 85 percent – are not manifesting psychopathological symptoms but very normal responses of movement in a positive direction.

Second, with regard to psychoneurosis, I am coming to the conclusion that true, authentic development begins always from so-called negativeness and so-called psychoneurosis.

From my observations, I began to elaborate a theory of positive disintegration that posits that mental health has nothing to do with narrow, rigid integration. If you are to develop yourself, you should go through disintegration, and that disintegration is normal and healthy, not integration. Surely after many steps through many levels, we can come in some cases to a "secondary integration" – a secondary level of harmony, after coming through conflicts, depressions, anxiety, inferiority feelings, guilt feeling, illusions, even hallucinations, and so on and so on.

Stanislav Grof:

My approach has been that of an experimental and clinical psychiatrist.

I've been working in a psychiatric research institute in Prague, Czechoslovakia, and I have a training in psychoanalysis and psychoanalytically-oriented psychotherapy, and I was specializing in psychotherapy of schizophrenics, which was using psychoanalytic principles but was more similar to the approach of Freda Fromm Reichmann's school of Chesnut Lodge.

During the last 13 years I have been interested in psychedelic drugs, especially how they can be used in psychotherapy for intensifying and accelerating the psychotherapeutic procedure.

Our institute was one of the places in Europe which developed a so-called "psycholytic" approach to LSD psychotherapy, which is different from the psychedelic approach. The psychedelic, as you know, uses large doses, usually in one or two exposures, in a special set and setting with a great religious/mystical emphasis, with the use of music, and so on. Whereas, our approach involves repeated administration of LSD, psylocybin, or other drugs, within a psychotherapeutic framework, using the techniques which are used in different schools of psychotherapy.

When I started with LSD about thirteen years ago, we were very much impressed by the fact that the same dosage used in different persons can produce an extremely wide range of experiences. We saw people who, for example, on a high dose of LSD didn't experience any perceptual phenomena, but the whole LSD session was experienced like a physical illness; they were somatizing all the time. We saw other people who experienced the whole LSD session as a sequence of sexual orgasms, or sexual tension, without having any other phenomena. Some of the subjects regressed into childhood and they reported complex reliving of traumatic childhood experiences. We had some of the subjects who experienced schizophrenic-like episodes. And then, we had a few subjects who experienced what seemed to be genuine mystical, religious experience.

So we were impressed by this fantastic range of clinical pictures which a single dose of a single drug can produce in different people, and we oriented our research toward an explanation of these phenomena.

We worked at the beginning with patients whom we knew in great detail —with whom we spent many hundreds of hours in individual and group psychotherapy. We knew their life situations, and so on. And then we gave them LSD. We wanted to find out whether we can understand something about their reaction to LSD, using all this information about their background.

And finally, during this kind of work, we developed what we call the psycholytic approach, because we felt that this can be useful, not only for diagnostic purposes but also as a very effective therapeutic technique.

Our last experience has been based on more than 50 cases in different clinical categories. We wanted to have a wide range of clinical diagnoses, patients in different diagnostic categories, and we treated them with the psycholytic approach. In other words, after we established psychotherapeutic contact with them, we went on with repeated LSD sessions, the number ranging anywhere between 15 and 90 or 100 sessions for each individual patient.

We made very detailed protocols of the sessions, and also of what was going on between the sessions, and we wanted to find out whether we can understand something about the underlying dynamics of the exposure to LSD.

And, you know, after some sessions, people can feel wonderful and feel purged, reborn. After some sessions they can have an experience of hangover. And after some sessions you can get something like a psychotic decompensation, or a freakout. So we were very much interested to see if we can understand something more about: In what kind of persons this happens? Under what circumstances? Or, is it related to some specific material from the LSD sessions?

Now, our present understanding of LSD is that it's more or less a non-specific catalyzer which brings up whatever is in the personality. And that this procedure of repeated LSD sessions actually is a sort of sequence of successive revealings and integrations of deeper and deeper layers of personality. We saw our patients going through what seemed to be typical Freudian material, reliving of childhood experiences, working through all kinds of hangups and so on. And going through the agony of birth. And going back through intra-uterine experiences. And in the advanced stages of LSD treatment, having what they described as Karmic experiences – going into past lives, having mystic or religious experiences, archetypal experiences, experiences which seemed like those of a collective racial unconscious, going back to different cultures: Egypt, Indian.

Now, what can this kind of experience with repeated administrations of LSD contribute to the problem we would like to discuss in this meeting?

You might be interested in what happens to schizophrenics if they are exposed to 80 or 90 LSD sessions within a therapeutic framework. We saw very dramatic therapeutic changes in the patients after certain characteristic experiences of disintegration, which we might discuss in greater detail.

George A. Kelly, Ph.D.

[From: *The Psychology of Personal Constructs, Volume One: A Theory of Personal Constructs.* New York: W. W. Norton & Co. 1955, pp 103-104.]

Summary of Assumptive Structure

FUNDAMENTAL POSTULATE AND ITS COROLLARIES:

a. *Fundamental Postulate:* A person's processes are psychologically channelized by the ways in which he anticipates events.

b. *Construction Corollary:* A person anticipates events by construing their replications.

c. *Individuality Corollary:* Persons differ from each other in their constructions of events.

d. *Organization Corollary:* Each person characteristically evolves, for his convenience in anticipating events, a construction system embracing ordinal relationships between constructs.

e. *Dichotomy Corollary:* A person's construction system is composed of a finite number of dichotomous constructs.

f. *Choice Corollary:* A person chooses for himself that alternative in a dichotomous construct through which he anticipates the greater possibility for extension and definition of his system.

g. *Range Corollary:* A construct is convenient for the anticipation of a finite range of events only.

h. *Experience Corollary:* A person's construction system varies as he successively construes the replication of events.

i. *Modulation Corollary:* The variation in a person's construction system is limited by the permeability of the constructs within whose ranges of convenience the variants lie.

j. *Fragmentation Corollary:* A person may successively employ a variety of construction subsystems which are inferentially incompatible with each other.

k. *Commonality Corollary:* To the extent that one person employs a construction of experience which is similar to that employed by another, his psychological processes are similar to those of the other person.

l. *Sociality Corollary:* To the extent that one person construes the construction processes of another, he may play a role in the social process involving the other person.

Comment

The author and Baskin Publishing Co. invite you to share in the space below your responses to ODYSSEY: *A Psychotherapist's Journey Along the Cutting Edge.*

[You may order copies of this book using the order form on the reverse side of this page. Cut out or duplicate and mail to Baskin Publishing Co., P.O. Box 7842, Eugene, OR 97401-0032.]

_____

_____

_____

_____

_____

_____

_____

_____

_____

_____

_____

_____

Name: _____

Address: _____

City: _____ State:_____ Zip: _____

☐ I would appreciate a response from you.

☐ Please send information about Odyssey System activities and publications.

Order Form

To Order by Credit Card: Call Toll Free 1-800-858-9055

Please send _____ copies of ODYSSEY: *A Psychotherapist's Journey Along the Cutting Edge.*

I understand that if I am not satisfied, I may return these books for a full refund – for any reason, no questions asked.

Price List:

1 to 2 books:	$24.95 each
3 to 5 books	21.95 each
6 or more books	18.95 each

Plus Shipping:

☐ Book rate: $2 for the first book plus $1 for each additional book. (Surface shipping may take three to four weeks)

☐ Air Mail: $3.50 per book.

Payment:

Make check or money order payable to Baskin Publishing Co. No C.O.D. orders.

Send order to:

Baskin Publishing Co., P.O. Box 7842, Eugene, OR 97401-0032.

Please deliver my books to:

Name:_____

Company Name:_____

Address:_____

City:_____State:____Zip_____

Enclosed is my check ☐ money order ☐ in the amount of $_____

Comment

The author and Baskin Publishing Co. invite you to share in the space below your responses to ODYSSEY: *A Psychotherapist's Journey Along the Cutting Edge.*

[You may order copies of this book using the order form on the reverse side of this page. Cut out or duplicate and mail to Baskin Publishing Co., P.O. Box 7842, Eugene, OR 97401-0032.]

_____

_____

_____

_____

_____

_____

_____

_____

_____

_____

Name: _____

Address:_____

City: _____ State:_____ Zip: _____

☐ I would appreciate a response from you.

☐ Please send information about Odyssey System activities and publications.

Order Form

To Order by Credit Card: Call Toll Free 1-800-858-9055

Please send _____ copies of ODYSSEY: *A Psychotherapist's Journey Along the Cutting Edge.*

I understand that if I am not satisfied, I may return these books for a full refund – for any reason, no questions asked.

Price List:

1 to 2 books:	$24.95 each
3 to 5 books	21.95 each
6 or more books	18.95 each

Plus Shipping:

☐ Book rate: $2 for the first book plus $1 for each additional book. (Surface shipping may take three to four weeks)

☐ Air Mail: $3.50 per book.

Payment:
Make check or money order payable to Baskin Publishing Co. No C.O.D. orders.

Send order to:
Baskin Publishing Co., P.O. Box 7842, Eugene, OR 97401-0032.

Please deliver my books to:

Name:_____

Company Name:_____

Address:_____

City:_____State:____Zip_____

Enclosed is my check ☐ money order ☐ in the amount of $_____